The Shopify Story

The Shopify Story

How a Startup Rocketed to E-Commerce Giant by Empowering Millions of Entrepreneurs

Larry MacDonald

Published by ECW Press
665 Gerrard Street East
Toronto, Ontario, Canada M4M 1Y2
416-694-3348 / info@ecwpress.com

Cover design: David A. Gee

LIBRARY AND ARCHIVES CANADA CATALOGUING IN PUBLICATION

Title: The Shopify story : how a startup rocketed to e-commerce giant by empowering millions of entrepreneurs / Larry MacDonald.

Names: MacDonald, Larry, author.

Identifiers: Canadiana (print) 20240358678 | Canadiana (ebook) 20240361334

ISBN 978-1-77041-749-6 (softcover)
ISBN 978-1-77852-296-3 (ePub)
ISBN 978-1-77852-299-4 (PDF)

Subjects: LCSH: Shopify Inc.—History. | LCSH: Lütke, Tobias. | LCSH: Electronic commerce—Canada.

Classification: LCC HF5548.325.C3 M33 2024 | DDC 381/.14206571—dc23

This book is funded in part by the Government of Canada. *Ce livre est financé en partie par le gouvernement du Canada.* We also acknowledge the support of the Government of Ontario through the Ontario Book Publishing Tax Credit, and through Ontario Creates.

PRINTED AND BOUND IN CANADA

PRINTING: MARQUIS 5 4 3 2 1

Contents

Introduction vii

1 At the Epicenter: Tobias Lütke 1
2 Prelude to the Launch 9
3 Lift-Off! 17
4 Turbulence and Tailspin 25
5 The Turnaround 33
6 The Boost from Venture Capital 48
7 Shopify Gathers Speed 61
8 The Shopify Environment 75
9 Empowering Entrepreneurs 90
10 Retail Operating System I 96
11 CEO of the Year 105
12 Listing on the Stock Market 112
13 Retail Operating System II 122
14 The Heroism of the Engineers 133
15 Escape Velocity 143
16 Entering the Big Leagues 154
17 COVID-19 at Warp Speed 161
18 Thriving on Change 170
19 Staying Alive 183
20 Rebooting the Engine 193

Epilogue: Wrapping Up 204
Acknowledgements 215
Notes 217
Index 257

May 21, 2015: Shopify executives ringing the NYSE Bell on their IPO Day. First row, left to right: Craig Miller, Joe Frasca, Harley Finkelstein, Tobi Lütke, Russell Jones, Cody Fauser and ——. Back row, left to right: Jean Michel Lemieux, ——, ——, Toby Shannan, Daniel Weinand and Brittany Forsyth.

Introduction

After launching in June of 2006 a software platform that enabled entrepreneurs to easily set up and run online stores, Shopify Inc. turned a profit for the first time during the financial crisis and recession of 2008 and 2009. This was rather remarkable: the bankruptcies of U.S. financial institutions were pushing the global financial system to the brink of collapse and most companies were spiralling downward during a sharp recession — yet Shopify was thriving.

Shopify's spurt of growth, along with financing from venture capitalists and some smart moves by Chief Executive Officer (CEO) Tobias Lütke, led to a period of rocket-like growth up to the Initial Public Offering (IPO) in 2015. The upsweep after the IPO was also breathtaking: Shopify's annual revenues shot upwards from 2015 at an annual rate of 60% to reach $5.6 billion in 2022, beating the consensus forecasts of brokerage analysts for 24 consecutive quarters.[1] (Shopify keeps its accounts in U.S. dollars; all dollar figures in this book are in U.S. currency unless otherwise stated.)

Shopify, then headquartered in Canada's capital of Ottawa, increasingly was viewed as a technology powerhouse, well on its way to joining the ranks of past Canadian tech champions, notably Nortel Networks and BlackBerry. Among other honours, Lütke was named Canadian CEO of the Year by the *Globe and Mail* in 2014, voted Entrepreneur of the Year by the Canadian Venture Capital Association in 2016 and presented with the Meritorious Service Cross by the Governor General of Canada in 2018. Shopify was named Canada's Smartest Company by *Profit* magazine in 2012, a finalist for Startup of the Year at the Canadian

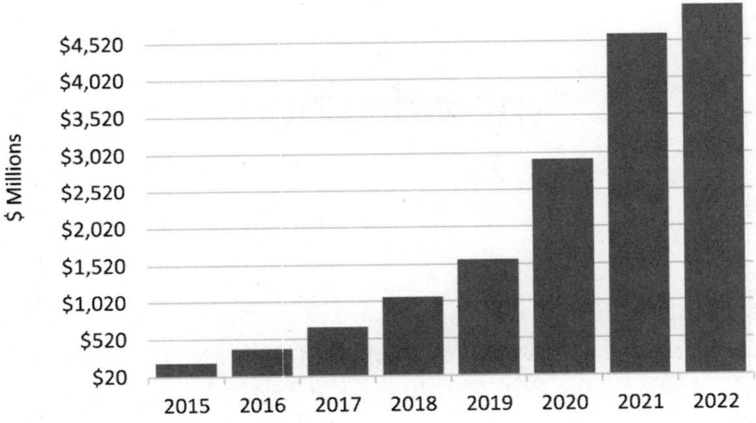

Data source: Shopify *Annual Reports*

Startup Awards of 2012, Employer of the Year at the Canadian Startup Awards of 2014 and one of Canada's Most Innovative Companies by *Canadian Business* in 2015.

Shopify's swift expansion stirred excitement among institutional investors, mutual fund managers, stockbrokers and individual investors. They bid up the price of its stock listed on both Canadian and U.S. stock markets — so much so that by early 2020, Shopify was the most valuable company on the Toronto Stock Exchange — surpassing leader Royal Bank of Canada, a financial institution with a workforce of 85,000 and 150-year history.

As the COVID-19 virus raged throughout 2020 and 2021, the world hunkered down at home. Again, when calamity struck, Shopify flourished. In-person shopping shifted to online shopping and Shopify's growth went ballistic. Investors kept scooping up shares: from the IPO in 2015 to the high in November 2021, the stock price increased by more than 5,000%.

By 2021, there were over two million stores on Shopify's platform, according to Shopify's 2021 *Annual Report*. Over half of the stores were

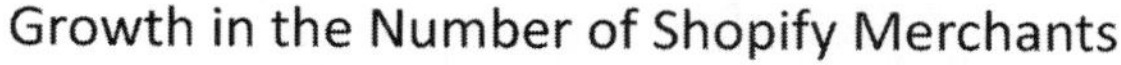

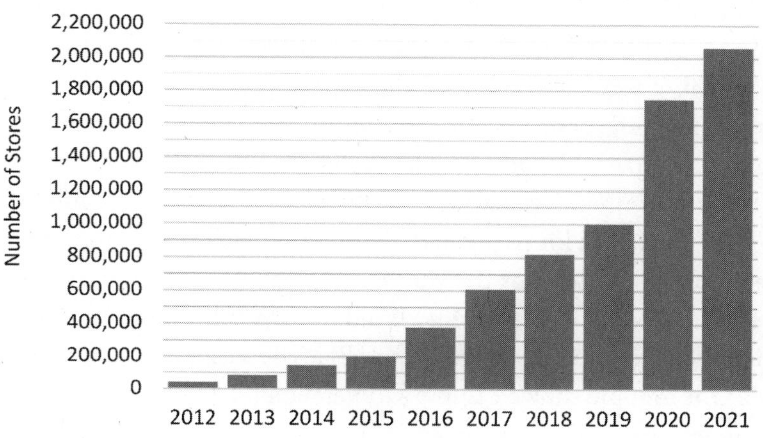

Data source: Shopify *Annual Reports*

launched in the United States. A high percentage of the launches were also in the United Kingdom (7.6%), Canada (5.7%) and Australia (5.1%).

In the beginning, mainly small and medium companies subscribed to Shopify, but as the years went by, larger companies increasingly signed up. The small, medium and large companies on the platform sold their products in more than 175 countries around the world, distributed as follows: North America (55%), Europe, Middle East and Africa (25%), Asia Pacific, Australia and China (15%) and Latin America (5%). According to a Deloitte study, Shopify merchants supported five million jobs in 2021, which represented the largest workforce in the world.[2]

Despite dramatic growth in its revenues, Shopify earned a profit in only a few quarters after going public in 2015. Investors did not mind. They were on board with the view that when it came to commercializing new technologies, companies needed to emphasize growth over earnings. There were so many expansion opportunities in which Shopify could invest; if they were not quickly seized, competitors would grab them and gain market share for themselves. As one Shopify executive explained: "We're trying to leave as little oxygen in the atmosphere for anyone else and trying to capture as much growth for ourselves as possible."[3]

When COVID-19 eased in 2022, consumers returned to in-person shopping and e-commerce fell back to its long-term trend, moderating Shopify's torrid growth pace during the pandemic. Making things more challenging, pent-up demand and supply-chain bottlenecks caused inflation to spike and central banks to sharply hike interest rates.

The stratospheric valuations of technology companies imploded; Shopify's stock was hit particularly hard, tumbling by 75% from its high in late 2021 to the lows of the summer of 2022. Coverage of Shopify in the media became less flattering. Pundits raised the spectre of another Canadian tech star succumbing to the BlackBerry and Nortel Networks curse. One graphic showed Lütke submerged up to his glasses in a sea of green goo, apparently drowning.[4]

Canada seemed to be engaging once again in what author Robertson Davies called its "tall poppy syndrome," that is, the inclination to cut down whatever rises above the crowd. In response to the media coverage, Lütke said on X (formerly Twitter): "We have to get rid of our tall poppy syndrome if we hope to ever become a country where the best and brightest come to build."[5]

People tend to conflate the performance of a company with its stock price but the ups and downs on the stock market are also affected by the mood of investors. Despite the tumble in its shares, Shopify itself continued to perform reasonably well, considering the macro environment. Monthly recurring revenue from subscriptions rose by 7.3% during 2022 to $109.5 million; the value of merchant sales rose by 12.5% to $197.2 billion.[6]

If Lütke is successful in his goal to create a 100-year-old company, more long-term growth lies ahead for Shopify. What fascinates him is the long game of building an enterprise that is an improvement on the versions that exist today.

There does seem to be a tailwind in Lütke's favour, at least for much of the current decade. According to eMarketer, world e-commerce is projected to continue growing by more than 10% annually to reach $8 trillion in 2026.[7] The growth potential in North America particularly appears significant: in 2022, e-commerce was little more than 15% of total retail sales in the United States[8] whereas e-commerce's share of total retail sales in China was more than double the U.S. percentage.[9]

In the fall of 2024, Shopify will have been in existence for two decades since it was first incorporated. Whatever the future holds, there is a story to tell about Shopify's past stellar growth. As such, this is a corporate history about the people involved and the milestones along the way. It is also an account of the factors behind the growth, and what lessons and insights may exist for business managers, employees, programmers, policymakers and investors. Entrepreneurs may also find lessons, insights and inspiration because the story of Shopify is about starting and growing businesses.

We may ask, how did Lütke, who had started out as a junior programmer, take the reins at Shopify in his mid-20s and lead the company to such meteoric growth? Was it skill or luck, or a mix of both? Does his example dispel the notion that MBA graduates are needed to scale startups? Is there a formula, or at least some nifty moves, for replicating such an outcome?

Not to be overlooked is the executive team that assisted Lütke. They and Lütke not only accomplished something amazing but made billionaires and multimillionaires of themselves, thanks to their holdings of Shopify shares and options received as part of employee remuneration. How did they find a seat on the rocket ship and then steer its flight?

There is also the question of how Shopify might fare going forward. We can't predict with certainty from Shopify's first two decades if it will see the next century as Lütke envisions. However, there could be some heuristics that give us hints of what may happen over the remainder of the 2020s, and perhaps beyond.

At the Epicenter: Tobias Lütke

It has been said that the brains behind Shopify is Tobias Lütke. He was there right from the start, as the Chief Technology Officer for the first two years and thereafter as the CEO, using his vision, unique management style and product expertise to guide the company through the tricky shoals of technological innovation and industry competition.

AN UNPROMISING START

Lütke's youth gave few hints of the heights to which he would rise. Born in 1981 and raised in Koblenz, Germany, he was a poor student just scraping by with minimal effort. When he was diagnosed with a learning disability, his dad, an internist, and his mom, a teacher, allowed him to be medicated for a time. After Grade 10, Lütke left high school.

His disinterest in school might have had something to do with computers. When he was six, his parents gave Lütke an Amstrad CPC (sold under the Schneider brand in Germany). Soon after he received it, his parents took a photo of him sitting at the personal computer with a chess game on the screen. But he particularly liked the Pac-Man and Space Invaders games.[1] As he got older, Lütke discovered that a computer magazine printed the coding for basic video games; he typed them into his computer and played them.[2] As he approached his teens, he began altering the code to change how the games played. He later learned that this was an activity called programming.

"My parents couldn't ground me as punishment for bad behaviour — I was all too happy to spend time in my room on my computer," Lütke posted on November 18, 2018, on X. Indeed, there were times spent confined to his room. He recalled one instance in the early 1990s: "I was grounded for weeks after my parents got the phone bill for me downloading the *Doom* shareware [computer game] from an American [Bulletin Board Service] over a dial-up modem."[3]

Another fun thing for Lütke while growing up in pre-Internet Germany was the Demoscene. This was a collection of festivals and competitions where people brought their computers to a large auditorium and created computer art. Also cool were the LAN parties in the 1990s, where techies would meet up and plug their PCs into a local area network (LAN) to participate in multiplayer computer games. After the latency problem on the Internet was solved in the mid-1990s, he played games online. He was good enough to become a competitive gamer and win a tournament or two.

THE APPRENTICE

At the age of 16, Lütke enrolled in Germany's national apprenticeship program to train as a programmer at a subsidiary of the industrial conglomerate Siemens. Apprenticeship programs in Germany are different from apprenticeships and co-op work in North America. They have more on-the-job training, with one day of the week reserved for classes at a vocational school. Certification is obtained by passing an exam at the end of a two- or three-year period.

As an apprentice, Lütke discovered he did not have dyslexia or ADHD in the clinical sense. "I was simply a kinesthetic learner," he wrote in his blog. "I could not understand or come up with solutions to problems I have never had. At my vocational school, I knew the problems we were solving. I had been in those situations. It was great! My self-esteem and confidence improved quickly."[1]

Lütke became not only an accomplished programmer but also an advocate for apprenticeship programs later in his life. He believed they gave him a head start compared to youths who go straight into college or university after high school. The latter end up with knowledge that is more theoretical, and their work experience does not really start until their 20s — much later than Lütke started working. As he wrote in his blog: "In Germany, leaving high school for an apprenticeship is not out of the ordinary . . . it is likely one of the main reasons for Germany's success. . . . Countries struggling with high dropout rates and lackluster job creation would be wise to give their students a similar choice."[2]

A major influence during his apprenticeship years was his supervisor and mentor, Jürgen Starr, a 50-something middle-level manager with a ponytail, leather jacket and a loud BMW motorcycle that he rode to work looking more like a member of a motorcycle gang than an employee of Siemens. A nonconformist through and through, he was in charge of "skunk works," the projects not necessarily approved by management but allowed to continue because of the creativity unleashed and potential for disrupting existing technologies.

Starr was a blunt speaker who pulled no punches. One thing he did especially well was "calling people out on bad ideas in plain language," Lütke said. Starr was nonetheless respected at Siemens because he knew his stuff and was usually right about things. Some of Lütke's management style originated from Starr: "Jürgen created an environment in which it was not only possible but easy to move through 10 years of career development every year," Lütke blogged. "It is a method and an environment which I am fiercely trying to replicate at Shopify."[3]

Often, when Lütke arrived at work in the mornings at Siemens, he would find on his desk a printout of the code he wrote the day before, covered with Starr's red marks correcting errors and omissions. This taught Lütke not to let his ego get in the way of learning and personal growth. He learned that getting feedback was a gift — not a putdown. Relatedly, Lütke came to believe the best work environment was one where everyone felt free to speak openly about what they and others were doing well or not well. Get to the root of issues and find solutions fast, then move on to other matters. For technology-focused companies, it's important to keep growing and adapting quickly, or obsolescence may be their fate.

Starr also tried to push people out of their comfort zones to learn new skills: Lütke was very comfortable with just working at a computer. To expand his horizons, Starr scheduled Lütke to go on trips with him to install software tools for clients. Then, just before the meeting, Starr would say he had another appointment and Lütke had to meet the client on his own. The adolescent Lütke initially felt overwhelmed — but he nevertheless went to see the client and when it somehow turned out well, came away not only relieved but with a sense of accomplishment. After a few more experiences like this, the uncomfortableness was replaced by a newfound confidence and the satisfying feeling of expanding his horizons.

"Everyone loves feeling comfortable," Lütke once said of the experience. "But it's actually completely useless. It's during that period of discomfort that intense learning and growth happen." This experience was to shape his view of the role that a CEO should play. As he told Trevor Cole in a November 27, 2014, *Globe and Mail* article: "So what I'm trying to create is an environment where almost everyone around me feels uncomfortable all the time, because I'm dragging them to the next box [level of performance]."[4]

ENTERING THE WORKFORCE

When Lütke finished his apprenticeship, he entered the workforce as a programmer. In a 2013 interview with Jason Calacanis, host of *This Week in Startups*, he disclosed that when he was working at Siemens, his work as a coder came under question. "I got one of those letters from them saying your performance isn't up to par and I was terribly shocked by that because I thought of myself as a really good programmer."[1] Then he realized that maybe Siemens had a point because he was playing computer games at night instead of getting enough sleep.

It also appears Lütke may have worked early in his career as a programmer in the adult entertainment industry. In 2012, a discussion arose in the *Hacker News* forum about working as a coder for the porn industry — there was a concern that it would be difficult afterward to get hired elsewhere. Posting on March 24, 2012, under the "xal" handle that he uses on *Hacker News* and Reddit discussion boards,[2] Lütke advised readers not to worry about getting a job afterward. How did he know? As he wrote in the post: "I worked in Porn early in my career and made the transition. I also actively try [as CEO of Shopify] to recruit people with this background."[3]

So much screen time during his youth had left its mark: after marrying in his 20s, his wife was to playfully describe him to a reporter as "an immigrant to the human condition."[4] His conversation was often at an intellectual level that some would need to pause and reflect on. For example, in the early years of Shopify, a fellow executive reported that some days they went to the pub together after work because, as Lütke said: "I like to meet people in their most idiomatic-appropriate location."[5] *Bloomberg News* editor Brad Stone remarked in 2021 that when he interviewed Lütke, the Shopify founder made statements such as: "I know how to exoskeleton my time," and "I fundamentally find nondeterminism more interesting than determinism."[6] *Cerebral* is certainly a word that has been applied to Lütke.

Some people thought Lütke was a genius. Lew Cirne, a founder and senior executive at software firm New Relic Inc., had dealings with Lütke and came away impressed: "It was clear to me the guy was a genius." What also made an impression was his humility: "That level of brilliance often comes with arrogance," Cirne added, "but Tobi never tried to make it about him being smarter than anyone else in the conversation."[7]

Standing five-foot-10 inches and wearing glasses, Lütke's physical stature was described by a journalist in 2014 as "slender, almost elfin in aspect." He wore a "newsboy" cap over a head of thinning hair during his 30s, before switching to a shaven-head look in his early forties. Perhaps the most distinguishing feature of Lütke's appearance was his steel-blue eyes, or "vivid-blue eyes," as one journalist described them. Depending on the lighting and setting, they could have an arresting quality.

"I've never set out to become rich," Lütke said in a December 2019 interview for Dan Martell's *Escape Velocity Show*. "I have very cheap hobbies. As long as I have a gaming PC . . . and a good laptop to do my work on, that's all I really need."[8] While he could be happy with just a laptop, that didn't mean his lifestyle was completely ascetic. For example, he learned to play the guitar during Shopify's early years and afterward raced cars at the Calabogie Motorsports Park near Ottawa or the Canadian Tire Motorsport Park near Toronto.

But computer games remained an enjoyable pastime. After the busy startup years of Shopify, he had more time for the occasional indulgence — and was even seen in 2019 on twitch.tv, a website that streams live video games. Gaming has certainly meant a lot to him. But it's not just a fun way to spend time. He also gives gaming credit for enabling him to become a successful CEO. Let's examine this interesting thesis. Could there be some plausibility to it?

GAMING AS PREPARATION

Preparing to become a CEO by playing computer games is not something usually found on the syllabus at business schools. Yet Lütke credits his youthful preoccupation with computer games, especially *StarCraft*, for a great deal of his success as a corporate executive: "I firmly believe that I learned more about building businesses from playing *StarCraft* than I've learned from business books," he wrote on X in April 2018.[1]

StarCraft is a futuristic sci-fi strategy game about two alien species and a wayward colony of earthlings residing in a remote part of the Milky Way, where they collect, combine and deploy resources to build up their economies and armed forces to compete for survival against each other. It requires managing many different inputs with imperfect information; the game is fast-paced, such that players win or lose depending on how they allocate their attention. Their focus is a limited resource that needs to be managed wisely to gain an information edge.

In addition, many of the resource-management decisions in the game are balancing acts between competing priorities, for example, current versus future needs, macro versus micro requirements, defence versus offence and so on — all performed within a constantly evolving environment wherein execution can result in imperfect outcomes. In short, *StarCraft* in many ways was like a simulation of the role played by senior executives managing an enterprise, he argued. As CEO of Shopify, he said:

> When you just watch the game, it looks like you make decisions between extracting resources, investing in expansion . . . that alone is a lesson that I think *StarCraft* players are already better at than a lot of people who end up getting MBAs. Both give you the same kind of decision matrix, except in an MBA it's through business case analysis. You just get a more intuitive feel for this through video games.[2]

As Lütke and others believed, executive skills could be learned from computer games — because of a phenomenon called transfer learning. The book *The Talent Code*, by Daniel Coyle, talks about this.[3] A classic illustration of how transfer learning works is provided by Brazilian soccer players, said to be the best in the world. As children, they played pickup games in smaller spaces with fewer players, and this gave them more touches on the ball than players on regulation-size pitches in Europe and around the world.

In real life, strategic corporate decisions on what direction to pursue and where to allocate company resources are not made with great frequency. But in an evening of *StarCraft*, poker, chess or bridge, these kinds of decisions can be practised by the bushel. The games are a way to have fun yet also to program the brain so it is prepared for those critical moments in sports or business when a player or company needs to make choices that will decide the outcome.

Not surprisingly, Lütke has taken flack for his pro-gaming views. He countered with: "Parents get upset about my [post on X in favour of] *StarCraft*. But think about it this way. Would you be upset if your kids were playing chess all the time? If I had [posted] about that, would you be vilifying me? What's the difference here?"[4]

Scientific studies published in peer-reviewed journals have found that not all computer games are a waste of time or harmful; in fact, many develop creativity and other useful traits. A paper entitled "Real-Time Strategy Game Training: Emergence of a Cognitive Flexibility Trait," published on August 2013 in the *PLOS ONE* journal, found that playing *StarCraft* and complex real-time strategy games can help improve brain agility and multitasking. "Our paper shows that cognitive flexibility, a cornerstone of human intelligence, is not a static trait but can be trained and improved using fun learning tools like gaming," noted Dr. Brian Glass, of the School of Biological and Chemical Sciences at Queen Mary University of London.[5]

True, there are a number of violent computer games that may justifiably be deemed objectionable, but there are also many games besides *StarCraft* that can have a positive impact — for example, *Minecraft* (building structures). Another is *Factorio*, in which an engineer marooned on an alien planet survives by gathering resources to create tools, machines, technologies and factories to build a vessel for returning home. Lütke has played this strategy game with his children for the lessons it teaches in resource management and building logistics networks. It's also one of the games that Shopify staff can expense; Lütke feels its similarity to the challenges facing the company makes the game useful for practising problem-solving skills capable of dealing with Shopify's real-world issues.

Gaming was indeed very important for Lütke. In fact, it not only filled his youthful leisure hours and laid the foundation for becoming CEO, but also brought Lütke the love of his life.

Prelude to the Launch

Fiona McKean was to play an important role in the Shopify story. It is probably even fair to say that Shopify likely would not have happened without her.

ENTER FIONA MCKEAN

The daughter of Canadian diplomats, McKean had grown up in Ottawa and several countries around the world. She met Lütke in the online fantasy game *Asheron's Call*, playing from Ottawa while he played from Germany.[1] Separated by six time zones, Lütke stayed up late at night to play. They chatted and went on quests together, their avatars fighting virtual monsters on journeys within the multiplayer game. In the real world of continents separated by the Atlantic Ocean, the vibes between the two were good.

Lütke flew to Canada for a winter holiday and to meet McKean at the Whistler ski resort in British Columbia. She was about the same height and age as Lütke, wore horn-rimmed glasses and had her blonde hair cut short. Personality-wise, McKean was "50% Geek, 50% Nerd," as she described in her bio on X. Lütke was smitten.

Alas, vacation time was over and he had to fly back to Germany; McKean had to study for her undergraduate courses in history and English literature at the University of Ottawa. After departing, they maintained a long-distance relationship online. But parting was such sweet sorrow that when McKean completed her bachelor's degree, she went to Germany to work and be with Lütke for nearly a year.

In 2002, she returned to Ottawa to study for a master's degree at the Norman Paterson School of International Affairs, a top training ground for people seeking careers in the foreign affairs department of the Canadian government. Lütke followed her to Ottawa, intending to support himself as a remote worker for a German company. "It was cool that I was still being paid by a German company even after I moved to Canada," he told the Mixergy podcast.[2]

When McKean was working on her master's degree, Lütke's assignment with the German company dried up. Not that he minded. The software tools were uninspiring and the coding was "the driest of the dry kind of stuff." In fact, he was feeling burned out. Yet, he wanted to stay with McKean. He could not get a job in Canada because he didn't have a work visa, but there was no law against starting a business. He was mulling over becoming an entrepreneur, and perhaps it was taking too long because McKean told him: "Look, I'm super busy because I'm finishing this degree. You should find something that makes you super busy. We don't have kids; we don't have a lot of costs. Now's the time to jump. So I'll jump with you."[3]

Lütke thus became an entrepreneur. The McKeans' dinner table was where it began. There, he met Scott Lake, a friend of the family. Lake was 12 years older, athletic and a venture capitalist who made friends easily. They shared a common interest: snowboarding. This led to trips to the ski hills and a plan to sell snowboards online. Lütke had just bought a snowboard for himself after doing some in-depth research, so he felt he could leverage his product knowledge to sell snowboards on a website. Lake could take care of the business side of the store, to be called Snowdevil (a snow devil is a vortex of swirling snow created by wind gusts).[4] The company was incorporated on September 28, 2004, under the name 4261607 Canada Ltd.

"At the beginning, there was no grand plan," Lake said. "We just said let's do e-commerce, let's sell some snowboards."[5] Lütke was going to set up the Snowdevil website using "off-the-shelf" software packages such as Miva, OsCommerce and Yahoo! Stores. He did not want to code a website from scratch because he was still burned out from programming and did not want it as a job, only as a hobby. He would be happy if he could just become a retailer and turn his passion for snowboarding into a source of income.

E-COMMERCE BEFORE SHOPIFY

Selling goods and services online was not all that new in 2004 when Lake and Lütke decided to set up Snowdevil. In fact, there had been many instances of e-commerce going back to the 1970s.

According to John Markoff's book *What the Dormouse Said: How the Sixties Counterculture Shaped the Personal Computer Industry*, the "seminal act of e-commerce" occurred on the ARPANET, a precursor to the Internet created in the 1960s by linking mainframe computers together. The network was to be used for failsafe communications in the event of nuclear war, and for sharing research between universities and government agencies. In 1972, some graduate students had other ideas and used it to arrange a cannabis transaction.

The first iteration of electronic shopping is said to have arrived in 1979, when a 72-year-old, white-haired U.K. resident, Mrs. Jane Snowball, pointed her remote control at a menu on the TV screen to order margarine, cornflakes and eggs. Michael Aldrich, an IT professional, made it possible by adding a microprocessor to a TV connected by a telephone line to a store's computer.[1]

In 1984, CompuServe's Electronic Mall was launched as a text-only online marketplace. Users pressed numbers on their keyboard to navigate through product lists arrayed against a featureless background on the monitor screen. A 1986 ad on TV promised that purchases would be delivered within a week; the fresh lobster in the ad presumably qualified for one-day shipping.

In the early 1990s, two events opened the floodgates to e-commerce. First, Tim Berners-Lee invented the World Wide Web as a way to share and access information on the Internet via hypertext, websites, browsers and other features. Second, an advanced version of the ARPANET fully opened up its network of linked computers to commercial use.

A blog post on the Shopify website declared that e-commerce first appeared in its truest form on August 11, 1994, with the purchase of a compact disc of Sting music from online mall NetMarket.[2] As the *New York Times* reported, it was "the first retail transaction on the Internet using a readily available powerful data encryption software to guarantee privacy."[3]

Pizza Hut in California set up PizzaNet as an e-commerce trial in 1994. The first order was for a pepperoni pizza with mushrooms and cheese. The *Los Angeles Times* wondered if PizzaNet was a harbinger of the dystopian future depicted in the 1992 novel *Snow Crash* — wherein Americans excelled at two things: writing software and delivering pizzas in less than 30 minutes.

In 1995, before they founded startup accelerator Y Combinator, Robert Morris and Paul Graham created Viaweb, a software tool for building online stores. They built their own computers to save money but spent $16,000 a month on a PR firm to get press coverage. It was worth every penny.[4] In 1998, they sold Viaweb for $50 million to Yahoo!, which renamed it Yahoo! Stores.

Jeff Bezos launched Amazon in 1995, to sell books online. However, Charles Stack came before him and launched Books.com in 1994.[5] Amazon branched out over the ensuing years to selling "everything," becoming the dominant e-commerce marketplace in North America. Books.com was sold to NetMarket in 1996 and now redirects to Barnes & Noble.

Another e-commerce firm birthed in 1995 was AuctionWeb, later renamed eBay by founder Pierre Omidyar. Omidyar hired the same PR firm used by Morris and Graham. It was worth every penny for them, too: eBay became a leading U.S. e-commerce firm.

Many more e-commerce-related websites followed: 3dcart (1997), PayPal (1998), eBid (1998), Volusion (1999), Zappos (1999), Tradera (1999), and StubHub (2000). Enthusiasm for e-commerce waned during the dot-com bust from 2000 to 2002, but it revived afterward with Squarespace (2003), eCRATER (2004), Big Cartel (2005), Esty (2005), Amazon Prime (2005), Wix (2006), Bandcamp (2007), Magento (2008), WooCommerce (2008) and BigCommerce (2009).

Many other e-commerce websites could be mentioned, some of the more notable being the large retailers Walmart Online (2000), Costco Online (2001) and Wayfair (2008). The first large retailer to build a custom e-commerce site was Victoria's Secret in 1998; the upfront cost was more than $5 million.[6]

An e-commerce firm outside of North America deserves mention: Alibaba Group (1999), in China. By 2021, the total dollar value of sales on its two e-commerce marketplaces, Taobao and Tmall, were $711 billion and $673 billion, respectively, according to Digital Commerce 360.[7] E-commerce in China was more developed than in the United States by 2021: Amazon's total sales that year of $390 billion were much lower than Alibaba's.

THE SNOWDEVIL INITIATIVE

During his early years as an entrepreneur, Lütke did not collect a salary. He lived with McKean in her parents' home. The couple stayed for quite a long time. "It was 2014 before we moved out," Lütke told the *How I Built This* podcast.[1] He was very grateful for the support provided by McKean's parents: "I can't believe the amount of patience and trust they had in me, but somehow they let me do my thing."[2] McKean's parents were indeed special people; they too played a pivotal role in the Shopify story.

Entrepreneurship was not something foreign to Lütke. His grandmother Erika ran a printing business in Koblenz; as a kid, Lütke would visit her to help out and watch the Letterpress churn out printed pages. He also ran some of his own enterprises as a youth. To raise money to buy more computer equipment, he bought items in bulk at wholesale prices and resold them to schoolmates in smaller batches at retail prices. Quite popular were the Magic Eye books, whose images turn into 3D pictures when looked at with unfocused eyes. Also, during his apprenticeship, he and some friends started a company to create a software program that processed and managed customer issues at call centers (which didn't work out).

To get Snowdevil up and running, Lütke lugged his laptop to the Bridgehead coffee shop on Elgin Street. He commuted by skating down the Rideau Canal in the winter and biking or longboarding the rest of the year. The coffee shop had Wi-Fi that he accessed for free and fixed when it went down. Seated amidst the patrons sipping their lattes and cappuccinos, he tapped away on his laptop and explored several software packages for online stores, including Yahoo! Stores. They didn't fit the needs of a first-time entrepreneur very well. They seemed to be meant for established businesses and were over-featured for his requirements. Moreover, the packages weren't that easy to install or customize. He nonetheless cobbled a website together.

To promote the Snowdevil website, Lütke and Lake used Google AdWords. This involved bidding for search terms related to snowboards, such as the name of ski resorts. When people googled terms like "Whistler ski resort," an ad for Snowdevil could appear near the top of the search listings. Back in 2004 and 2005, not many people were bidding for Google AdWords, so Snowdevil loaded up on the ads and got some good results.

In its first year, Snowdevil sold about 40 snowboards and turned a modest profit. The first sale, to someone in Pennsylvania, came soon after the store opened. It was a magical moment, the kind Lütke will never forget. He remembers what he was wearing and where he was at the time — he was just beginning his workday in Bridgehead on a day in November of 2014 when there was a "ding" sound from his laptop and an email came in with the header: "New Order!" The impact was profound: it wasn't just a new order but his first ever.

"I realized, in that moment, that I had gone from someone who did something kind of interesting to actually being an entrepreneur," he explained.[3] How immensely satisfying it was to see what his digital construct had done — it caused a commercial transaction to occur between two distant, anonymous parties and brought some money into his register. That "ding" sound turned out to be a clarion call to his life's work.

But plugging gaps in the Snowdevil website and rendering improvements was still an uphill battle. "The final straw was when I got a custom design made for my snowboard store and I couldn't get it to work; Yahoo!

Stores barely allowed me to change the background colour of the top frame," Lütke told *Signal v. Noise*.[4]

As a wave of disgust was sweeping over him, he got a message from his friend Daniel Weinand in Germany about an open-source coding language called Ruby on Rails. It was devised by Danish programmer David Heinemeier Hansson, who at the time had a gig at the software development firm 37Signals. Ruby on Rails was so new that there was not even a 1.0 version; the only version available was passed around as an attachment to an email. Lütke downloaded it and fell in love.

Ruby on Rails had a syntax that looked more like English, which decreased the "cognitive load" and time required to complete jobs. It assisted with debugging programs by flagging typos and offering suggestions to fix them. It also simplified the creation of web applications with default structures for coding, databases and web pages. One could perhaps say the framework was like a box of Lego with pre-fitted blocks of code that could be connected together to build a web application without having to do everything piece by piece. Lütke liked it so much that he realized he was not burned out because of programming per se; the problem was with the constricting languages that he had to use in the companies he once worked for.

With his newfound enthusiasm, Lütke spent mostly rapturous hours learning Ruby on Rails, contributing to the open-source community and crafting the kind of online store he wanted for Snowdevil. A few months later, after a lot of pizza and late-night coding, Lütke jubilantly posted to the Rails community:

> At long last, it's done. Snowdevil launched on 31.1.2005 after close to 4 months of the most intense but also fulfilling programming of my life. . . . This is the time where small businesses can compete or outperform big businesses just because of better tools. . . . I can't even put into words how thrilled I am that the first milestone is done, and the groundwork is laid out. . . . We have very ambitious plans for the Snowdevil codebase and great technical challenges are yet to come. I can't wait![5]

Meanwhile, McKean was doing well for herself, too. She obtained her master's degree in international studies and became a deputy director in Global Affairs Canada, the foreign affairs branch of the federal government. McKean then left the government in 2015 and became the operator/co-owner of The Opinicon after performing extensive renovations to the 120-year-old lodge south of Ottawa.

3

Lift-Off!

After his jubilant post to the Rails community, Lütke vacationed for a week in the Dominican Republic with McKean. While enjoying the sun and sandy beaches, the couple did typical touristy stuff like whale watching and cigar rolling. The highlight, of course, was when Lütke also proposed marriage (the wedding took place in 2007).

On their return to Ottawa, Lütke turned his attention back to Snowdevil. It was presenting another challenge: snowboard sales were melting away with the warm temperatures of spring. To become a year-round operation, Lütke and Lake considered diversifying into skateboards and surfboards. Members of the Ruby on Rails community provided a better idea: several of them had expressed interest in having an online store of their own like Snowdevil, and this made the two entrepreneurs think there could be a commercial opportunity in licensing their software. There appeared to be a gap in the e-commerce market: many aspiring entrepreneurs and small business owners wanted to have a customizable, easy-to-build online store without having to learn coding or spend a lot of money hiring programmers.

THE LAUNCH OF SHOPIFY

With his love of programming restored, Lütke plunged into developing a software for building and hosting online stores. He ran tests to see what Ruby on Rails could do and designed a blog-hosting platform called Typo (one of the first Ruby on Rails applications). It became quite popular and at one point had over 10,000 installations.

Lake produced a name for the e-commerce platform that Lütke was developing. He called it Shopify, which was an amalgam of "Shop" + "Simplify." The domain name, shopify.com, was available and they grabbed it in April 2005. Shopify was originally just the name for the e-commerce software product under development. The company's actual name on founding was 4261607 Canada Ltd., which was changed under articles of amendment on January 19, 2006, to Jaded Pixel Technologies, as derived from an online name generator. Snowdevil and Shopify were to be the first two product lines under the Jaded Pixel banner. But Shopify was so successful that it claimed all of the executives' attention and left no time for Snowdevil. On November 30, 2011, with the snowboard line long abandoned and no others in sight, articles of amendment changed the company name to Shopify Inc. Most people might agree that Shopify had a better ring to it than Jaded Pixel; maybe human intelligence has a chance against artificial intelligence after all.

In the beginning, Shopify was bootstrapped with Lake's and Lütke's savings, modest profits from snowboard sales and seed money from family and friends. For the first half of 2005, Lütke worked on the Shopify software. In August of 2005, he posted more good news on the Ruby and Rails forum: "My buddy Daniel [Weinand] just arrived in Canada last week. He moved back from Germany with his girlfriend who happens to be from the Ottawa region too — how weird is that?"[1] Weinand was happy to help Lütke out by taking on the role of user-interface (UI) designer. In so doing, he became the third co-founder of Shopify.

UI designers perform an important function. Programmers labour hard on a feature and want to see it included in the product, but the feature may have flaws or limited utility or may degrade system performance. UI designers are needed to ride shotgun. They bring in people and observe them as they try out the latest version of the software. Another approach was to use usertesting.com, whereby a designer watches people online to see how they react while using the interface. Having Weinand's help with this task "was a massive luck event for us," Lütke disclosed. "He has made sure that the software stayed very easy to use."[2]

The first workspace for the three co-founders continued to be the Bridgehead coffee shop on Elgin Street, where Lütke had first settled in. Besides having high-speed connectivity, it also had electrical outlets at every table and customers were permitted to stay and work on their laptops if they bought something when they came in. It also looked like they had to keep fixing the Internet connection whenever it went down. "Heaven!!!" posted Lake in a Shopify blog during 2005.[3] In late 2005, Lake, Lütke and Weinand changed their workplace to the second floor above the coffee shop, after performing extensive renovations.

When the decision was taken to build the Shopify software, a release date for the fall of 2005 was set. However, the coding was all-consuming. Not only was there an e-commerce platform to develop but also open-source software to develop for use in support of Shopify's functions. The supporting software included: Opinion (forum software), Active Merchant (integrating payment gateways and shipping) and Liquid (a templating engine). As a result, the delivery date was pushed back several months. A casualty was Snowdevil: there was not enough time to deal with its trickier problems, particularly outsourcing fulfillment to the third-party logistics firms of the day.[4] The postponement became permanent as Shopify's growth ratcheted up and absorbed the co-founders' energies.

Yet, setting up and running the Snowdevil website the year before had not been a wasted effort. It informed Lütke about what was needed to create Shopify, what was important to include and what was not. "It is incredibly powerful if you solve the problem that you actually have yourself," Lütke told *Entrepreneur*'s Katherine Duncan. "It's really tough to develop a good product when you don't have very close proximity to the people who actually use your product. The closest proximity you can have to those people is to be that person."[5] Speaking years later to Sarah Niedoba in the August 2016 issue of *Canadian Business*, Lütke stated: "I can tell you what I would absolutely do again: I would still start by building a store myself and doing one year of just selling snowboards — paying attention to all the complications that come with that. I think there's nothing nearly as powerful in the world of business as having that experience."[6]

As he was going about his work on Shopify, Lütke posted updates to the Ruby on Rails forums and his blog on Typo. Weinand also posted updates to his online design communities. The buzz was building. The Typo blog-hosting system that Lütke built when Ruby on Rails first came out played a key role in attracting the initial customers. Each of Typo's 10,000 installations linked back to his blog, which gave it a high ranking in Google. Moreover, most of the Typo bloggers were from Ruby on Rails or other programming communities; as a group, techies tend to be in the vanguard of spreading awareness of new technologies to less technical groups, especially their family members and friends who often ask them for advice on computers.

"It was the biggest SEO [search engine optimization] scheme of all times, even though I didn't know it," Lütke told an interviewer in 2010. "My weblog got a lot of readers. Those readers were fantastic for launching Shopify later on because I already had an audience. . . . One of the biggest ways of helping launch our product in 2006 was having an audience that we built from the technology we used through Typo."[7]

In the months before the launch of Shopify, another valuable addition to the team arrived. Cody Fauser was a University of Alberta graduate with a bachelor of science in computer engineering, and well-versed in Ruby on Rails — good enough, in fact, to author several Rails manuals, such as *Rails 3 in a Nutshell: A Desktop Quick Reference*. He had come to Ottawa and was working at a job when he emailed Lütke for a chat. Fauser also loved snowboarding and shared a German heritage with Lütke, so it perhaps was not surprising that the commonality in backgrounds and interests led to Fauser joining Shopify.

A landing page was set up on the shopify.com domain. It invited visitors to leave their email addresses if they were interested in knowing when the site would be ready. A company logo, featuring a green shopping bag with a large white *S* on it, was also designed. There was one last promotional boost from a blurb on the Ruby on Rails homepage, and then a blast of emails went out to the several thousand people who had left their contact info on the landing page. A good number of them signed up to try out the Shopify website after it was launched on June 2, 2006.

With the launch, merchants could now set up an account and straight away build an online shop. It would take no more than two or three hours of mostly pointing and clicking with a mouse, without any call for skills in web development or programming languages. The package came with store templates that could be customized, order tracking in an RSS feed, inventory management and other functions such as image uploading and tagging.

This was something new and exciting for entrepreneurs. Carrie Bailey-Morey, owner of Callie's Charleston Biscuits, said: "Shopify helps my small business process an average of 100 orders per day with minimal effort thanks to the efficient billing and tracking system. I run my business on a part-time basis and I love that I can easily make changes to my Shopify website instead of relying on a third party."[8]

Website designers around this time also liked to put their customers into Shopify stores because of the "set it and forget it" aspect. Alternative offerings for building online stores required a lot of maintenance and updating after they were installed, which was a burden on website designers. "I love my clients, but the great thing about Shopify is that when the websites are designed and launched, I never hear from them again," remarked Jamie Sutton, who was working at Evolution Design in 2006 when he got his first Shopify customer. "It is that easy to use, and updates are handled seamlessly by the developers."[9]

FRESH FOUNDERS

Lütke discovered a great support group for entrepreneurs in 2006. Called Fresh Founders, it started that year as a place for young entrepreneurs in Ottawa to share struggles, insights and advice. A key organizer was Fluidware founder Aydin Mirzaee, a former Nortel Networks software engineer (trivia tidbit: his uncle was Lütke's dentist). Fresh Founders was a decidedly different atmosphere than the standard networking event populated by older entrepreneurs, and a bevy of lawyers, accountants and consultants dressed up in suits. It had more informal and conversational meetings, where the participants could learn things from each other, such as how to do marketing, raise money, hire staff and so on. In sharing their experiences, members often shed light on problems the others were wrestling with.

A large number of members went on to establish successful businesses. Sam Zaid's firm, Apption, was named by *Profit* magazine as one of Canada's fastest-growing companies; Luc Levesque sold his travel blog and platform to TripAdvisor and became a tech executive in Silicon Valley; Mirzaee's Fluidware startup was acquired by SurveyMonkey; and Paul Lem's Spartan Bioscience partnered with Canon to commercialize its DNA testing device. For Lütke, the exchange of ideas and social outings with like-minded individuals provided much-needed intellectual and emotional sustenance, grounding him further in the role of an entrepreneur.

Important connections were made, particularly with Harley Finkelstein, who was to later join Shopify and prove invaluable in developing the business side of the company. Another Fresh Founders member sold his firm to Shopify years later. And Levesque left his executive role at Facebook in 2020 to become Shopify's Chief Growth Officer. Lütke told the *Globe and Mail*'s Sean Silcoff in 2015: "I just loved it. There was something magical, it was hard to describe. Shopify wouldn't have happened without Fresh Founders."[1]

RAMPING UP

After the Shopify platform went live, the response was good. The workload grew and was partly crowdsourced: a call went out to users asking for help adding new features. One spot where this worked well was translating the checkout function into other languages. A lot of users were fluent in a second language and added a translation via a drop-down menu.

Still, the co-founders had to do much of the work themselves in the beginning. They handled customer support, marketing, programming, accounting and other functions. Lütke credited this hands-on stage with giving him the experience to screen for the best candidates. "Once you understand the job, it's so much easier to hire for it. Even after you hire for it, you have a much easier time actually talking with and engaging individuals who are doing the job, because you have a better common language with them."[1]

By 2007, about half a dozen people had been hired. Lake was serving as CEO, and Lütke was serving as Chief Technology Officer (CTO). Lake was a good person to have around at this point. As Lütke observed: "He was a massive help. . . . Group work is always like herding cats. You always need someone to sit down and say what are the things that are really important. That's the kind of thing Scott was good at."[2]

The second floor above the Bridgehead coffee shop was at first perfect for three people. Even for four or five. But with the ninth, it got a little crowded. "A day wasn't complete without blowing a fuse from using too much power, without pushing your chair back and knocking the person behind you over, or without having to make your phone calls in the hallway," blogged Shannon McKarney, then in charge of managing Shopify's affiliates. "We were bursting at the seams and definitely ready for a change."[3]

The Shopify team moved out in early 2008 to the second floor of a two-story building with about four times more space, stone walls on the inside and polished concrete floors. The location was on Rideau Street, a primary thoroughfare once lined with department stores built in the 1920s and 1930s under names like Freimans, Ogilvy's, Woolworth, Caplan's and Metropolitan. They had disappeared when the big department store chains moved into other parts of Ottawa in the 1960s and 1970s. Now, as Amazon, Shopify and other e-commerce firms expanded, many of these large stores were dealing with a similar fate.

The new location would need to be furnished. Both Lütke and Weinand agreed that it was important to design an office space that would bring out the best in staff. In 2008, Weinand was appointed Chief Design Officer (CDO) to lead this initiative. Being a musician, composer and photographer, in addition to his training in computer science, Weinand had a strong artistic streak and was in his element with this assignment.

There was not a particularly large budget at Shopify for designing office settings in 2008, which may have been just as well because the location on Rideau Street filled up quickly and fresh digs had to be found not long after settling in. The new spot was only a hop, skip and jump north to the second floor of Tucker's Marketplace on York Street. It was set up as an open-office concept with bright colours, warm lighting and computers perched on top of desks arrayed in rows across a polished hardwood floor.

There were two dozen staff at this location and four employees working remotely. More than 6,000 merchants were on the Shopify platform, registering annual sales of $100 million in 2009. Employees received up to 17 weeks of maternity/parental leave, full health and dental benefits, stock options, funding for travel to conferences and the latest Apple gear. Nearly everyone was in their 20s; there were daily stand-up meetings at Tucker's Marketplace to talk about what people were working on. On breaks or day's end, they switched to games like *Street Fighter IV*, *NHL Hockey*, *Guitar Hero II*, and "nuggeting" the interns (turning their backpacks inside out and placing the contents back inside). It was important for the team to have fun because it would be more conducive to creating great products, Lütke believed.

Turbulence and Tailspin

After Shopify launched, the customer base expanded and the workload increased. However, revenue growth remained sluggish. In fact, Shopify was nearly out of funds to meet payroll and a palpable fear of insolvency weighed on Lütke. He kept the matter to himself for a while so staff could stay focused on their projects while he worked on a solution. Team meetings continued to strategize on long-term projects even though there were only enough funds left for a few months.

SHOPIFY NEARLY GOES BANKRUPT

Lütke's father-in-law, Bruce McKean, was a compassionate person. As a young man just out of university, he spent two years in New Guinea volunteering with Cuso International, an organization dedicated to reducing global poverty. After working for the Canadian government, he held a position for several years as an adviser on sustainability and Indigenous issues; later he became involved in the field of mental health research. So, when his son-in-law was beset with financial woes, it was in his nature to help out; he loaned Shopify the money to keep it afloat for several more months in hopes a solution could be found.

It didn't take long. The problem was that the existing pricing model charged clients 2–3% of their monthly sales, which tended to attract small companies with little or no revenues — yet they created a workload that required hiring people. Few large companies joined because they usually needed more features than what Shopify then offered. A new pricing model was introduced and the recovery got started.

The new pricing schedule was a flat-fee subscription for each of the three tiers of service. For startups and small companies, there was a basic package at $29 per month; for firms with expanding and consistent sales, there was the regular package at $79 per month; for established firms with high volumes of sales, the advanced package at $299 per month would be of interest. With this change, revenues got a pulse. The monthly subscription fee gave small store owners more of an incentive to generate sales to cover the cost; for store owners with significant sales, it brought the cost down considerably.

Around this time, a Toronto-based angel investor in his 50s, John Phillips, showed up. Like the McKean family, Phillips played a big role in Shopify's success. He had previously worked as general counsel at wireless firm Clearnet Communications. After it was acquired by Telus in 2000, he became more focused on his family holding company, Klister Credit Corp., and invested some of his wealth in startups.

In the fall of 2007, Phillips had a meeting with an executive from a software company. The executive mentioned that while doing an online search, he had discovered a company called Shopify, which had an "elegant" website and was looking for funding. This mention, plus the fact Phillip's "parents were in Ottawa and he needed an excuse to go there to visit them," led to visiting Shopify.[1] He ended up investing $250,000 in Shopify and later recalled leaving his first meeting with Lütke "thoroughly impressed by his acuity, clear and deep thinking, and resolution."[2] He also liked that the software was already built and attracting revenues (after the pricing had been straightened out).

Lütke portrayed Phillips's investment as a stroke of good luck. It may well have had an element of good fortune, but it didn't come out of nowhere. In the early days, Shopify didn't have the resources or expertise for marketing its product, so Lütke's substitute strategy was to make the platform as good as possible: if a product was really good, it would generate its own advertising through word-of-mouth endorsements — as obviously was the case when Phillips got a tip from the software executive.

After receiving the investment, Lütke paid back the loan from his father-in-law and kept Shopify going. His father-in-law continued to help out by serving as Shopify's chairman from 2007 to 2010; his mother-in-law also lent a hand, doing payroll and accounting. Nonetheless, the brush with bankruptcy was a harrowing experience. Friends and relatives had invested in his startup, and they came close to losing their savings.

The experience had a deep impact on him, to the point where it was a difficult topic to talk about. When asked about it in 2010 during a Mixergy podcast, the normally candid Lütke uncharacteristically replied: "We won't go there."[3] Some gentle probing by the host did get Lütke to open up. Mixed feelings were evident. As he first said: "I would never do friends and family investment like this again." He just could not bear the thought of having them lose money on account of him. But he added that he was grateful for the experience because it made him very motivated to live up to the trust placed in him. "Making this the best investment of those people's lives is now my goal," he elaborated. "It definitely pushed me to work harder."[4]

CEO DEPARTS — LÜTKE STEPS IN

During this period, Lake decided to resign as CEO of Shopify (he remained on the board of directors until 2010). He missed being a venture capitalist and wanted to get back to helping new companies start up. Another reason, apparently, was that he wanted Shopify to raise some venture capital to transition to a growth company. However, Lütke at the time liked having a "lifestyle company" that stayed small and crafted great software, although there were times he seemed to be in favour of expansion. "I think Scott was frustrated by me changing my position so often," he said.[1]

When Lütke started at Shopify, he was happy to be the CTO. He was a programmer by trade and coding was his universe. He was okay with treating the rest of the business as a black box. The coding and technology side was what he was good at, and wanted to do. He just didn't feel comfortable taking on the CEO role himself, so a search was commenced for another person to replace Lake. "I just didn't want to become the pointy-haired boss in the Dilbert comic!" he was to exclaim during a 2019 podcast with *The 4-Hour Workweek* author, Tim Ferriss.[2]

He began interviewing prospective CEOs. His search led to a trip to see some Silicon Valley venture capitalists, who promised to line up some interviews with CEO candidates. Lütke also thought he could learn more about business by talking to the venture capitalists.

Obviously, there was the possibility of raising funds. But Lütke wasn't that excited about it, since he was still thinking of Shopify less as a growth company than as a small business. When it came to money, he seemed more concerned about keeping his expenditures low on his trip to California's Silicon Valley: he stayed overnight at a youth hostel and used a bike bought on Craigslist to get to appointments. Lütke was such a newbie that he had no pitch deck to present at the meetings with the venture capitalists. As described in the *Globe and Mail*:

> [Lütke] listened to their questions about Shopify's attrition rates and conversion rates and "funnel" (the various means by which a company attracts the attention, and secures the commitment, of new customers). . . . He had no idea what they were talking about, but he wrote down the terms. Then he went back to the hostel he was staying in and looked everything up on Wikipedia. He would read up on how to calculate contribution margin ratio (the amount by which sales exceed variable production costs), then go to Shopify's database to get the numbers. "Oh," he'd think, "that's an interesting way to look at the business." Then, at the next meeting, he was able to answer one more question.[3]

The venture capitalists presented him with some interviewees for the CEO job, but Lütke didn't hire any. The venture capitalists liked what they saw in Shopify and offered term sheets and capital injections. The trouble was that the offers were conditional on Shopify moving to California, which Lütke was not prepared to accept. For one thing, his wife and her parents had roots in Ottawa, and Lütke himself was more at home in Canada (which he felt was like a European version of the United States). He also thought Shopify could hire talent from the Canadian "Silicon Valleys" near Ottawa, Montreal and the Waterloo area. So there was no deal.

One of Phillips's first interventions helped solve the problem of finding a replacement for Lake. After several dead ends were reached, Phillips urged Lütke to take the CEO job himself, saying: "Tobi, you'll never find someone who is going to care as much about Shopify as you do."[4] The comment resonated with Lütke, and he decided that it was time to commit to stepping outside his comfort zone as a coder to become CEO. With Phillips providing support, it certainly was worth a shot. As well, Ruby on Rails expert Fauser was on hand to take over as CTO when Lütke vacated that role. In April of 2008, Lütke became CEO of Shopify.

"When I took over as CEO, I had to essentially get an MBA in a couple of weeks," he said.[5] Lütke asked some associates to recommend a few good business books. The most frequent suggestions were *High Output Management* by Andy Grove and *Influence: The Psychology of Persuasion* by Robert Cialdini. He read them and felt like he had hit paydirt. Years later they were still in the top 10 of his favourite business books.

What appealed about Grove's book was how the author, a former CEO of Intel, portrayed running a company like an engineering task. This made the process "less scary to me because engineering I understand," Lütke told Ferriss during a podcast.[6] It equated the business executive's task to being like a waiter (which Grove had been at university). A waiter has to constantly prioritize tasks on the fly — should he go greet customers arriving at the door, take an order at an occupied table or bring food to another group, and so on? The business executive's job, in essence, was to select, direct and closely monitor company resources. There were basically five performance indicators for executives to track: 1) expected sales (to tell how many staff are needed), 2) inventory levels (to make sure orders are filled), 3) equipment condition (make sure ovens, etc. are working), 4) workforce (find replacements for sick staff) and 5) quality (find out if customers liked their meal).

Cialdini's book presented six principles of persuasion and showed Lütke that people are flawed and can be influenced — including when it came to buying products and services. For example, the first principle was reciprocation: if you do a favour for someone without expecting a reward, they may feel more like returning the favour. Another was to cultivate relationships in order to have more influence.

Lütke also embraced the CEO role because he liked the idea of being his own boss. "The reason why I did it was because I thought it sounded amazing not having to answer to anyone," he told Ferriss. "I wanted to make my own technology decisions and these kinds of things. And I wanted to see what I could do. I wanted to challenge myself. So, I said, 'This is the right time in my life.'... I will learn a ton. There is no way this could be a failure on a personal level other than in the way that maybe people lose money."[7]

Still, the transition was not easy. Dealing with computers was neat and tidy. They do exactly what you tell them. And coding can be one of those flow activities where the hours just speed by, followed by the gratification of getting a program to work and deliver a result. Business, however, was chaotic and messy. The connection between effort and reward was not as clear-cut. Lütke had to spend days going to meetings and reading reports and not doing any programming. Initially, it felt like he wasn't doing anything productive. Only coding gave him a sense of accomplishing something back then.

It took many months to rewire his mindset to see that all the conferencing, monitoring and setting of goals was also a useful activity. Phillips lent a hand: he considered it his job to go into Lütke's office once in a while and get him to clear everything off his desk. Lütke needed to spend his time thinking big thoughts and looking ahead. The CEO shouldn't have any actual work to do. "He has [people] to do that," Phillips pointed out. "And if he meddles in it, he'll cause a problem."[8]

GLOBAL FINANCIAL CRISIS AND RECESSION

Because Lütke had been busy looking for a new CEO and familiarizing himself with the world of business, things were moving slowly at Shopify. He ran the business conservatively, on a cash basis, taking few risks. By his own admission, he was hampering the growth of the company. "The time I took speaking with mentors, reading, learning, that did constrict the growth of the business for a while," he told *Canadian Business* magazine.[1]

The years 2008 and 2009 were a difficult time in the world. Large tranches of subprime mortgages went into default and U.S. house prices crashed, pushing the global financial system to the brink of collapse with the failures of Lehman Brothers, Bear Stearns and other large financial institutions. The world economy and stock markets were also spiralling downward during the financial crisis. Lütke initially thought his company was toast.

But then something magical happened in the midst of all the gloom: subscriptions to Shopify took off. Companies looking for ways to cut costs during the economic meltdown found sweet deals by replacing their expensive e-commerce websites with Shopify's stores priced at a fraction of the cost. It also turned out that the people losing their jobs and sources of income thought they could get back on track by starting an online business.

Trisha Trout was one such case. Her family not only lost its sole source of steady income but her husband passed away just as the economy was collapsing. Trout had been a homemaker focused on raising her kids and had no real job experience, so it was doubly difficult for her to find a job during the recession. She and her two teenage sons had to sell their house and most of their possessions to pay off debts. Life insurance payments were coming in, but the five-plex apartment purchased by her husband before he died turned out to be a money pit that swallowed up a lot of it.

The only income she had earned during her marriage was a trickle coming in from a soap-making hobby. She had studied different aspects of the craft to become good enough to sell her soap at the local farmer's market. With the insurance money winding down, she returned to the farmer's market. It was gratifying to see her customers hadn't forgotten her. She also expanded to other local markets, and her son helped her set up an online store, Prairie Sage Soap. Her income picked up and several years later, Trout was happy to report:

> The best part of running my business is just the knowledge that I'm able to support myself. I'm not wealthy, but I make enough to enjoy life and help others here and there. . . . Having the focus of this business has been the thing that has kept me going through all the tears and lonely times. In many ways, this business has become my best friend and therapist all rolled into one. Having a small business requires focus, which is just what a grieving person needs to carry on.[2]

Meanwhile, as people opened up stores on Shopify, revenues poured into Shopify's coffers, cash flow gushed and profitability emerged. Phillips invested another $500,000 in 2009 and joined Shopify's board of directors in 2010. He liked Lütke's skill in reading people and getting the most out of them. "It is staggering how good he is with people," Phillips said. "He is absolutely heroic."[3]

In addition to the financing, Phillips played an important, behind-the-scenes role for many years as a mentor to Lütke during a critical time in his development as a business executive. Phillips had a great deal of business wisdom to pass on from his many years of experience, and as Lütke said: "He was there at many important parts of the Shopify journey and was full of good advice."[4] In another interview, Lütke again expressed his gratitude for the support Phillips provided: "Apart from allowing us to meet payroll for the first year, he has spent countless hours teaching me all the things I needed to know about running a company. Without him, we simply could not have survived the years and would not be around today."[5]

After the struggles and near bankruptcy of Shopify, the wave of new subscribers that rolled in during the financial and macroeconomic turmoil was most welcome. One of them was to become a major account: Tesla Motors (selling accessories). This upswing in fortunes was a huge morale booster. It proved to be the start of a multiyear expansion of epic dimensions.

5 The Turnaround

The dramatic improvement in Shopify's finances during the global financial and economic crisis of 2008 and 2009 brought a much-needed improvement in perspective at Shopify. Along with some astute moves by Lütke, Shopify's rebound in sales and earnings marked the beginning of its growth trajectory.

THE API AND OTHER ASTUTE MOVES

By 2008, Shopify executives were getting a weekly report summarizing customer feedback. Among other things, it contained many suggestions for adding new features. As the months ticked by, the list got longer and it was becoming apparent that Shopify didn't have the resources to build all of them into the platform within a reasonable time frame. Besides, many of the recommended features would not be useful to all of the merchants but of value only to some. And even if Shopify had enough resources, incorporating all the features could present users with an overwhelming range of choices and potentially degrade the uptime, speed and other performance metrics of the system.

The solution was to build an Application Programming Interface (API) that allowed third-party developers and designers to create apps and themes that could be plugged into the Shopify platform. Merchants could then click on and activate apps according to their individual needs. Completed by Lütke and Fauser in June of 2009, the company's news release nicely summed up the rationale for the API:

> E-commerce is a highly individualized business. Every store wants to offer a unique buying experience but providing too many features makes the software cumbersome and difficult to use. The Shopify API solves this by allowing merchants to install exactly the features they need to get the most out of their store.[1]

The API was a masterstroke that helped Shopify pull ahead of rivals. As experienced programmers, Lütke and Fauser were aware of the benefits of an API. The first wave of apps added by developers would enhance the value of Shopify's offering and attract more subscribers; this in turn would give third-party developers a larger market to sell into and an incentive to build more apps for Shopify. This second round of apps would add another layer of value that elicited more merchant subscriptions — and so on. Once this flywheel got going, it could keep feeding on itself and produce an upward spiral in growth.

However, offering an API did not automatically lead to a virtuous growth cycle. If a competitor already had a substantial customer base, developers would gravitate toward it and ignore companies with smaller client bases. But Shopify was one of the first companies to get started and it gave the flywheel several pushes by running contests, generously sharing revenues with partners, and letting them dialogue with merchants in Shopify forums about the apps they needed. An energetic go-getter was also hired to canvass developers.

The initial version of the Shopify App Store had a menu of about a dozen third-party apps, including PixelPrinter (simplified printing invoices), PowerReviews (enabled customer reviews), FetchApp (for selling digital goods), Mapify (gave the location of customers' purchases), and BaseSync (a tool for syncing a store's products to Google Merchant Center). By 2013, the total number of apps from all sources had risen to 100, climbed past 2,000 by 2018 and past 8,000 by 2021. They turned out to be a great way for merchants to customize their online stores, as highlighted by an increase in the average number of apps a merchant used, from one in 2013 to six in 2018.

Because Shopify was quite generous in sharing the revenues from installed apps with developers, its partner ecosystem ended up taking home far more revenues. For example, in 2021, the partners earned $32 billion, nearly seven times what Shopify earned. Lütke and his executive team were okay with this because as former Microsoft CEO Bill Gates said, it is a sign of a platform with staying power in the market — like the Windows operating system was in its heyday. Another e-commerce company could theoretically develop a better platform for online merchants but still not win the competitive battle because Shopify had so many more third-party utilities installed that its platform still had a greater total value.

Rivals such as Volusion, BigCommerce and Magento were also creating APIs and building partner ecosystems but "these have seen limited uptake," reported Bessemer Venture Partners in 2010.[2] Creating a platform was not easy to do because "you are leaving a lot of [income] that you could easily take for yourself on the table," Lütke told the *Masters of Scale* podcast. "You are investing it into your own future by giving it to other people. And that is very hard to do for most businesses."[3]

Another smart development was the launch in April 2010 of a new Shopify Theme Store. It showcased professionally designed templates so Shopify merchants could choose "a beautiful and unique look" for their online store. The templates were easy to install, customizable and quite affordable. "Where a custom-designed theme might cost in excess of $1,500, Shopify themes started at just $80 — a one-time cost with no ongoing monthly or annual fees," noted a Shopify press release.[4]

Setting prices in the theme store was a bit tricky. When designers were allowed to set any price they wanted for their products, Shopify found that competition within the group drove prices to rock-bottom levels — as a result, designers were exiting or providing low-quality storefronts. Lütke solved this problem by introducing floor prices, which brought about an improvement in quality and quantities.

In May 2010, a free mobile app, Shopify Mobile, was launched in the Apple App Store. Coming just as smartphones were taking off, it was a game-changer for Shopify, providing a new source of robust growth. Shopify Mobile was a game-changer for merchants too, allowing them to monitor their online store from remote locations. While away on errands and holidays, they could use their iOS mobile devices to check sales, shipments, inventory and other analytics. It was also easier for 9-to-5 workers to run a business as a side hustle — they could check in on their store while on a lunch break.

CROSSING THE CHASM

The Build a Business contest was launched in early 2010 and staged annually up to 2017. It was a big contributor to the company's success, attracting a lot of publicity and expanding the subscriber base by awarding lavish contest prizes and perks. When a Shopify executive was asked how important the contest was, he replied: "Are you familiar with the Geoffrey Moore book *Crossing the Chasm*? What the contest did was to allow us to cross the chasm from the early adopters in the Ruby on Rails crowd to mainstream users."[1]

The idea for the Build a Business competition originated in the back room of a Las Vegas hotel in 2009. It was there that Lütke met Ferriss. In the speaker's waiting room behind the presentation stage of a Ruby on Rails conference, Lütke told Ferriss that he loved everything about his *The 4-Hour Workweek* book except that Ferriss kept mentioning he was using Yahoo! Stores for his online food-supplement business. "You really should have used Shopify," Lütke boldly asserted.[2] The admonishment did not fall on deaf ears. Months before, when doing an edit for the revised edition of his book, Ferriss had polled more than 50,000 X users on what was the best e-commerce platform, and the most consistent answer was Shopify.

After the conference ended and the pair returned to their respective hometowns, they continued talking over their mobile phones. The two had a mutual interest and it turned into a collaboration. Ferriss was advocating in his books such lifestyle hacks as location-independent livelihoods, entrepreneurship and the outsourcing of routine tasks — things Shopify wanted to also facilitate. Lütke and Ferriss both agreed that it was time to spread awareness of Shopify and give people a nudge to overcome the inertia of starting a business. In return for his advisory services, Lütke agreed to give Ferriss shares in Shopify[3] (it was reported he sold in 2015 at a good profit but missed out on the stock's appreciation in the following years[4]).

In short, it was time to run a promotional campaign for Shopify. But how? Both men were competitive — Ferriss was once a world champion in tango dancing, and Lütke had won computer-game competitions — so it was perhaps not surprising that they came up with the idea to hold a competition as a way to raise Shopify's profile. The competition would reward whichever new entrepreneur could grow their business the fastest on Shopify within a certain period of time.

But what kind of prize would be offered? Both men remember when the light bulb went on. Lütke was lounging in a boat near his island cottage at a lake south of Ottawa, and Ferriss was pacing up and down a street in San Francisco, in front of a Thai restaurant he intended to enter for lunch. The conversation over their phones went like this:

"What if we give away a MacBook Pro notebook as a prize in the contest?" Lütke asked.

"That's too nerdy," replied Ferriss. "Not everyone is into notebooks like you, Tobi. If anyone is going to notice, you got to go big, like 100 times that in price."[5]

So they decided that Shopify would put up $100,000 as a grand prize to be won by whoever could grow their business the most on the Shopify platform during the first half of 2010. Another $20,000 in consolation awards would be handed out, for a total giveaway of $120,000. This was nearly all the funds Shopify had in the bank.

As one of the biggest grand prizes ever offered in a business competition, the $120,000 gained a lot of publicity for Shopify. Yet Lütke was still uneasy with the risk that draining the company's bank account could bring Shopify back to the brink of insolvency. Ferriss, on the other hand, was confident. Encouraged by his optimism, Lütke plowed on with the preparations.

The set-up task took months of legal and administrative wrangling to complete. One of the problems was the different legal frameworks for contests in various locations. The lawyers kept asking if Build a Business was a game of chance or skill — because the applicable laws and regulations in any district hinged on this important distinction. Lütke was uncertain what the reply should be, whether the contest was a game of chance or skill. "The intellectually honest answer is that it's chance," he told Ferriss. "You just cannot predict all the things that will happen. Sure, Shopify has been enormously successful but 99% of it was chance."[6]

Due to all the legal complications, Shopify ended up running the 2010 contest only in the United States. Just before it was announced on January 1, 2010, Ferriss published a glowing post about Shopify and the Build a Business contest on his widely followed blog, declaring "that Shopify offered the easiest-to-use, full-service platform in existence." He added: "From Pixar to Tesla, Pamela Anderson to Amnesty International, I saw slick design after slick design, all of which could be set up in minutes. . . . Tens of thousands of online stores have been created with Shopify. . . . I know a Fortune 500 employee who's quitting because his Shopify store makes more than $1,000,000 a year. Not bad for a side gig!"[7]

At the *New York Times*, where Ferriss's book had risen to the top of the bestseller list, an article appeared in early February of 2010 on Shopify's business competition. It was a big boost, too.[8]

The outsized prize money might have been a financial concern in the beginning for Lütke, but as it turned out, the $120,000 was not such a stretch after all. The sum was amply covered by the subscription fees the contestants paid over the six-month period. To break even, the contest needed to attract 600 new entrepreneurs to the Shopify platform; when it ended in June, the contest had attracted 1,300 new subscribers. The contest was a great success all around.

The winner in the first year was DODOcase. At the time, iPads were new products and DODOcase realized they needed cases — just like mobile phones had theirs. They arranged for bookbinders to make some attractive Moleskine-like cases; then they distributed fliers to people waiting in line at Apple Stores to get new iPads. They also promoted their products with pictures of famous people, like President Obama, holding iPads with DODOcase covers on them.

After 2010, the Build a Business contest ran annually until 2017. It was opened to entrepreneurs from Canada, Australia, the U.K. and other countries. Besides richer monetary prizes, winners got mentoring sessions over dinners or at resorts with gurus such as Ferriss, Seth Godin, Mark Cuban, Gary Vaynerchuk and Arianna Huffington. Toward the later years of the contest, winners were treated to lavish visits with celebrity entrepreneurs — for example, a week with Richard Branson at his private island in the British Virgin Islands or a week with Tony Robbins in a resort on the Fiji Islands.

A DIVERSE TEAM

Another key intervention by Phillips came in 2010. Noticing the executive team was made up of individuals with similar backgrounds (Lütke, Weinand and Fauser), he urged Lütke to hire executives with more diverse qualifications to generate a variety of viewpoints that would help with decision-making and growth. This suggestion struck a chord with Lütke: "I made one change based on one comment by John, and it massively impacted the company."[1] Lütke hired three new executives in 2010, two in 2011 and one in 2014. Who were these new executives and what was their path to seats on the rocket ship?

Brittany Forsyth

Brittany Forsyth was the first to be hired in 2010, as employee number 22. Originally, her job was office manager. For her, it was supposed to be temporary. She wanted to get her foot in the door and then volunteer for human resource (HR) functions at Shopify to add work experience to her college training so she could be hired at a major corporation. It never occurred to her that the tiny company she was using as a stepping stone would grow to be so big that it would give her the career that she sought in HR. She ended up working at Shopify for the next 11 years, as Head of HR and Chief Talent Officer.

"When I joined in 2010, I remember telling Tobi I wanted to do HR," Forsyth told Unicorn Labs in a 2022 interview.[2] She remembered that his response was to ask: "What is HR . . . heart rate?" Forsyth explained

HR meant human resources and described what the functions were. She began doing "HR stuff" after office hours for free and later ended up heading the HR department.

In her youth, Forsyth always had a tight group of friends that "would move forward together." With her cheerful personality, she often found herself leading the group, and when she took jobs afterward, she usually started at the entry level and rose to supervisory positions. At Diabetes Canada, she started on the phones calling for donations and then became the supervisor for the shift and, in turn, manager. She also worked at a bar as a hostess, then rose to be a bartender, followed by manager. "I always went in with extreme curiosity, a drive to do more and just a high level of respect and care for the people around me," she told Unicorn Labs. "And I think those things kind of allowed me to lead." But the first step "was just leading myself," she added. "It was finding and doing the work, then presenting it; so, if you're in a role where you want to be a leader, take that initiative, be a self-starter."

Harley Finkelstein

Harley Finkelstein was ebullience and hustle personified. He has been described as a "power extrovert." Finkelstein himself said it was his "chutzpah" that brought him business success. He spoke in blocks of paragraphs as polished as if they were written — and, as some have remarked, at a speed faster than any other person they had heard yet still clear enough to understand. His childhood friend Benjamin Crudo called him "a frickin' force of nature."[3]

Finkelstein grew up in Montreal. In a 2021 interview, he told Crudo that his schoolteachers left comments on his report cards to the effect that he had a surfeit of energy and struggled to sit still in class. He was usually one of the shortest boys in his classes, and even as an adult, stands at five feet and four inches — or five feet and five inches on a good day.

On the cusp of becoming a teenager, Finkelstein wanted to be a disc jockey but couldn't find anyone to hire him. He created his own job by starting a business providing disc jockey services at bar mitzvahs and birthday parties. He had made hundreds of appearances by the time the business wrapped up in his early 20s.

About halfway through high school, Finkelstein moved with his parents to Florida. After finishing high school there, he returned to Montreal to attend McGill University. During the first term, however, his mother called with some bad news: Finkelstein's dad had gone bankrupt. His parents couldn't help pay for their son's university classes anymore, so he had to return home to Florida or else fend for himself in Montreal.

He chose to stay in Montreal and find a way to pay for university and send money to his family. He did DJ gigs on the weekends and tried working in a café, then a travel agency, but it still wasn't enough money. He next thought about starting a business. After asking a lot of people for advice and getting nowhere, he got a break: a friend on the student council told him that McGill bought printed T-shirts in large quantities to sell in the campus bookstore and to hand out during orientation.

Finkelstein bought a cheap screen-printing machine and learned how to operate it, only to learn McGill administrators were happy with their current supplier of T-shirts, a large and proven manufacturer. Getting desperate, he went into overdrive with his hustle and started calling the student council daily, asking for an order of any size. Whenever he heard of a request for a proposal (RFP), he was the first to show up — not just with a written proposal but also with actual samples of the T-shirts, printed with the required logos.

He pledged 24/7 service and on the first RFP presented his quote at cost. At last, he got an order for a few hundred T-shirts. He delivered them days early, with some extra T-shirts thrown in for good measure. The day after delivery he called to make sure his customers were happy. Over the next three years, he built up the business until it was supplying more than 50 universities across Canada by the time that he graduated with a BA in economics.

His plan after university was to pursue his printed T-shirt business full-time, but a mentor and family friend, Phil Rimer, persuaded him to get a law degree instead because it would be like a finishing school to become a good entrepreneur. Furthermore, Rimer, a lawyer himself, would be teaching at the University of Ottawa's law school, so Finkelstein would not be alone if he came to Ottawa. In 2005, Finkelstein entered the university's joint law and MBA degree, while continuing to run his T-shirt business on the side.

How right Rimer was about law school. The professors used the Socratic method in the classroom, asking students at random — whether or not their hands were up — to report on the assigned readings. It was great practice in gathering essential information quickly the night before from voluminous readings, speaking persuasively in public and thinking on one's feet. Moot court further refined his debating skills.

In fact, Finkelstein said he found his law courses to be better preparation for business than his MBA courses. As he was to find out, the skills he developed as a communicator were to stand him in good stead for his role at Shopify handling business development and external relations.

While at the University of Ottawa, Finkelstein wanted to find other entrepreneurs to hang out with. They were his tribe, his kind of folk. He reached out to some business incubators to ask if there was a group somewhere and was referred to the Fresh Founders, which met regularly at a downtown Ottawa café.

It was there that he and Lütke first met. Finkelstein became intrigued with Shopify as a solution for his own business. By setting up an online store, he wouldn't have to skip a lot of classes to go meet with existing and potential customers. His online store, Smoofer, was Shopify's 137th.

Finkelstein found that Smoofer could compete against retail giants like Walmart, even while he was sitting in class or preparing for tests and assignments. His strategy was to identify towns with a movie theatre but no shopping malls or other places selling printed T-shirts. If the theatre was showing blockbuster movies like those from the Batman series, he would then buy Batman-related Google AdWords for that town, so when local residents looked online for Batman movies and merchandise, they would see his ads displaying T-shirts with Batman logos and characters sublicensed for that area.

Finkelstein also squeezed his suppliers. At first, third-party fulfillment companies refused to take his shipments because his T-shirts orders were below their minimum shipment requirement. After much calling around, he struck a deal with one shipper by promising to commit to a two-year contract if they gave him six months to grow his business to their minimum.[4]

Finkelstein also tried to get Shopify to give him a fee break when his suppliers were late restocking his inventory. But Lütke's billing system didn't have an option for prorating, so he was confronted with a decision: whether or not to build this feature into the platform. "I had this super squeaky wheel of Harley over here. Am I going to invest? Because it was basically me and four other people working on the engineering of Shopify," as he told Dan Martell on the *Escape Velocity Show*.[5] Lütke decided it was just easier to make Finkelstein's account completely free.

After Ottawa U., Finkelstein went to Toronto to article at a law firm. But it wasn't his kind of environment. He began to look forward to weekends and dread Mondays. Meanwhile, when Phillips advised Lütke to bring in new faces to the executive team, Lütke thought of Finkelstein. True, the latter had pestered him until he got free access to Shopify. "Frankly, he sent me more emails than any other person ever," Lütke revealed. "But he was just enthusiastic, absolutely enthusiastic, and also relentless . . . that guy was such a pain in the butt but if he was on my side, he could be somebody else's pain in the butt."[6] So Lütke and Finkelstein ended up talking, and Finkelstein started at Shopify on December 9, 2010.

Finkelstein began as director of business development and general counsel, then moved to the Chief Operating Officer (COO) position in 2016 and to President in 2020. His parents may have been disappointed in the beginning over their son's abandoning law for a small, unknown company, but that sentiment surely changed to pride as his career progressed at Shopify.

Toby Shannan

On the same day, December 9, 2010, as Finkelstein was hired, so was another key addition to the executive, Toby Shannan. He was "a warm, bearded, bear of a man," as an interviewer described him in 2014.[7] Lütke first met Shannan when he was interviewing for the Shopify CEO job. Lütke began the interview by talking about Shopify and the CEO role.

Shannan was impressed with how knowledgeable he sounded and within minutes suggested Lütke should consider taking the CEO job himself. Shannan subsequently became Shopify's Chief Support Officer (CSO), in charge of customer service, and then in 2020, he became COO, at which point he had close to 3,000 staff under his wing.

Shannan grew up during the 1960s in Perth, a small, blue-collar town south of Ottawa. Already six feet and two inches tall by Grade 9, he gravitated easily toward sports and has fond memories of playing football under the field lights on Friday nights. However, his parents were part of the hippy counterculture. His mom was a convert to the Age of Aquarius and his stepdad had long hair, a PhD in English literature and drove around town in a converted ambulance. He was a U.S. draft dodger who brought "10,000 books" with him, along with fellow draft dodgers, Buddhists and an assortment of other individuals that made for quite a "cosmopolitan" group.

There was no electricity or running water in the house until Shannan was 10 years old, so anyone wanting to read at night had to use candlelight, as he told *This View of Life* in 2020.[8] Still, childhood friends remember Shannan as the boy who could read in kindergarten.

In their "buttoned-down" small town in eastern Ontario, his nonconformist parents stood out, yet Shannan managed to also keep a foot in the local community thanks to being a high school jock who distinguished himself in sports. Shannan slipped into college with the help of his athletic abilities and planned to major in philosophy but sports and women remained his preoccupation — plus, he was "lazy and drank too much." When his girlfriend became pregnant, he did the right thing and got married, then went to work for his biological dad, building luxury log and timber-frame homes at nearby lakes. After his second child was born (final count: four kids) in his mid-20s, Shannan completed a "short technical certificate" in the late 1990s, just as a technology boom was gripping the Ottawa region thanks to the success of Nortel Networks and other tech companies. This led to a succession of sales positions in tech companies.

At the age of 29, he started his own tech company and raised some money. This changed his life for good because he was able to say he was a company executive on his resume, which he leveraged "into a couple of things, most of which failed as tends to happen with entrepreneurship."[9] Around 2002, he met a scientist and helped him commercialize a kit for taking DNA samples from saliva, now used at many genome companies. As he was turning 40, he came into contact with Shopify when it consisted of just half a dozen or so people, and after his interview with Lütke, ended up on the executive team. In the fall of 2022, in his 50s, Shannan retired from his executive position but remained on the board of directors.

Craig Miller

In 2011, Shopify filled another senior executive position, Chief Marketing Officer (CMO), with Craig Miller. He became the Chief Product Officer (CPO) in 2017 and left Shopify in 2020.

Miller studied electrical engineering in the late 1990s at McGill University, in his hometown of Montreal. In his spare time, he used SEO, Google AdWords, and affiliate marketing — then in their infancy — to create GeoCities websites ranking at the top of search engine results. He threw enough "spaghetti against the wall" for the affiliate links to bring in a six-figure annual income. It was a surreal experience coming home from engineering school every day to find his mailbox crammed full of cheques paying that much money for his referrals, as he told Brandon Chu on the podcast *The Black Box of Product Management* in 2021.[10]

After graduating from McGill in 2005, the lean and bespectacled six-foot, five-inch Miller put aside his engineering career and turned his lucrative side hustle into a full-time business. It grew to a size he couldn't handle on his own; to gain some experience hiring and managing people, he decided to go work for another company. Online classified ad company Kijiji was just starting up in Canada and was looking for a developer/business analyst. Miller sent in his resume. Kijiji at that time was also separately advertising a community get-together at a local Montreal pub, and Miller decided to join them for some Belgian beer. No one showed up except two people — two-thirds of the Kijiji workforce at the time.

After Miller sat down and told them he had applied to their job posting, an impromptu interview unfolded over beers. Within two weeks, Miller had moved to Toronto to become Kijiji's fourth employee. He applied his SEO skills to build up Kijiji's traffic from virtually nothing in 2006 to a top-10 website in Canada. In 2010, a Shopify recruiter contacted Miller through LinkedIn and asked if he would be interested in becoming their executive in charge of marketing. He informed the recruiter that he likely was not the marketing person they needed because he had never taken a course in the subject or done media promotions.[11]

But the recruiter was persistent and Miller agreed to go and meet the Shopify team. Miller loved the atmosphere at Shopify's headquarters. But upon returning to Toronto, he sent back an email turning down the job because he had just bought a house in Toronto and didn't want to leave family and friends. His message charitably included a P.S. that listed ideas for boosting Shopify's profile in online searches. A week after returning to Toronto, Miller got a call from Shopify saying it would be okay for him to work remotely from Toronto. Miller thus came on board as CMO and head of the newly created Toronto office. "Always be good to people," Miller later reflected in a *Medium* post in 2015, entitled "The P.S. That Changed My Life." "Always. Even if there's nothing in it for you."[12]

Russell Jones

By the time Russ Jones became Chief Financial Officer (CFO) of Shopify in 2011, he had worked for over 30 years as a chartered accountant and finance executive. During the 1980s and 1990s, he held managerial and director roles at telecom companies Mitel Networks and Newbridge Networks in Ottawa. He then served as the CFO at Watchfire Signs (a maker of digital signs), co-founded a company that hired out interim chief financial officers on contract to early-stage technology companies and was CFO from 2007 to 2011 at financial services company Xambala, located in the San Francisco Bay Area.

Joseph Frasca

Prior to joining Shopify in May of 2014 as Chief Legal Officer (CLO), Joe Frasca had begun his legal career as an associate at Skadden, Arps, Slate, Meagher & Flom LLP from 2004 to 2008. His focus was on corporate mergers and acquisitions. These were small deals but they groomed him for his shot at the big time: the spinoff of EMC's subsidiary, VMware, to raise nearly $1 billion. EMC wanted to retain control of VMware, which Frasca and his colleagues arranged by developing a dual-class share structure with one class having multiple votes attached to each share. His work on the deal led to a position with EMC from 2008 to 2014 as Senior Corporate Counsel, where he worked on a number of M&A deals and joint ventures.

The Astronauts

To paraphrase former Google and Meta Platforms executive Sheryl Sandberg's famous career advice: "Get on a rocket ship. When companies are growing quickly and they are having a lot of impact, careers take care of themselves. When companies aren't growing quickly or their missions don't matter that much, that's when stagnation and politics come in."[13] The executive team in place for their fast-paced careers at Shopify had come together. The six new hires joined the old guard of CEO Lütke, CTO Fauser and CDO Weinand; they were all still on board for the IPO in 2015.

As the executive team was being assembled, another important development at Shopify was unfolding in the background. It was discussions with venture capitalists to raise the funds that would provide the fuel to power Shopify's rocket engines.

The Boost from Venture Capital

When business picked up in 2009 and Shopify's cash flow turned positive, it was grounds for optimism. "You know what?" Lütke said to himself. "I think this is a growth company."[1] As a test of this possibility, he split a $50,000 marketing budget over five different trials. If any of the five were a success, it would be a sign to go ahead. All five were successful. By wide margins. This trial-and-testing approach for growth ideas was to be used many times in the years ahead: as Lütke told an interviewer in 2013, "The mechanism we've settled on for trying to build a business that is fundamentally good at thriving in chaotic environments is to experiment a lot and just try a lot of stuff."[2]

The success of the five trials in 2009 was a definitive sign that the time had come to switch to a growth business. "We'd began to understand our business, not completely, but at a deeper level . . . and how to spend a dollar here to make $1.80 on the other side," Finkelstein told *The Tim Ferriss Show* in 2020. Lütke put the results in an Excel spreadsheet to show the venture capitalists. The problem was there weren't too many venture capitalists in 2010 who understood Shopify's opportunity in e-commerce.[3]

But there was one: Bessemer Venture Partners. A year earlier, it had posted a white paper online and Shopify executives had found the document quite useful.[4] It gave them the formulae and terminology for understanding their business, and the metrics for gauging how well it was doing — for example: monthly recurring revenue (MRR), average revenue per user (ARPU) and customer lifetime value (CLTV). So there was a venture capital firm out there that understood what Shopify was doing. Since Shopify was already growing and profitable, perhaps it shouldn't be too hard to convince Bessemer to lead a Series A funding.

$120 MILLION

Bessemer, with two other partners, FirstMark Capital and Felicis Ventures, came through with a Series A financing of $7 million in December of 2010. In return for injecting capital, Bessemer got a 20% ownership stake, two of the five positions on the board of directors and the right to force a sale after six years.

Before agreeing to fund Shopify, Bessemer had sent one of its partners, Alex Ferrara, to do a company assessment. He was "incredibly nervous" because it was his first time leading an investment for Bessemer. When he was finished with his analysis, he presented an October 2, 2010, report, "Shopify Memo," to the other Bessemer partners. It summed up what Shopify had become at that point:

> Shopify sells a simple . . . solution that enables a business to quickly set up and run an online retail store. A typical customer signs up using their credit card and is up and running in a few hours with no long-term contract. Shopify targets small- and medium-sized businesses and at-home capitalists (e.g., eBay and Etsy sellers) . . . with the goal of servicing these customers as they scale to become larger customers with more sophisticated needs. Shopify has also managed to sign-up a number of large businesses like Pixar, Amnesty International and Tesla Motors at higher price points.[1]

It took Ferrara three round-trip flights to Ottawa before he finally decided to present Lütke with a term sheet. Why the hesitation, aside from being the lead on an investment for the first time? Because few venture capitalists then believed that software businesses targeting e-commerce for small- and medium-sized businesses were good investments. Many turned

Shopify down. Its total addressable market was thought to be too small, which may have been the case if one just looked at existing businesses. As it turned out, the addressable market was much larger once Shopify's system emerged because it removed many of the technical barriers and frictions that entrepreneurs had found hard to surmount in creating online stores.

Despite his qualms at the time over market size, Ferrara could not ignore Shopify's impressive growth rate. As he wrote in his report:

> With limited marketing, customers have increased from 5,500 a year ago to nearly 10,000 today. Over the same period, monthly recurring revenue has grown from $164K to $438K. Across all Shopify-powered stores, the annualized total dollar value of orders facilitated through the Shopify platform (including certain apps and channels for which a revenue-sharing arrangement is in place in the period, net of refunds, and inclusive of shipping and handling, duty and value-added taxes), otherwise called Gross Merchandise Volume (GMV) was roughly $132m. The business is profitable and largely bootstrapped, having raised just $1 million to date and having $1.3 million of cash on its balance sheet with no debt.... Over time, the average revenue per customer was increasing . . . driven by rising transaction fees as Shopify's customers grow their own businesses and the increase in number of customers opting for higher-priced plans.

Ferrara was impressed with the management. "Lütke . . . is a young, first-time CEO who is thoughtful, has good product and management instincts," he wrote in his report. He did not feel there was any immediate need to replace him as CEO but they needed to ensure that he had more senior talent around him. The business desperately needed a VP of Marketing. This latter recommendation was what led to the hiring of Miller. Bessemer also recommended hiring a CFO, which led to bringing Jones into the company.

Ferrara didn't see any need to relocate Shopify out of Ottawa to Silicon Valley in California or some other place. He didn't mention that a thriving technology sector had built up in the Ottawa region around Nortel Networks over the previous decades and although Nortel went out of business in the 2000s, it left behind a pool of tech startups and skilled technology workers. But he did mention: "With Tobi's reputation among the developer community, the company has been able to recruit some of the best development and design talent in Ottawa at 60%-70% of the cost of similar talent in Silicon Valley or New York."

As the coming years would show, there was more to Shopify than lower labour costs. Turnover rates in Shopify's workforce would be much lower. Whereas the average tenure at Silicon Valley firms was 18 months, at Shopify it turned out to be more like 5 to 10 years — which meant the company could invest more in developing its employees.

The Shopify API was a big selling point. "This approach is a big competitive differentiator for Shopify," Ferrara concluded. He also noted that acquisition cost per customer ranged from $175 to $225 and was covered in seven to nine months on a churn-adjusted basis (churn is the number of customers that cancel or don't renew their subscriptions). Shopify retained roughly 75% of its new customers after three months and just over 50% after 12 months. Once stabilized, monthly churn ranged from 3% to 5%. The latter churn rates "likely scared off other investors," noted Ferrara. But Bessemer was okay with it because Shopify didn't have to pay a lot to get customers and "the customers that do stick around end up making up for the ones that churn."

The market for e-commerce software was crowded, but Bessemer believed that Shopify was best equipped to meet the growing preferences of small and medium businesses for mobile commerce, web-based inventory management and point-of-sale e-commerce systems. Of the main rivals present in its market segment — eBay ProStores, Amazon Webstore, BigCommerce and Volusion — the latter was deemed the most formidable. Although it had a pricing point and feature set similar to Shopify's, its offering required some programming to customize. In the mid-market niche, Magento Commerce was the leading open-source e-commerce product, but typically required some technical skills for implementation and operation. On the high end, the offerings were Escalate, IBM, ATG, and Demandware; they offered a superset of Shopify's features, but installation and maintenance were even more complicated and expensive.

Two months after winning the Series A financing, Shopify was heralded in the *Ottawa Business Journal* by Bruce Firestone, founder of the Ottawa Senators NHL hockey team and entrepreneur-in-residence at the University of Ottawa's Telfer School of Management. He said it was a good move for Shopify to secure customers and become cash-flow positive before seeking venture capitalist money because it gave them the leverage to obtain financing without sacrificing too much control. Shopify didn't need the money to survive; they only wanted to use it to invest for a higher return, as their market experiments indicated was possible. Having launch customers also helped make the Shopify product offering more robust because of the product adjustments made in response to customer feedback. Lastly, it didn't hurt that Bessemer Ventures was well connected in Silicon Valley: "This makes business development at Shopify a lot easier when the firm can get first-hand introductions to tech titans such as X, Facebook and Google," Firestone wrote.[2]

Firestone was spot on pointing out that one of the benefits of signing with a venture capitalist is the contacts they can provide. Around the time of its Series A financing, Shopify wanted to find a merchant selling at scale to test the resiliency of its platform, and when Aydin Senkut of Felicis Ventures heard, he immediately put Shopify in touch with Rovio, one of the companies in his investment portfolio. Rovio had scored a big hit with the Angry Birds plush toys, one of the hottest sellers of the season. Within a week or so, they had started a store on Shopify, and millions of Angry Birds toys were sold, providing Shopify with one of their first big sales blowouts to prove the scalability of the platform.

The Series B round came quickly. Mark MacLeod, an executive at startup Tungle, was helping Shopify with raising funds and recalled attending a Shopify board meeting shortly after Series A. There was talk of going for a Series B financing and before anything was decided, the Bessemer directors at the meeting said: "Hey, wait, give us some time to get back to you." They wanted to present a proposal right away and "basically came back with an offer we couldn't refuse."[3]

Within 10 months of the $7-million Series A funding, Shopify closed a $15-million Series B funding from Bessemer Venture Partners, FirstMark Capital, Felicis Ventures and Georgian Partners. Shopify's growth rate after the Series A financing had picked up steam and "just took off to a degree that is almost comical," Lütke said in a 2019 interview.[4] "The venture capitalists are still talking about those times as something they've never seen before . . . they wired the [Series B] money before we even started talking about it. It's like [they said], 'You need more money. You didn't raise enough money because the numbers were so good.'" It turned out to be a great move for Bessemer, too. "Shopify was still its largest cash-on-cash return, and that is because they doubled down," MacLeod said in a 2021 interview.[5]

Shopify was still experiencing rapid growth when a Series C of $100 million was announced in December of 2013, led by the venture capital arm of the Ontario Municipal Employees Retirement System and global private equity firm Insight Venture Partners. The previous rounds of venture capital had been used to power Shopify from two dozen employees to 300 employees supporting 80,000 online stores with sales of $1.5 billion. The Series C would help Shopify maintain this growth, and adapt to new channels then emerging for e-commerce, such as mobile phones and tablets.

Other venture capital firms participated in the Series C, including Bessemer. Its involvement in all of the venture capital financing rounds also helped Lütke hone his management skills. He learned from Bessemer that a big part of running a startup is picking the right "compass metric" to serve as a gauge of performance. Like a compass, it gives the team direction. When calculated at weekly intervals and disseminated to key personnel for review at short weekly meetings, it can be an effective way to maintain the focus and alignment of staff on growing the company.

When Shopify was deriving most of its revenues from subscriptions prior to 2014, Lütke's chief compass metric was Committed Monthly Recurring Revenue (CMRR), as borrowed from Bessemer Venture Partner's Cloud Computing Law #2. CMRR equals monthly revenues from all active customers *plus* in-progress sign-ups and upgrades for subscriptions *less* in-progress downgrades and terminations (i.e. churn) of subscriptions. Shopify's goal was to increase weekly CMRR by 3%. An email would go out early Monday morning reporting on what percentage growth was achieved the week before; the reported figure had a red *X* placed next to it if it was below target or a green checkmark if the target was achieved.

Every Thursday, there was a quick funnel meeting, attended by those who had a direct impact on the CMRR number. Everyone present shared two things: what they had learned over the week and what they were going to do differently next week. As Lütke summed it up in 2013 on his blog:

> This is the motor of a fast-growing multimillion-dollar venture-backed business. Our growth comes from a combination of choosing the right time intervals (1 week), the right compass metric (CMRR), and the right perspective (week over week growth). There is only a minor amount of support scaffolding built into this structure: one email and one meeting a week. Everything else flows from that.[6]

HYPERGROWTH AND COACHING

As Shopify deployed the financing from venture capitalists into its various commercial opportunities, staffing levels skyrocketed at the firm. While this meant Shopify could capture much greater growth and gain market share, executives and managers faced challenges keeping up with the sudden escalation in the number of their employees. On top of this, much of the managerial staff was young and inexperienced, so the influx was doubly overwhelming.

One solution to the hypergrowth was to bring in coaches. It got started with Fauser in 2011. He did not have prior experience as an executive, so managing such big, expanding teams didn't come naturally. To adapt, he hired an executive coach by the name of Cam Gregg, who had previous managerial experience at IBM and other companies. When Lütke and other senior executives saw the benefit for Fauser, they too started having sessions with Gregg. This was the start of Shopify's coaching program.

After some weeks had gone by, a decision was made to hire an in-house coach on a full-time basis. This would give the coach a better understanding of the inner workings of Shopify and help them fine-tune their advice. This arrangement worked out well enough that Shopify hired a team of full-time coaches. By 2016, there were a dozen on the payroll — forming what was called the talent acceleration team.

Several of the Shopify executives found the coaches particularly useful. Forsyth received support and encouragement from four consecutive coaches for most of the time she was at Shopify. Another beneficiary was Finkelstein. In an October 7, 2016, article for *Forbes*, he wrote about the coaching program and how it helped alleviate his managerial problems.

When he joined Shopify, he felt he would be a good executive because of his prior experience running businesses. But that "misplaced confidence in leading a team came to an abrupt end." A year or so into his job at Shopify, he was, in his words:

> managing a half-dozen people, and much to my surprise, not everybody thought the same way as I did. It was challenging when people weren't always able to see the big picture right away and sometimes got caught up in details. At the same time, I didn't trust others to do their jobs so I ended up micromanaging them. Worst of all, I was taking my problems home with me, putting strains on my relationships.[1]

One of his earliest revelations was to appreciate the difference between leading and managing. He understood the former; it came naturally for him to get up at a podium and give a rah-rah speech to rouse the troops. Managing was, however, more of a long-term process that required enormous patience and building up trust to be in a position to get everyone on the same page and performing as expected.

This part was not necessarily easy for an entrepreneurial person because they are used to resolving a lot of things on their own, which was "just quicker and more efficient than teaching someone else," Finkelstein said. He could get away with a do-it-yourself approach when starting out with a small team, but by 2016, he had more than 1,000 persons working under him. It was with the help of his coach that he was able to adopt the view that he had "to invest in people and put faith in their abilities." But there was a lot more to it, as he noted:

> As a young entrepreneur, if I walked into a room and everybody agreed with my ideas, I felt great. But working with a coach has allowed me to see the value in differing opinions and working styles. I work best under pressure and in a slight state of chaos, but others are more cautious by nature and question big risks. Working with a coach, I've learned, well, the art of empathy: the ability to put myself in someone else's shoes and accept differing points of view. And you know what? I now have tremendous appreciation for those who question and challenge me on some of my plans. By poking holes, the end result is often 10 times better. Today, when I walk out of a meeting and everybody agrees with me, I get really nervous.[2]

Years later, in 2020, Finkelstein was to say on *The Tim Ferriss Show*: "But I have to say, if I had to distill down one of the things that has allowed me to get to where I am at this point with my career and certainly helped me lead Shopify, coaching is up there in the top three or four things that I've done."[3]

Finkelstein remained a staunch advocate of executive coaches. They can be used as sounding boards, a safe place to talk about things that are working or not working. Many of them had a great deal of experience working as senior managers and executives in the corporate realm — and that background can be valuable to new managers. The coach that Finkelstein first connected with was Gregg. Finkelstein could mention a problem and Gregg would respond by describing a similar situation he had faced and how it was solved.

SHOPIFY THE VENTURE CAPITALIST

After the API was created, Shopify began investing in some of its third-party developers and designers to help them build their tools. As they rode Shopify's coattails and grew with the platform, the partners became more valuable companies — as did Shopify's stakes in them. The investments not only helped its partners build their tools but also generated substantial capital gains for Shopify.

As more investments were made in its partners, the collection of private equities held by Shopify grew in size. For many years, information on the holdings was piecemeal and intermittent. But that changed in June of 2023 when Shopify launched the Shopify Ventures website to display all its holdings in one place.[1] Here is what the group looked like then:

Financial Services — innovation in financing, spending and payments processing

- **Affirm:** "buy now, pay later" fintech company
- **Bench:** bookkeeping software with live bookkeeping advisers for small business
- **Codat:** API integrates systems used by customers of small businesses
- **Diem:** cryptocurrency firm
- **Melio:** simplifies payment of invoices
- **Nomba:** banking and payment services for small businesses in Nigeria
- **Pipe:** provides financing against future revenues
- **Stripe:** payments processing

Marketing Technology — advancing tools that help merchants attract customers

- **Disco:** collaborate with 1,000-plus brand partners to drive collective growth
- **Gorgias:** a highly rated helpdesk for merchants

- **Klaviyo:** marketing based on customer data (e.g. recommending similar products)
- **Single:** content-driven (video, music, NFTs, etc.) shopping experiences
- **Supergreat:** beauty fans reviewing products, sharing routines and shopping daily drops
- **Tapcart:** helps e-commerce brands on Shopify build mobile apps in hours
- **Triple Whale:** manage/automate analytics, attribution, merchandising, forecasting, etc.
- **Wati:** WhatsApp API platform that automates marketing, sales, service and support
- **Yotpo:** text messages about special offers, flash sales, loyalty/ reward programs, etc.

Global Commerce — smarter logistics solutions to de-risk and speed up shipments

- **Flexport:** logistics and fulfillment network
- **Global-e:** offers international online shoppers a seamless localized experience
- **Loop:** offers a platform to reduce the cost and hassle of handling returns
- **Shippo:** best rates and tracking for shipments plus discounted shipping labels

Commerce Infrastructure — making it easy for merchants to create enjoyable digital experiences

- **Crossing Minds:** AI-powered product recommendations and personalized shopping
- **Sanity:** app for Hydrogen and Oxygen to add immersive content to custom storefronts
- **Thirdweb:** developer toolkit for blockchain apps such as games, NFTs and marketplaces

- **WalletConnect:** suite of APIs that enhances interoperability across blockchains

This collection of investments looks like the kind of portfolio that a venture capitalist might assemble. But Shopify was likely better positioned to spot the winners. Being a major player in the burgeoning e-commerce sector, it had intimate knowledge of the industry; its software also gathered data that could identify developers with the more successful apps.

Two Shopify holdings, Affirm Holdings and Global-e Online, went public on the stock exchange in 2021, generating unrealized capital gains totalling more than $2 billion for Shopify. Since these two holdings were now valued in a public market, accounting rules allowed their unrealized capital gains to be included in earnings statements. Thus, most of the $2.9 billion in net income reported in Shopify's 2021 *Annual Report* was due to these two partners.

Unrealized capital gains can turn into unrealized capital losses in other years, as happened in 2022 with Affirm Holdings and Global-e Online. However, over the long run, the portfolio as a whole should yield a positive return given its diversification and the projected long-term growth rates for e-commerce.

In late September 2023, another of Shopify's private equity investments, Klaviyo, did an IPO.[2] With this listing, Shopify had three publicly traded companies in its investment portfolio. The vast majority remained private companies. If and when any of them are listed on the stock exchange, their capital gains or losses can be included in earnings reports. Consequently, the impact of the portfolio on reported financial results could become substantial over time.

Because the share prices of Shopify's public investments are affected by sentiment in the stock market, Shopify's reported earnings may not often reflect its operating performance. A better notion of the latter would be provided by the numbers reported for Shopify's operating income (which excludes unrealized capital gains and losses).

As portfolio holdings are sold, the receipts should climb well into the billions of dollars. From one vantage point, this harvested income will recoup much of the revenue that was passed over to the partnership ecosystem. From another, the gains realized from the portfolio have the potential to be a significant source of financing for future growth opportunities.

7

Shopify Gathers Speed

As financing flowed in from Bessemer and other venture capitalists, Shopify's executives got busy with their projects. They knew they would have to stay on their toes. Lütke, like his mentor Starr at Siemens, liked to nudge staff out of their comfort zones so they could grow and become better versions of themselves. Indeed, they needed to be better versions of themselves just to keep up with Shopify's sizzling pace. As Lütke put it in an email to staff: "The red-queen race of Shopify's historic 40% or better growth is that everyone has to show up at least 40% better every year to qualify for our current jobs."[1] In other words, just as the Red Queen told Alice in *Through the Looking-Glass* that she had to run to stay in the same place, Lütke was telling staff they needed to continue learning and developing to keep up with Shopify's growth.

In 2014, Finkelstein was asked what it was like working for Lütke. He replied: "Tobi has consistently pushed me. . . . Once I get good at something, lo and behold he walks into this office and says, 'You built that, and now you should take care of this thing. . . . Build a system for thousands of third-party agencies around the world to refer business to Shopify. Done? Now focus on increasing sales tenfold. Now scale up this third-party app store. Make it a hundred times bigger than it was.'"[2]

Finkelstein rose to the challenges, which led to a close rapport with Lütke. When asked in 2020 about his relationship with Finkelstein, Lütke replied: "We have worked very, very closely together now for a decade, and we have never had couple's counselling or something like that. [Laughs.] It's very intuitive for us when to go with one of our ideas because this is what a relationship with a 100% [trust] battery looks like.... It's very rare that you can get there in the world of business."[3]

Finkelstein also put his speaking skills to work carrying out public functions associated with the CEO role so that Lütke could focus on his strength in technology and product development. As Lütke said, they would be more productive as "spiky stones" specializing in their strengths rather than well-rounded "river stones" handling all aspects of their positions.

In a way, the relationship between Finkelstein and Lütke was reminiscent of the relationship between BlackBerry's co-CEOs Mike Lazaridis and Jim Balsillie. Shopify benefited from having two dedicated individuals at the helm much of the time, one specialized in the business side and the other in the technology side. But at Shopify, there was a clear chain of command with the buck ultimately stopping at Lütke's desk. Lazaridis and Balsillie were at times like two generals in command of the same army, so sometimes it was working at cross purposes — as appeared to be the case portrayed in *Losing the Signal: The Untold Story Behind the Extraordinary Rise and Spectacular Fall of BlackBerry*, the 2015 book by Jacquie McNish and Sean Silcoff.

AGILE BUSINESS DEVELOPMENT

Finkelstein's first big assignment was to grow the partnership ecosystem. An early convert was Kurt Elster of Chicago; he had started his own business, Ethercycle, developing websites for local businesses — then switched in 2011 to building just Shopify stores. Over in Manitoba, Jay Myers and three of his friends thought they could earn some weekend beer money in 2012 by designing a few apps for Shopify — and were still at it years later as a full-time business (Bold Commerce), with 150 staff. In the Shopify Affiliate Program, the members included Sarah Chrisp, a YouTuber who shared tips for running e-commerce websites; Nathan Chan, CEO of *Foundr* magazine, which profiled entrepreneurs; and Adrian Morrison, founder of the eCom Success Academy, which trained Shopify merchants.

But signing up partners was not easy in the beginning. Few were keen to join because Shopify's platform did not have at the time a huge number of merchants to buy their apps and themes. "You have a classic chicken-and-egg problem," Finkelstein told the *Greylock* podcast. "[Developers and designers] are not going to build unless there are a lot of merchants and we are not going to get a lot of merchants unless the product gaps are filled."[1] Moreover, the problem had to be solved quickly before rivals could grow a larger subscriber base and lure third-party developers, designers and affiliates with greater opportunities to profit.

Cue Finkelstein. His hustle wasn't so much the kind that blitzes with cold calls and pounds the pavement door to door. Trained as a lawyer, he knew the value of research to uncover leads and build relationships. He also had a way with words and could be persuasive.

Finkelstein gave an example of one win. "There was a European sneaker company on Shopify that badly needed some sort of online shoe-size converter," he said. Rather than spend time beating the bushes to find a developer who could build an app, Finkelstein and his team did some checking around. They discovered "that there were a bunch of third-party app developers in London who had just built these free tools online, including one where you put in your U.S. shoe size and got the European shoe size — so we contacted them and said, look, just take everything you built and put it into the app store."[2]

Finkelstein also found inspiration in an approach Lütke was using to speed up the coding process, labelled Agile Software Development. Finkelstein adapted it to the field of business development, naming his version Agile Business Development. It called for more agility — that is, less dwelling on procedure, extensive documentation and contractual negotiations — to "get shit done" faster. Done is better than perfect, went one of the mantras.

The ability to pivot was important, Finkelstein disclosed in a 2011 interview with Mixergy.[3] During the process of soliciting partners, there may be a gulf between what they and Shopify want, so a pivot in Shopify's stance would be needed to meet in the middle. Also, during discussions with a partner, information may surface about other opportunities — so, it was good to stay mindful of them and ready to pivot.

Finkelstein told the story of learning about an app designer who was infringing on Shopify's intellectual property. Since Finkelstein was also legal counsel at the time, it was up to him to send a cease-and-desist letter. Usually, such missives have a threatening tone to them, but Finkelstein decided to be agile and send a more friendly request. As it turned out, the developer complied and the channels of communication remained open for a discussion about building apps for Shopify, which the developer agreed to do.

Agile Business Development was also about avoiding those term-sheet discussions that dragged on for months and months. Finkelstein's rubric specified that, essentially, three main communications, whether by email, phone or in person, should be sufficient to close. The first step was the "tickle," emailed to the CEO. It simply said: Here's an idea; we think it's pretty cool. If you're interested, let us know. Often that results in the CEO replying by email and copying one of his or her staff to follow up on the proposal. The second step is the "sizzle" presented to convey what the deal is about and the advantages for both sides. Finally comes the "pivot and close," where the two sides have laid out what they want, then move toward the middle ground where their interests align.

Simplicity was another aspect. Some companies with large legal departments, especially government agencies and publicly traded companies, may present terms sheets with dozens of items because they want to cover every contingency. Finkelstein will tell them he is okay with the first three or four. The rest can be tabled for discussion at a later date, say six months down the road after both parties have "beta tested" the arrangement and decided if they want to continue or need to renegotiate. This speeds up the process because prospective partners feel they are not locked into anything. They can go back to their superiors to say the deal is not ideal but it could turn out to be good — and it if doesn't measure up, it can be renegotiated in six months.

In the case of partnering with app and theme developers, it was an easy matter to say, "Let's whittle down the terms and go to beta testing via the API to see what the response will be like on the platform." It was the same for partnering with payment processors around the world: they could plug into Active Merchant, Shopify's open-source payment gateway library.

When a deal could not be tested on the platform, other measures were required. One was to start out with a small deal if a bigger one was not possible at the time of negotiations. A small deal can provide the client with proof of concept and later be leveraged into a more substantial involvement.

Finkelstein was also a driving force behind the annual Build a Business contest. On this front, his approach of doing some research and forming relationships relied on finding a "centerpiece."[4] This is something that Shopify and a prospect have in common and can be the basis for a conversation. It personalizes the process and keeps an unsolicited contact from feeling like a cold call.

Shopify wanted to get more celebrity entrepreneurs to be mentors in the second year of the Build a Business contest. On the wish list was Seth Godin, a dot-com entrepreneur, marketing strategist, bestselling author and long-time blogger; another was Gary Vaynerchuk, a successful serial entrepreneur who became a bestselling author, inspirational speaker and Internet personality. Both were superstars and likely very busy; getting them on board would be a challenge. "If I cold called or emailed them, I'm probably going to get an assistant and the likelihood of them actually doing something with us was probably going to be quite low," Finkelstein said.[5]

Finkelstein and his team found out that Godin and Vaynerchuk were each about to release books. Finkelstein could see that their core messages were about entrepreneurship and they were going to be published around the same time as the second iteration of Build a Business. The centerpiece, then, was their books coming out at the same time as Shopify's contest.

Finkelstein reached out to let them know their book themes tied in nicely with Shopify's contest and to ask if they would be interested in a quick chat about teaming up. Shopify's contest would help them promote their books and vice versa, they could help promote the contest. And that is what led to Godin and Vaynerchuk participating in the contest as mentors.

A SECRET GROWTH HACK

Shannan led the client support team for many years, starting at the end of 2010. Lütke praised Shannan 10 years later for the way he "created and scaled one of the secret ingredients of Shopify." This view had gained currency in other quarters as well. For example, in a February 2022 edition of the *Where It Happens* podcast, the host called Shopify's support team one of its "secret growth hacks."[1] Arriving at the same conclusion many years before was Bruce Firestone. As he wrote on February 15, 2011, in the *Ottawa Business Journal*, Firestone built his own Shopify store "in less than 10 minutes." There was a problem with a back-end function, so he sent an email to Shopify customer service at 5:50 p.m. on a Saturday. He got a reply back at 5:57 p.m., made the change to get his store working and was ready to take his wife to dinner at their appointed time of six p.m. To Firestone, it was plain to see that the "company . . . has made customer service one of its 'secret weapons.'"[2]

In the first year or two of Shopify, there wasn't much of a budget for hiring customer support staff, so Lütke, Lake and Weinand filled in and responded directly to customer inquiries. This extensive exposure to the front lines left Lütke with the view that customer service was a function to be taken seriously. When he was interviewed on *The Tim Ferriss Show*, he told a story that highlighted the extent to which he would go to ensure customer satisfaction:

> Here's the kind of interaction that happened all of the time . . . someone would send me an email saying, "I cannot imagine you're calling yourself an e-commerce system and you don't even have this feature." I'm on the other side of this email, and I'm starting to write an essay about what went wrong, and it's clearly not coming together, which then means I spend the entire night and implement the feature. I deploy it in the morning, and reply to the customer's email: "What are you talking about? It's right here."[3]

For many tech companies, service departments merely help customers with the technical aspects of getting a product working. Shopify wanted to do more. It created a support team not only to help merchants overcome technical problems but also to provide an abundance of content on its website in the form of articles, blog posts, guidelines and so on — all aimed at providing tips on how to use the Shopify platform and tools to get the most out of it. It was always important for Shopify to promote the success of its merchants because then it did well too.

Beyond this level of support, the customer service team also provided advice on the challenges of running a business. "When you're talking to entrepreneurs, in many cases, what they need is just a voice at the other end of the line to tell them to keep going and to give them some tips about something they hadn't thought about yet," Finkelstein told *Where It Happens*.[4] Many of the support staff were entrepreneurs themselves and had experiences relevant to those calling in, so they were usually empathetic and able to help resolve business problems.

The customer service reps, or "gurus" as they were called within Shopify, mirrored in many respects the makeup of the merchant community calling in. Recruiters were more likely to offer guru jobs to people in their 20s or early 30s with previous experience as online entrepreneurs commercializing a hobby, doing a side hustle or even running a full-time online business. Technical qualifications weren't terribly important. "We don't tend to hire too many industry insider experts," Lütke said in an August 4, 2017, Motley Fool interview.[5] "We tend to hire a lot of high future potential people." The result was a diverse group of young adults in the early stages of their working years; hires in 2017 and 2018 "included a beauty consultant, cook, photographer, television news traffic coordinator, arts center manager, graduate in English literature, magazine editor and multiple retail clerks," reported the May 28, 2018, edition of the *Ottawa Citizen*.[6]

Shopify's "talent acceleration teams" and Shannan met with the new hires to groom them for their roles as client support staff. They were further encouraged to run a Shopify business on the side if they were not already doing so. Talking to a guru would not feel like dealing with a clerk reading off boilerplate responses — or putting you on hold for 15 minutes while they talked to their supervisor about what to advise you. Most gurus were knowledgeable about the platform, enthusiastic about the entrepreneurial lifestyle and motivated to help other members of the "tribe" with their problems. "Our guru team has genuine human conversations," said Shannan. "We want every contact with our merchants to be engaging and ultimately add value to their business."[7]

Once client-service staff were trained and ready to field merchant inquiries, they usually went to work out of their homes, an arrangement that started several years before Shopify adopted remote working in 2020 for the whole company. They assisted clients by telephone, email, chat and video conferencing with a wide variety of issues such as online advertising, billing, and design — often guiding them to software apps, subscription upgrades and other aspects of Shopify's platform that could help them. And since the gurus could view the back-end of the merchant's account, they might see other ways to optimize a business that the merchant was not aware of — for example, the guru might see that the merchant was getting a lot of visitors coming from Instagram or Pinterest, so they'd recommend looking into monetizing those channels more.

Furthermore, recordings of selected interactions between gurus and merchants were reviewed (with the merchants' consent) during internal meetings on Slack or at town hall get-togethers. The purpose was twofold: first, to help the gurus improve the support they provided to clients; and second, to explore customer feedback on what features could be added to the platform to better serve customers.

In the early days of the support group, a problem arose. The orthodox approach to running call centers was applied and Shopify's customer service staff worked individually on their own to communicate with customers, all remotely and under the direct supervision of Shannan. The traditional view then on call centers was that "leadership should have as small a footprint as possible," Shannan told the *This View of Life* podcast in 2020.[8]

But after a while, it became apparent that the staff "were miserable." This was not good for their sake or the company because unhappy staff on the front lines can affect the quality of service to customers. Shannan thought the dissatisfaction could be fixed by putting the gurus into small teams. "Sometimes the only consolation of working in a corporate environment is the socializing — sure, there is the paycheque, but you put up with everything else because you are surrounded by other people you tolerate and are friendly with," Shannan said.[9]

So, to remove the isolation of working individually, the gurus were reorganized into small teams of approximately nine members and one leader. They would still be working remotely but would be connected together through Google Hangouts or Zoom for a half-hour, unscripted jump-off meeting in the mornings, a team wind-down session at the end of the day and even an end-of-week social hour or two with a beer or glass of wine. Shannan called this a "hub and spoke" arrangement, with the spoke being where the gurus lived and the hub where they came together.

The switch to small teams for Shopify's support staff "made a huge difference," Shannan reported. "The people looked after one another and we were able to scale up without people feeling alienated." When the division had grown to 1,400 people, the level of engagement was measured via surveys, and the gurus had the highest scores within the company.

In the early years, Lütke and Shannan had gone once a week to a pub after work to share ideas on running Shopify. They both read business books for ideas, some of which Shannan would present in his annual meetings with company employees. One especially influential book for Shannan and Lütke was *Team of Teams: New Rules of Engagement for a Complex World* (2015), authored by General (retired) Stanley McChrystal. As commander of the Joint Special Operations Task Force confronting al-Qaeda in Afghanistan, McChrystal had organized his troops into small groups with local autonomy. But this presented a problem, and McChrystal's solution was instructive for Shannan.

While McChrystal's units on the ground were more agile, the other agencies involved in the campaign — the CIA, National Security Agency, State Department and others — were focused on their missions, operating in separate silos that blocked or slowed down the transmission of information between the silos. A technique McChrystal used to break down the walls was to give liaison roles to his best personnel and embed them in the other agencies to build trust, understanding and communication.

Shannan was able to use this tactic to improve coordination within Shopify. For example, his support team was receiving complaints from merchants about some aspects of Shopify's product line; the feedback was catalogued and sent to the Shopify product team, who were receptive during the meetings. But afterward, little changed. The client support team tried different ways of presenting the data but that was a dead end too. Shannan then was allowed to place some of his best people in the product teams to give them deeper context on what was going on. As soon as this human element was introduced, the product people responded.

Not to be overlooked was Shopify's website: the amount of information was (and still is) encyclopedic. The Help Center had sections on creating marketing campaigns, shipping products to customers, migrating from another platform, performing analytics on how one's business was doing and the Experts Marketplace (where third-party agencies could be hired to help with building a business). Then there were several other sections: a blog amply filled with posts, business courses/lessons taught by seasoned entrepreneurs, guidelines in the form of how-to articles, Shopify Community forums for sharing ideas, lists of free tools, weekly podcast interviews with entrepreneurs and e-commerce experts, a business encyclopedia, community events calendars, research reports on trends in e-commerce and a section for referencing Shopify Editions (semi-annual reports on upgrades to Shopify offerings).

The client services team performed a critical role in supporting merchants. As the number of merchants on Shopify's platform soared, so did the size of the customer support. By 2018, it had over 3,000 employees, then about a third of Shopify's total workforce. Moreover, its contribution to Shopify's success involved not only customer relations but also came in handy when Shopify switched to remote working in 2020, and the client services division provided a ready-made template to follow for implementing remote working across the rest of Shopify.

MARKETING OUTSIDE THE BOX

When Miller was hired as CMO in 2011, he had no training or experience in conventional marketing methods. He was just really good at SEO, as the superlative growth of Kijiji demonstrated. His first assignment at Shopify was refining and extending Shopify's SEO so it could better guide traffic through the haystacks of online data to the Shopify needle.

As part of defining the team's mission, Miller rebranded his group in Toronto as the "growth team." Explaining why, Miller told *McGill News* in 2018: "When you call it a growth team, everyone knows exactly what the goal is."[1] It was not marketing. It was doubling subscriptions, then doubling them again, and doubling yet again and again until Shopify got big enough to list on the stock market. A listing could give employee remuneration a big boost through stock ownership plans; this was the Big Hairy Audacious Goal (BHAG) for motivating staff, a concept enunciated by Jim Collins and Jerry Porras in their 1994 book, *Built to Last: Successful Habits of Visionary Companies.*

As his work on fine-tuning Shopify's SEO moved to completion, Miller's focus shifted from helping people find Shopify to getting more people *wanting* to find Shopify. The idea was to do what Nike had done with running shoes: at one time, they constituted a niche market for athletes but then became popular with the general population. For Miller, broadening popularity and increasing demand for Shopify's services did not call for billboards and TV ads but meant continuously improving the platform to reduce pain points for entrepreneurs, so that more of the general population would find it easier to start a business.

"We talked about removing friction and barriers to entry, and those are the types of projects I was basically involved in for a long time,"[2] Miller said. For example, one project he worked on was Shopify Shipping, introduced in the United States in September 2015. Merchants could use it to print U.S. shipping labels with two clicks of the mouse instead of having to go through the more labour-intensive process of setting up a UPS account and integrating it with Shopify.

Shopify Shipping also partnered with USPS to provide Shopify merchants with discounts of up to 60% on shipping labels, as well as free home pickup of prepaid shipments and/or no waiting in line at USPS offices. This was followed by a Canada Post partnership of a similar nature and then, in October of 2017, a partnership with DHL Express, which enabled small companies to ship to international destinations in more than 200 countries at a cost equivalent to what large companies paid. Shortly after that, a partnership was signed with UPS. Shopify Shipping added a new feature in September 2018 called Locations, which allowed business owners to allocate and track shipments of products they ordered for their inventory — relieving merchants of the time-consuming process of manually tracking inventory on "long spreadsheets."

Miller's other projects included Shopify Email and Shopify Ping. Shopify Email creates marketing campaigns with a drag-and-drop editor and customizable templates that pull in branding, products, and prices from a store. Shopify Ping lets merchants conduct customer conversations from different services within one app, as well as send products, discounts and new orders.

Looking back in 2022 on his years in marketing at Shopify, he posted on X: "I spent very little time & money (read $0) on brand or brand marketing. Instead, I focused on digital, attributable, direct marketing." The same day, he added on X: "People would invariably ask why I didn't buy billboards, TV commercials, event sponsorships, and other crap to 'build our brand.' I'd cheekily tell them that I got free brand impressions via the millions of ads [from Shopify merchants] on Google and Facebook that people saw . . . each day."

Miller's outside-of-the-box perspective on the marketing function was similar to that of Andrew Chen, a partner at venture capital firm Andreessen Horowitz and author of *The Cold Start Problem*, a book on startups. Chen argued "that coding and technical chops are now an essential part of being a great marketer" for online companies.[3] Online companies such as Pinterest, Zynga, Groupon, Instagram and Dropbox went "from zero to tens of millions users in just a few years" by integrating into platforms that had hundreds of millions of users, like Facebook. Airbnb was another case. With its Craigslist integration, the company created a way to post an Airbnb listing that a traditional marketer would not have come up with — instead, it took a marketing-minded engineer.

THE BACK OFFICE

CFO Russ Jones, CLO Joe Frasca and Head of HR Brittany Forsyth were not in the spotlight much. But they still made important contributions to Shopify.

Jones's extensive experience in finance helped get Shopify's accounts ready to go public. One of the first steps was to move to a fiscal year ending in December and report the accounts in U.S. dollars, using U.S. GAAP rules. He knew that young tech firms sometimes end up doing an IPO, and having the accounts in U.S. dollars and GAAP rules would be acceptable to Canadian investors but also appeal to investors from the United States.

When Jones joined Shopify in 2011, it was an early-stage company headed by a young programmer still learning the ropes as a CEO. "I got the impression initially Tobi wasn't sure what a CFO did," Jones told *The Role Forward Podcast by Mosaic Tech.*[1] "Shopify had gone looking for a CFO because one of the venture capitalists said, 'Okay Tobi, I'll invest in your company but you have to promise you'll use some of the money to hire a finance person.'"

The amusing episodes, according to Jones, included Lütke calling account receivables "negative payables" and speaking of something puzzling called "revenue leakage." The latter turned out to be a discrepancy between the amounts that were invoiced and the amounts that showed up in the bank. Jones rolled up his sleeves and for about a week went through the payments step by step, checking details such as the transaction fees taken out by the credit companies and banks. He ultimately discovered that the "leakage" was nothing nefarious, just a timing issue: the dates on the invoices were different than the processing dates of the credit card companies, so a transaction invoiced near the end of one reporting period could be recorded by the credit card company in the next reporting period. Once this was all straightened out, the process was automated so it would be easier to add new revenue sources as the company grew.

"I think a lot of finance teams make the mistake of just doing something to get the job done and say later on they'll put in the right processes or the right controls and then all of sudden they're trying to go public and get a warning entered on their prospectus about poor financial controls and stuff like that," Jones explained.

He also thought it was important for growth companies "to ask if a process can scale up and if the answer is no, then fix it as soon as you can." He had previously been at another growth company and learned that "if you're not careful, finance can become a roadblock to scaling up a business — the right systems and processes have to be put in place early on."

Frasca had a lot to contribute as well. He led the legal team and made sure all the i's were dotted and t's crossed on legal documents needed to run Shopify — especially when it came to the IPO and acquisition of other companies. His legal department was also responsible for representing Shopify in court on matters such as patent infringements. Forsyth handled personnel, namely functions such as payroll, training programs, appraisals, and employee communication. Weinand continued to specialize in creating workplaces to bring out the best in employees and teamed up with Forsyth in shaping Shopify's culture and recruiting. Fauser and his legions of programmers did the heavy lifting down in the depths of Shopify's code base.

It took some time to get going, but Shopify was now on an even more amazing leg of its phenomenal journey. The crew was at their stations, navigating unknown climes and unfamiliar landscapes. It helped that much attention had been paid to crafting an operating environment that could inspire them during the voyage.

The Shopify Environment

In Shopify's early years, Weinand and Lütke wanted to shape the work environment to bring out the best in its employees. For the two co-founders, this priority went beyond designing the interior of an office. It also included workplace culture, recruitment and engagement. Before dealing with these dimensions, however, let's examine an aspect rather unique to Shopify's environment: the location of its offices.

THE CITY'S HIPPEST SCENE

In May of 2011, the topic of office location came up for discussion during a Shopify luncheon at a restaurant in Ottawa's ByWard Market. "There was some talk to move out to the burbs where there is a ton of space to grow and work alongside other large high-tech companies [in Kanata]," wrote a co-op student, Anna, in her blog. But Lütke put a damper on the notion. He was of the opinion that "downtown Ottawa represents Shopify's culture and style," Anna added. "To move away from that wouldn't be in sync with the company's values and image."[1]

The company's blistering pace of growth compelled it to relocate its headquarters five times within its first 15 years; all the selected locations were in the Elgin Street and ByWard Market corridor of downtown Ottawa — one of the trendiest parts of the city. It was filled with restaurants, outdoor patios, nightclubs, street malls, comedy shows, museums, shops, grand hotels, Victorian-era brick buildings and towers clad in glass, concrete and metal.

In this area, there was also the posh National Arts Centre for evenings out to operas, symphonies, Shakespearean plays, and shows by magicians, hypnotists and other top billings. Behind it, leisure craft docked on the Rideau Canal, which flowed north to the locks between Parliament Hill and the Château Laurier hotel, then down into the Ottawa River. In front of the National Arts Centre was the National War Memorial with its tall granite arch, at the base of which more than two dozen statues of infantry, cavalry, pilots, sailors and other combatants strained forward toward some unseen battlefield.

Throughout this bustling corridor during the day, throngs of tourists, office workers and locals coursed down the sidewalks for lunches, coffee and shopping. Revellers filled them to overflowing at night. Nearby were apartments to rent or condos to buy, all within walking distance of Shopify and virtually every amenity. There was a vibe to the place that would appeal to Shopify's young workers, many of whom were fresh out of university.

More than 20 kilometres away to the west was the Kanata technology park once dubbed "Silicon Valley North." Nortel Networks, Mitel, and other past tech stars once ruled the roost there. But the location was not Shopify's kind of place: the ambiance was — well, non-existent. Picture a sedate slice of suburbia divided by boulevards of cars speeding past strip malls, gas stations, Tim Hortons, fast-food joints and the squat office buildings of several dozen tech companies.

OFFICES IN PARADISE

When Shopify's office at Tucker's Marketplace got too crowded, it moved to several floors of the S.J. Major Ltd. heritage building, further east on York Street. This time Weinand had a much bigger budget thanks to the infusion of cash from venture capitalists. He went all out in creating what must have seemed like an employee's paradise. Journalist Mark Anderson visited the Shopify offices at the S.J. Major building in November of 2012. In a *Profit* magazine article, he marvelled at the decor and perks:

> The workspace itself looks like a cross of a sci-fi movie set, an avant-garde art gallery and a Toys "R" Us outlet. Floor-to-ceiling chalkboards line the hallway and are covered with murals, doodles and slogans. . . . The offices and conference rooms are named after video games and are elaborately decorated, employees receive annual allowances to tart up their spaces as they see fit. . . . Staff also get memberships to one of Ottawa's toniest health clubs, catered gourmet lunches each day, $250 a year to spend on sports gear . . . and a maid service that's dispatched twice monthly to clean employee homes.[1]

Although the settings and fringe benefits might have seemed rather extravagant, Shopify needed to attract and retain talented staff to be as appealing as Google and Facebook as a place to work — even more so to make up for cold Canadian winters! Perhaps some U.S. talent would be lured north but the hope was to also entice Canadian talent to stay in Canada. Lütke had found on his trips to tech hubs in the United States that a surprising number of executives and engineers were from Canada, so perhaps Shopify could stem some of the exodus. Besides, when Lütke looked at successful tech companies operating outside of Silicon Valley, a common thread seemed to be that they were usually the best place to work within a large metropolitan area.

In addition, Lütke and Weinand believed that the physical space in an office could nudge employees toward good behaviours in a way that would be more effective than rules, posters and procedures. For example, there was a problem with getting employees in the lunchroom to return their dirty dishes to be washed. What finally did work was putting the trolley for dirty dishes next to the exit so that it would be very easy for employees to drop them off on their way out. "If you want a river going down a mountain to go by a town you can't post a sign . . . you will have to dig a ditch," Lütke told Shane Parrish, host of the *Knowledge Project Podcast*.[2]

The office design can also have an impact on how well staff do their work. "If someone is in an inspiring space full of great design, where everything just works so well, your own craft is going to be significantly affected by this," Lütke told Parrish.[3] For example, it was discovered that the office kitchen had a poorly designed dispenser, with three buttons that had to be held down to get hot water to pour out. It was replaced with a sleeker design that had just one button. "I ask everyone to do world-class software . . . but if you arrived in the office and the first thing you do is get the hot water for your tea and you face some crazy user experience . . . then I can't really ask everyone to do better," Lütke added.

In 2014, two years after the journalist's visit to the S.J. Major building, Shopify had again grown so much that it needed to relocate to a larger venue, which turned out to be the six floors of the Performance Court office tower on Elgin Street. The floors were meticulously designed around specific themes — comic books, transportation hubs, a gangster hideout, an urban street landscape, back alley digs and a cottage retreat. The gangster floor, for example, was set in the 1920s in Chicago and included a poker room and library with a rotating bookshelf leading to a hidden boardroom.

Among the other embellishments throughout the floors were a yoga studio, a gourmet kitchen serving free lunches, a massage parlour, a nap room, arcade games, Ping Pong tables, a slide ending in a ball-pit room, a soundproof go-kart and skateboard track, meeting rooms that looked like a giant sauna or artist's loft, and an indoor backyard deck with artificial grass. Of course, there was a beer keg for Friday afternoon get-togethers. Floor layouts had open concepts for small groups of about six programmers to foster interaction and teamwork but there were also quiet rooms and nooks for introverts to work and think in solitude. The corner rooms were not for senior executives but places for project teams to meet.

Lütke's office looked like a ski chalet with a fireplace. It had snowboards displayed on the walls and shelves, some of which had been retrieved from Snowdevil's old inventory or repurchased from customers who had bought back in 2004. Weinand surprised Lütke with the decor. "I didn't actually know what my office was going to look like until the day we moved into the new place," he told an interviewer in 2016.[4]

Finally, in 2018, the ever-expanding Shopify leased just under 20 floors in the Plaza 234 office tower on Laurier Avenue West, a stone's throw from Performance Court. It was an occasion for another retrofitting. As Lütke said to *Signal v. Noise*: "I firmly believe that the only way to get a great product is to have a company that is having fun. If your corporate culture is nondescript, you will end up with nondescript software."[5]

SKIP THE SHIT SANDWICHES

As Shopify's growth took flight, the task of nurturing its core values was handed to Weinand with his appointment in 2012 as Chief Culture Officer (CCO). He would work on this assignment in collaboration with Forsyth while retaining his duties as CDO.

In an interview for the *Hazel Blog*, Weinand said the definition of culture that resonated with him was: "Culture is the beliefs and willing behaviours of a group of people."[1] With the right beliefs or values, a company didn't have to direct or monitor employees very much; nor did it need to formulate a lot of rules and procedures. Employees would on their own initiative be looking for ways they could contribute and add value. At a 2019 Core Summit Conference, Lütke riffed on Shopify's culture:

> Everyone in the company knew that — wherever possible — we would resist creating excessive process and rules. Instead, we wanted everyone to use their best judgment, bring their own authentic selves to work, and add little bits of their own lived experience. Then, everyone in the company simply trusts that, against the backdrop of all that is happening, great judgment ends up winning, and people make good choices. The truth is, though, that this started at around 20 people, but it continued to work for us at 40 people, 400 people, and even now at 5,000 people.[2]

Having core values can be a way for a large company to retain many of the positive aspects of a startup, Lütke and Weinand felt. Without a lot of rules, procedures or close supervision, employees had more autonomy to get stuff done. Having a greater say in performing jobs could also release creativity and productivity while providing job satisfaction.

What were Shopify's core values? One was: "We value people who get shit done," to use the phrasing from Shopify's early *Annual Reports* and IPO Prospectus (it is believed Shopify enjoys the distinction of being the only company to get the word "shit" into its prospectus). In later *Annual Reports*, the phrase was replaced with the toned-down equivalent, "We value people who are impactful."

Staff were given latitude to deliver results and told not to be afraid to take risks. As Lütke told *Motley Fool* in 2018, failure "is not a bad word at Shopify. . . . We usually refer to it as a successful discovery of something that didn't work."[3] On the *Disruptors* podcast in 2021, Forsyth added: "New hires are empowered by telling them they are going to fail and it's actually okay. Failure is part of the learning process. We talk a lot about these mental models and create a psychological safety zone that gives them permission to experiment, fail, change their mind."[4]

Within Shopify, negative feedback was not to be interpreted as a put-down. Employees were urged to give and welcome honest opinions so everyone got better at their craft and issues didn't fester. Lütke and Weinand found that Canadians were too nice, so they needed encouragement to participate in more direct communication.

Feedback was best served directly to avoid dilution of the impact needed to promote growth. "I am not a fan of the popular 'shit sandwich,'"[5] Weinand declared (shit sandwiches give negative feedback between two slices of positive feedback). "We need to be able to openly talk about issues," he added. For those viewing negative feedback as a personal affront, the recommended reading was Carol Dweck's *Mindset: The New Psychology of Success*, a guide to converting fixed mindsets into growth mindsets.

However, disregarding the feedback and chronically repeating mistakes or habitually failing to deliver projects ran one's "trust battery" down with superiors and co-workers, which could lead to closer supervision or poor ratings on evaluations. The "trust battery" was charged at 50% when people were hired, as Lütke said; every time they worked on a project, the trust battery was charged or discharged based on what transpired.

Probably the second-most important cultural value at Shopify was "thrive on change." At its core, Shopify's culture embraced staff who were not only resourceful and adaptable but also "antifragile," meaning they emerged better than before from trials (recommended reading was Nassim Nicholas Taleb's book *Antifragile: Things That Gain from Disorder*). If they saw a tidal wave coming, they grabbed their surfboards — and maybe even ended up more skilled at doing some tricky flips or rolls on the whitecaps. Software firms like Shopify needed such sturdy individuals on board because of the frequent disruptions in new technologies. If a new thing was emerging, it needed to be quickly investigated and addressed; teams should be ready to switch to new tasks virtually at the drop of a hat, even in the midst of a project.

Shopify's culture also valued people who were "committed learners." Emerging stronger from upheavals and keeping up with the company's rapid growth required continuously learning new things and getting comfortable with the uncomfortable transition periods. Often recommended to employees for reading and discussion were the books from the Shopify Book Bar.[6] The over two dozen books on innovation, design, leadership, business organization and other related topics were well read — to such an extent that "people have accused Shopify of being a book club thinly veiled as a public company," Lütke told *The Observer Effect* in 2020.[7]

"The core competency of our business needs to be how to thrive in chaos and how to react quicker than anyone else," Lütke told Calacanis during his *This Week in Startups* podcast.[8] To promote adaptability, Lütke applied Chaos engineering and periodically subjected Shopify to random disruptions." For example, he would log into Shopify's server farms and turn off random servers, to make sure the company was prepared in the event servers actually crashed. The tests created an environment where staff would feel that things going wrong was not such a rare thing, leaving them more prepared to cope with Black Swan events. Resiliency can be lost when everything goes right for a long time and complacency sets in.

The other traits that Shopify's *Annual Reports* mentioned as valuable were building for the long term, making great decisions quickly and being merchant-obsessed. The latter was particularly important. Indeed, during Shopify's early years, there was not as much focus on making a profit as there was on helping merchants grow their businesses. Shopify's mission was to make commerce better for everyone; that was a mission worth pursuing not just for the company but also for the global economy itself. Entrepreneurs drive economic growth, innovation, job creation and a lot of other variables related to our living standards; becoming a full-time or part-time entrepreneur can also be a necessity for many or a way to self-actualize and obtain independence for others.

To increase empathy for entrepreneurs, Shopify employees were encouraged to run their own Shopify businesses on the side. As a dutiful Shopify employee, Daniel Patricio decided in 2015 to start a Shopify store called Bull & Cleaver, selling a South African–style beef jerky called biltong. He had come to Canada from South Africa with his family when he was a teen and could not find biltong anywhere, so he thought he could make some money providing South Africans in North America with this delicious treat. He ran some Facebook ads when the South African team was playing in the 2015 Rugby World Cup, and business soared. By October 2021, Bull & Cleaver's sales to South Africans *and* North Americans were delivering $30,000 a month in income. That's when he quit his job to be a full-time entrepreneur. Shopify didn't mind — such departures were part and parcel of its effort to cultivate a kinship with entrepreneurs.

Shopify also values diversity. "I can directly measure the quality of a meeting by how different the people are," Lütke told Parrish in 2019.[9] For decades, Canada has been promoting a multicultural society and Shopify is a quintessentially Canadian company in this regard. With uniformity, "you end up losing something that makes companies really much better," Lütke declared.

RECRUITMENT: KEY TO SHOPIFY

When Weinand was given the CCO role in 2012, it included responsibility for recruitment. The hiring process could be used by Weinand and Forsyth to screen employees for the likelihood that they would be a good fit with the company's core values. To this end, the interview process placed a lot of weight on getting to know the applicant through their "Life Story," which was simply a conversation about their interests, passions, key decisions and major turning points in life.

It could be said Shopify's core values resemble the traits of an entrepreneur in many respects. So it's even better if the applicant has had actual entrepreneurial experience or their personal history exhibited a strong inclination toward it. On the other hand, certain personality types rarely get through. "For instance, we ban any office politics and thus try to avoid adding people who in their previous jobs, worked towards their own personal gain rather than their team's," Weinand told the *Hazel Blog*.[1]

Through the Life Story technique, Shopify wanted to uncover events in the job seeker's life that demonstrated they were likely to fare well at Shopify. For example, was there a positive reaction to unexpected upsets? When CEO Lütke was interviewing for an executive assistant, the applicant who got the job told him about a trip he took to Europe; he went there with a band to help his friend organize the tour because he liked doing that sort of thing (That's good, thought Lütke). But then the bassist didn't show up. The band could have packed it in or played without the bassist even if the performances would be subpar. Instead, the organizer learned how to play the bass lines himself and filled in during the performances. "You're hired," Lütke told him.[2]

When CMO Miller was interviewing a candidate in 2015 and learned he was working a successful side hustle selling selfie sticks online, it was a big factor in awarding the job. This applicant, Brandon Chu, had discovered that bestsellers on amazon.com tended to become bestsellers on amazon.ca with a lag, so his successful gig was arbitraging that lag. At Shopify, Chu went on to become a vice president responsible for the partnership ecosystem.

Finkelstein, too, was keen on hiring people with entrepreneurial tendencies: "When I'm hiring, I don't want the person who played on the tennis team," he explained to *Canadian Business* in 2016. "I want the person who created the tennis team. I don't want the person who participated in some charity; I want someone who created a brand-new charity. I look for people who are self-starters — people who have a bit of a founder mentality."[3]

When it came to interviewing programmers, craftsmanship was an important aspect. For Lütke, the Life Story segment became a way to distinguish between left- and right-brained coders. Left-brained ones were scientific types that could write lots of complicated code with speed. But Lütke preferred the right-brained ones because they were the creative types that could produce elegant solutions requiring much less coding. So, when the Life Story segment asked programmer candidates what they did for fun, Shopify was hoping to hear something creative, like playing a musical instrument or doing photography as a hobby.

Often, the executives didn't need to conduct interviews to know if someone would be a valuable addition. In October 2019, Lütke saw a message on X from Kyung Ryoo, a pro gamer who had racked up wins in StarCraft tournaments from 2010 to 2015. Ryoo was 30 years old at the time and had retired from professional gaming to get a degree in software engineering and his X message said he was looking for an internship for the summer of 2020. Within a day, Lütke replied and said he would be happy to hire Ryoo as an intern. "Your StarCraft accomplishments are enough of a CV. Place is yours if you want it," he added.[4] Later, he elaborated in a Reddit forum: "It's insanely hard to become a pro in StarCraft, significantly harder than it is to get a degree. So I feel like this should be highly valuable on a CV."[5] Ryoo accepted the intern position.

However, Shopify's biggest source of proactive recruitment was "acqui-hiring." This term refers to acquiring certain startup companies not just for their technical expertise but also to bring their founders into the Shopify fold so they would become product managers running a particular area of the company with a considerable amount of freedom. Lütke was well acquainted with the poor track record in the industry of acquiring other companies, so his acquisitions were conditional on the staff in the acquired company welcoming the opportunity to become part of Shopify. Some of the founders joining Shopify included:

- Daniel Debow, VP of Product, founded the startup Helpful.com
- Satish Kanwar, VP of Product Acceleration, started Jet Cooper
- Glen Coates, VP of Product, founded Handshake
- Carl Rivera, VP of Product, co-founder and CEO of Tictail

- Mike Schmidt, Head of Shopify Collabs, founded Dovetail
- Kaz Nejatian, COO, founded Kash

In fact, much of Shopify was made up of fairly autonomous teams run by former founders. Some of the founders arrived, as mentioned, after their startup was acquired, while others were failed founders who had subsequently joined Shopify. The failed founders actually played an important role. They "ended up being an amazing source of talent for Shopify," Chu remarked during an April 2021 *Black Box of Product Management* podcast. Many of those who "made it through to leadership levels were ex-founders and we liked to joke, but it was totally true, that our gold mine was finding failed founders . . . they had been through that founder experience and had the weight of everything on them, so they often kind of had a chip on their shoulder and wanted to prove themselves."[6]

In short, bringing in so many entrepreneurs and startup founders was likely a big reason why Shopify was able to scale up to a large size yet maintain a startup culture and entrepreneurial mindset to get stuff done as a culture-driven organization. As Finkelstein replied to a question raised at a conference in 2019: "One of the keys to our success . . . is that nearly every team that you're on at Shopify feels like a startup."[7]

Often, people who cleared the Life Story segment of their interviews didn't have all the boxes checked for technical skills and experience required by the position. This was to be expected since Shopify was not based in a primary talent market, like Silicon Valley, where there is an ample supply of fully qualified workers ready to hit the office floor running. However, job tenures in those primary markets averaged 18 months, much shorter than the 5 to 10 years in secondary talent markets like Ottawa, Toronto, Montreal and Vancouver. Since they would be staying for a while, this meant Shopify could still hire staff who were short of resume-type credentials but long on potential, then invest in training them up to their potential.

It's not like most interviewees were badly lacking in qualifications, either. Ottawa is close to Canada's major metropolitan areas of Toronto and Montreal; within this corridor are more than 15 million inhabitants. In the Ottawa region itself, there were in 2018 more than 1,500 technology companies and the highest per capita concentration of scientists and engineers in Canada. Shopify's offices were also close to several universities, so high-potential employees could also be found through internships and campus recruiting. Every time Lütke met a professor, he asked which of his students were amazing and hired them quickly.

To give a boost to recruitment, Shopify began seeking partnerships with Canadian universities to set up its Shopify Dev Degree program. In 2015, the first to sign up was Carleton University, about a 10-minute drive from Shopify's Ottawa headquarters. The Shopify Dev Degree was more of a hands-on approach, similar to the apprenticeship system in Germany. Each term, students spent a good part of their week working on a team alongside Shopify employees while taking university courses during the rest of their week. Academic credits were given for work performed at Shopify, and graduates received an accredited degree in computer science within three to four years. "On top of this, we will pay your tuition and give you a competitive salary and vacation," noted the Dev Degree website. "That's over $160,000 (CDN) in total financial support."[8]

But for those seeking to work at Shopify, the Life Story technique was a key tool for screening candidates. In a post to his blog, Josh C. Simmons described his experience applying for engineering jobs at two top U.S. technology companies and Shopify. At the U.S. companies, he had to solve algorithm problems during his interviews. "My hunch with those companies was that it wouldn't have been a major issue if I was videoing in from the State Penitentiary . . . as long as I solved the algorithms correctly," he commented. On the other hand, during his interviews at Shopify, Simmons found the "Life Story was a refreshing and free-ranging conversation that felt humanizing." He landed a job at Shopify and observed in his blog post: "The people were phenomenal. I think assholes are pretty effectively filtered out during the Life Story round."[9]

ENGAGEMENT

Another focus for Weinand and Forsyth was nurturing engagement in order to promote job satisfaction, productivity and employee retention.

It began with the onboarding process: the orientation period was several weeks long, much longer at Shopify than at most other companies.

Afterward, new employees were placed on small teams of 6 to 10 co-workers, at least one of whom was a seasoned veteran capable of serving as a mentor. Working as part of a supportive, small team made work feel less daunting and more personal — like being in a startup or on a journey solving challenges with friends. To further assist with employee development at all levels, coaches on a talent acceleration team provided support in various ways.

Shopify had several channels for promoting the flow of information throughout the organization. A centerpiece was the weekly town hall meeting, where employees met with executives and were informed about what was going on at the board and executive level. Included were Ask Me Anything (AMA) sessions where anyone could ask an executive a question. These meetings and sessions also allowed the executives to "really understand what are the pent-up issues, where is the anxiety and what people are wondering about," as Finkelstein told FUBU founder Daymond John.[1]

"What I like most about Shopify is its transparency . . . leaders at Shopify are open and honest about our roadmap, success, failures and exciting milestones," posted Shopify intern Anna on her blog *Life @ Shopify* in February 2013. "We are in the loop; we know what's going on and we are encouraged to voice our opinions."[2]

Contributing to the flow of information were the internal podcasts Lütke and Finkelstein put out every two weeks for staff. They gave the history and context of past topics or issues involving the company and why decisions were taken. The podcast was particularly useful for getting staff up to speed on what Shopify was doing in pursuit of its objectives.

One initiative boosted the spirit of innovation and experimentation: Hack Days. Every quarter, employees got to take a break from their regular duties to work on whatever they wanted for two days as long it was of benefit to Shopify. One completed project messaged the receptionist whenever the beer keg got low so a refill order could be submitted before the trauma of it going dry. Other Hack Days projects found practical use on the Shopify e-commerce platform, including a "point-of-sale system, flash-sale app (Frenzy) and carbon-offsetting option at merchant checkouts," as Meghan Rosen noted.[3]

Another important initiative was Unicorn, an internal messaging channel for employees to share developments in the projects they were working on, and to thank co-workers for their help and/or contribution to an assignment. Shopify split 1% of company revenue evenly among employees so they would each have a bonus budget from which they could transfer dollars to other employees who had helped them with a problem or did a good job on something important to the company. The bonuses were paid out quarterly to recipients through payroll.

Unicorn rewarded those people who had expertise and shared it with co-workers to help them solve problems — which gets company work done sooner and raises the knowledge level within the office. Unicorn was also a good way to reward those who made quiet but significant contributions to helping others. It's easy to spot them in small companies but less so in big companies. Lütke cited the case of a Shopify recruit who looked promising during his interviews but was underperforming during his probationary period. When his Unicorn was checked, it turned out he had a large number of people thanking him for his help. "This was his own way to integrate into the company and it was tremendously useful," Lütke said.

Unicorn was launched during the startup days as an attempt to stay aligned as a team. Everyone was working hard and solving problems, but to prevent duplication of effort or going off in different directions, Shopify needed people to self-report on their work. "The trouble was, we couldn't get anyone to share their accomplishments," Lütke noted in a blog post. He and Weinand couldn't understand why. Then it occurred to them that it wasn't part of Canadian culture to "brag" about the good things one had done. So Unicorn was part of the solution to draw this information out.[4]

"Unicorn is what . . . really helped us get through this 30 to 70 employee death valley, which is very hard to get through," Lütke said at a Business of Software conference. "It's the time when your company realizes, we can't all go to have lunch anymore and talk everything over. You don't know what the people in sales might have accomplished, especially if you are in development and so on."[5]

Things like talent acceleration programs, Hack Days and the Unicorn channel were important instruments for making Shopify what it was. "If you want to become better as a company — build your people," Lütke told Dan Martell, host of the *Escape Velocity Show*. "Help your people have their breakthroughs . . . and eureka moments. . . . If you figure out ways to ratchet up the quality of thinking and decision-making within the company, in a consistent way, eventually it will become unbeatable."[6]

Empowering Entrepreneurs

Lütke and Lake had sensed in 2004 and 2005 that there was a commercial opportunity in e-commerce and set about acting on their hunch. In doing so, they landed on the leading edge of a paradigm shift that Hemant Taneja was to call "unscaling" in his 2018 book *Unscaled: How AI and a New Generation of Upstarts Are Creating the Economy of the Future*. The core idea was that new technologies were enabling small- and medium-sized businesses to compete against the large companies that historically dominated markets.

THE UNSCALING PARADIGM

Cloud computing was a major technological advance behind the paradigm shift. It began to take shape in the 1990s and went mainstream in the early 2000s with the launch of Amazon Web Services, which made unused computing capacity on Amazon's servers available to outside parties on a pay-as-you-go basis. Google, Microsoft and other major tech companies followed with offerings of their own in the ensuing years. This business model became known as "software as a service" (SaaS); it gave businesses the ability to access a range of software services without having to make a large expenditure on IT infrastructure and programs. When Shopify was launched in 2006, it too was a SaaS provider.

The requirement for expenditures on hardware and software was one of those huge barriers that made it difficult to become a retailer. Surviving against a giant like Walmart was a problem too: the latter could open an outlet in a town and put a third to half of the local retailers out of business because it had the scale and capital resources to acquire (among other things) new technologies such as barcodes, Radio Frequency Identification, sophisticated logistics, inventory management and direct connections to suppliers.

If the ability to rent computing power is combined with the ability to "rent ways to reach consumers via social networks and search engines, rent production from contract manufacturers, and rent distribution through FedEx and UPS," as Taneja argued, businesses using SaaS platforms could level the playing field — or even tilt it in their favour.[1] Finkelstein had discovered this when he was in law school: his printed T-shirt business, Smoofer, flourished in the shadow of Walmart by purchasing digital ads in towns where the retail colossus was absent.

Moreover, as the subscriber base at a SaaS provider grew large, it could bolster small businesses in other ways. One was leveraging the collective size of the merchant base on the platform to extract large discounts from shippers, couriers and other suppliers of services to merchants. Also, the large database of transactions between merchants and customers stored on SaaS computers could be analyzed to develop ancillary services such as fraud detection and loans (e.g. Shopify Capital). Furthermore, as its reach went global, the SaaS platform enabled small merchants to go global too; niche products that were uneconomic in local markets could become profitable in global markets.

In addition, small businesses had access to a variety of digital tools that enhanced the efficacy of business operations. One example: the third-party cookies that made it possible to target digital ads to social media users based on their online interests (but killed in 2021 by Apple). Other examples of useful digital tools: the apps that enhance market research via A/B testing (visitors are directed to different versions of a merchant's web page to see which will lead to the most sales) and the apps for targeting, personalizing and automating email (and SMS) marketing campaigns.

Small businesses moreover got a boost from technological developments outside the domains of SaaS platforms. Of note were the online crowdfunding platforms that enabled many startups to raise capital. The most popular of these was Kickstarter. Founded in 2009, it has provided more than $7.5 billion in funding to over 245,000 projects (as of 2023). On Kickstarter, backers did not receive an equity interest — they could only receive incentives such as shout-outs, swag, or pre-order discounts. Another prominent crowdfunding platform, with some differences, was Indiegogo. Others, such as Fundable, let accredited investors take equity positions in startups. In 2016, Shopify added the Crowdfunder app, which accepted pre-orders as a way to validate an idea and fund it.

A retailer that went the crowdfunding route was Allbirds, a seller of superfine merino wool sneakers. Their product, which had an eco-friendly and pleasing minimalist design, was named "the world's most comfortable shoes" by *Time* magazine. The founder, Tim Brown, was a New Zealander whose first sneaker prototypes were dead ends — and just as he was about to give up, he was told: "Why don't you put it on Kickstarter so you can fail and get on with it?"[2] Within days, his 1,000 sneakers on Kickstarter were pre-ordered, providing a large infusion of cash and proof of interest. Allbirds then opened a store on Shopify in 2016 and their footwear became a smash hit with the help of influencers on TikTok, YouTube and other platforms (particularly the ones espousing carbon-neutral and renewable causes). They became so popular that Allbirds was able to list its shares on the Nasdaq in late 2021 and become a public company.

DIRECT TO CONSUMER

The new technologies made it much easier for businesses to sell directly to consumers. Not needing wholesalers and other middlemen, direct-to-consumer merchants enjoyed lower costs and could earn higher margins or lower their prices to boost sales. They could also provide customers with better shopping experiences and product information than box stores, by adding video, audio and written content to their website, as well as online chat. In addition, they could get to know their customers and be in a position to provide products that fit their needs better.

One of the early demonstrations was provided by Warby Parker, an online retailer of prescription glasses and contact lenses that started up in 2010 and in short order was disrupting market leader Luxottica. As an online retailer, Warby Parker sold quality eyewear at lower prices by cutting out middlemen such as optical shops and licensing companies. They also offered conveniences such as being able to try on frames virtually or through home delivery. Lastly, they followed a social entrepreneurship model, donating glasses to the needy for every pair sold.

There were also many examples among established consumer brand-name companies such as Heinz, Proctor & Gamble and Mattel. They too could increase margins and/or lower prices by cutting out the wholesalers and retailers in their supply chains. Direct-to-consumer merchandising also helped consumer-packaged-goods companies to combat the loss of sales to in-house brands developed by grocery stores and other retailers.

CELEBRITY MERCHANTS

SaaS providers gave pro athletes, film stars, creators and other celebrities an alternative to signing sponsorship deals with retailers and manufacturers. If they had a large fan base, they could instead open a Shopify store and sell directly to consumers. With this option, they often participated in the design of products and were in a position to authentically endorse them.

Finkelstein and Shopify welcomed many celebs onto the Shopify platform. One of the first to sign up was Kylie Jenner, a member of the Kardashian-Jenner family featured in the reality show *Keeping Up With the Kardashians*. She was also one of the most followed persons on social media; her Instagram account, in which she posted makeup tips and tutorials, had over 130 million followers. When she launched Kylie Cosmetics on Shopify, sales went through the roof. In fact, her listings of lipstick and lip-liner kits usually sold out within minutes (by the time she turned 21 in 2021, *Forbes* magazine had declared her the youngest self-made billionaire, unseating Facebook's Mark Zuckerberg, who did it at the age of 23).[1]

DROPSHIPPERS

Through dropshipping, SaaS platforms opened the door to entrepreneurship for just about anyone. With dropshipping, a merchant didn't have to spend time and money on inventory and fulfilling orders. They could simply focus on marketing their products and when an order came in, pass it to a manufacturer or wholesaler for shipping directly to the consumer. This made it very easy and inexpensive to give entrepreneurship a try; many people used dropshipping to try out different marketing approaches and/or products in search of a profitable business idea. "In my view, dropshipping is basically a great entryway into entrepreneurship for people that are risk-averse," Finkelstein told the *Guardian*.[1] If a marketing or product idea doesn't work out, the merchant still could continue to try other ideas.

Dropshipping took off in the 2010s when Chinese e-commerce giant Alibaba launched AliExpress, an app for shipping inexpensive products from Chinese manufacturers to global consumers. The low prices from China attracted a lot of customers. In 2015, the Oberlo app was added to the Shopify platform to expand the range of products for dropshipping; in 2022, Oberlo was replaced by the DSers, which provided even more choices.

A notable case where dropshipping and a creative marketing approach were used during the validation phase of a business idea was Gymshark, founded in England by pizza-delivery driver Ben Francis and his friend Lewis Morgan in 2012. In his teens, Francis had joined a gym and watched bodybuilders on YouTube to learn how to get results pumping iron. His workouts also gave him some business ideas.

His first idea was to sell bodybuilding supplements from an online store, using dropshipping to test it out. The effort was a flop. Francis next turned to fitness garments — at the time, they tended to be large and baggy. Something more streamlined and tapered would be better. He used his earnings from pizza deliveries to buy a sewing machine, which he set up in his parents' garage to make the clothes.

Lacking funds for traditional marketing, he sent free Gymshark apparel to personal trainers in London, asking that they mention the clothing online if they liked it — or if they didn't, give him feedback. Many of them gave his apparel good reviews. When the orders picked up, he outsourced fabrication and logistics to a firm in Asia; after accumulating enough capital, he took back control of the fulfillment and inventory process. In 2020, a private equity firm acquired a 21% stake in Gymshark, giving it a valuation of £1 billion.

As the ranks of dropshippers swelled, however, so did consumer complaints. Some surfaced in the media: "If you've purchased clothes from an Instagram brand that took ages to arrive, looked nothing like the photographs and were terrible quality, you've probably fallen victim to dropshippers," wrote journalist Sirin Kale in the June 14, 2020, *Guardian*.[2]

A guide to dropshipping by Corey Ferreira appears on Shopify's website. To its credit, the article presents a balanced picture of the pros and cons.[3] The pros include a low capital requirement, easy set-up, low overhead, flexibility in work location, and ease of scaling up. As for the drawbacks, the main one is low profit margins. "Because it's so easy to get started . . . many competing businesses will set up a dropshipping store and sell items at rock-bottom prices in an attempt to grow revenue. . . . This increase in competition will quickly hurt the potential profit margin in a niche," noted Ferreira. A second drawback: when the manufacturers or wholesalers mess up on delivery and product quality, it can reflect badly on the dropshipper, and they could end up dealing with irate customers, or worse, none. A third: it is hard for the merchant to differentiate or customize the products they are selling.

Retail Operating System I

In early 2013, Lütke announced to company employees that Shopify was going to transition to a "retail operating system." Similar to how computer operating systems deliver spreadsheets, word processing, apps, games and other tools to desktop computers and mobile devices, a retail operating system would deliver a wide range of tools that entrepreneurs could use for commerce, wherever it takes place. When Shopify first started, its focus was product-centric, on making it easy to create an attractive online store. Now, its focus was shifting to a mission, which was "making commerce better for everyone."

It would have been tempting to stay focused on online stores because they were delivering an exciting upswing in Shopify's revenues, and company staff was getting not only comfortable but good at meeting customer needs in this niche — whereas veering off in a new direction with an uncertain outcome would feel uncomfortable and unwise to many. On the other hand, Harvard professor Clayton Christensen had advised in his 1997 book, *The Innovator's Dilemma: When New Technologies Cause Great Firms to Fail*, that companies focused on satisfying customers' current needs should be wary of maximizing growth and profitability to the detriment of developing new and better ways to meet future needs of customers.

Helping merchants set up online stores was a good thing, but what they really wanted was to be successful and generate a profit; helping them do so would require Shopify to facilitate successful outcomes by removing barriers and pain points anywhere they are present. Moreover, in a rapidly evolving industry like e-commerce, the tools that merchants needed to be successful were also changing — so Shopify's product offering had to evolve to remain relevant.

CHANGING ENGINES MID-FLIGHT

Miller remembers the company meeting in 2013 at which Lütke announced his vision to "build the world's first retail operating system." It created quite a stir. "I remember the crowd leaving and saying 'Yeah, this sounds great. Let's build this retail operating system,'" observed Miller. However, in the following days, people were "kind of scratching their heads and saying, 'Well, what exactly is a retail operating system?'"[1] It became clearer in the months to come.

On August 12, 2013, one of the first utilities was released: Shopify POS, a point-of-sale device consisting of a wireless tablet for registering transactions within brick-and-mortar stores and syncing them with the transactions from an online store.[2] This feature came about because Shopify had noticed many of its customers with physical stores were spending a lot of money on systems integrators to synchronize their point-of-sale data with their Shopify online data. Shopify POS was a major point of departure for Shopify: because the company was now thinking about easing pain points for entrepreneurs, it was going "in a completely different direction" than simply being a provider of online stores.

With Shopify POS, the company was also greatly expanding its total addressable market by shifting to powering both online and offline commerce. The future of retail was not an either-or choice between online sales and in-store sales; it was more about the co-existence of both. The utility also opened up new ways of doing business: of note, salespersons equipped with iPads could use them anywhere on the shop floor to register sales right away, rather than send customers to line up and pay at a cash register. In 2014, Shopify POS was synced with Shopify Mobile, allowing merchants to use their smartphones to register sales inside their stores.

A second feature was also released the same day, August 12, 2013: Shopify Payments. It was an alternative to the third-party payment gateways (Visa, Mastercard, American Express, etc.) that merchants were using to process payments.[3] To launch this feature, Shopify formed a partnership with Stripe to use their technology. Fees were comparable with major credit cards: 2.25% to 2.9% of revenues.

Shopify Payments became popular with merchants because it resolved more pain points. It came bundled with store set-ups, which relieved merchants of the hassle of setting up their own payment accounts with a third-party service. For online stores already in existence, it could be activated with just a few clicks. There was also easier chargeback recovery and higher rates of converting shoppers into buyers (due to prepopulated fields, one-click purchases and other features, such as installments).

A third utility was released on February 4, 2014: Shopify Plus.[4] It started out as a white-glove service for merchants that had grown to a large size on the Shopify platform. It offered unlimited bandwidth, as well as additional storage and customization options. A key feature provided to clients was a dedicated account manager to assist with set-up, ongoing customizations, third-party integrations and other functions. Lütke and the other executives had become concerned that the firms growing to a large size on Shopify would feel they had to move to other platforms that specialized in large companies. Not only did Shopify Plus retain many of the larger Shopify merchants but it also attracted new subscribers who wanted a more customized product offering without the price tag and long delivery time frames of platforms catering to large companies.

A fourth feature was the launch, on March 31, 2015, of Multichannel Shopify, which gave merchants the ability to sell on social media websites and marketplaces through sales channels integrated with their Shopify dashboard.[5] After it was installed, merchants could advertise on these sites and the shoppers who clicked on the ads would be referred back to the merchant's website for more information or to take their order. It was quite convenient for merchants because it gave them access to multiple social websites from one spot on their dashboard. No setting up of separate stores on various sites was needed.

A fifth feature was introduced April 27, 2016: Shopify Capital, to plug gaps in bank lending to entrepreneurs and small businesses.[6] Banks tend to be more circumspect in lending to smaller business owners. They usually only agree to lend against the home equity or personal assets of the small businessperson, which can be a roadblock to obtaining sufficient funds. There usually is also a lengthy application process, credit checks and extensive paperwork.

Several other features were added to the retail operating system. They were mostly smaller-scale additions, such as: 1) Shopify Buy Buttons (2015) for merchants to sell products on websites other than their own, 2) the Frenzy mobile app (2016) for supporting flash sales, 3) Shopify QR codes (2017) for shoppers to scan codes on physical items with their phone camera in order to access the item in the merchant's online store, 4) the Arrive mobile app (2017) to let customers track their purchases from Shopify, and 5) Nest cams (2018) for merchants to remotely monitor the interior of their physical stores.

One of the more significant of the smaller-scale additions was Shopify Pay (2017), the consumer-facing, one-click checkout linked to the merchant-facing gateway service, Shopify Payments. Rebranded to Shop Pay in 2020, Shopify Pay stored buyers' payment, billing and shipping information to accelerate checkout with a simple "Buy Now" button on participating Shopify stores. Other benefits included: installment payments, loyalty programs, gift cards and upsell opportunities.

As the retail operating system unfolded, Miller's marketing responsibilities got more challenging. The transition "was a very tricky sort of thing to do, almost like changing the engines of a plane mid-flight," Miller declared during a *When It Clicked* podcast. "We were future-proofing the company but also trying not to lose our short-term customers."[7] The problem was that not too many merchants felt a need for a retail operating system just then. How does a person market a thing when many people don't yet feel a need for one, Miller wondered. Instead of trying to explain what a retail operating system is to a world that wasn't ready, Miller's solution for addressing both current and future needs of merchants was:

> Let's respond to what they're looking for, so if they're looking for a website hosting provider with a shopping cart, let's show up. If they're looking to sell on marketplaces let's show

> up; if they're looking to sell in retail stores, let's show up. And once we get them to start using Shopify, let's expose the broader strategy and platform to them.[8]

When any of the new utilities were not quickly embraced by the market, many Shopify developers, accustomed to the quick success of their past efforts, were disheartened. They felt that they had wasted their time. So a big part of the transition to meeting the upcoming needs of customers for Miller and other executives was keeping spirits up. Market adoption will just be a matter of time, they said. Such lags are to be expected. And for the most part, this was the case.

28,000 LINES OF JAVASCRIPT DELETED

In the back office, Fauser and his team were busy working on a major revamp of Shopify's software to increase the platform's capabilities in response to merchants' requests for new features (such as advanced refund management), and to support the greater demands of the envisioned retail operating system. It was a very ambitious coding assignment; Series A and Series B venture capital rounds were used to aggressively hire developers for the task. The upgrade, called Shopify 2, began in 2010 and took close to three years before the first release came out. Over this long interval, a phalanx of competitors, including Etsy, Weebly, Wix and Zaarly scooped up clients, leading Rip Empson to muse in *TechCrunch:* "There is now a long list of competitors in this space, and Shopify may not have helped itself by taking so long to push its redesign."[1]

Although Shopify's existing platform was still functioning while Shopify 2 was under development, perhaps it may not have been kept up to date as much as it should. But the Shopify 2 release was expected to turn Shopify into something more formidable than the offerings of its competitors. Moreover, with the $100-million Series C funding coming down the pipeline in 2013, there would be plenty of firepower for catching up.

In the planning stages, the project leaders for Shopify 2 decided to bypass more commonly used developmental frameworks in favour of a framework built in-house. As described in a company press release, Shopify 2 was "built using a cutting-edge JavaScript MVC framework called batman.js, developed in-house by Shopify and then released open-source."[2] Batman.js was written in CoffeeScript because Shopify was a Ruby on Rails shop and CoffeeScript looked familiar to Ruby on Rails programmers. For example, it shared the principle of "convention over configuration," which made its code more readable and faster to write. But this new framework increased the number of variables in play during the development phase and became a complicating factor.

Shopify 2 was released in April of 2013. Despite the lengthy gestation period, it became apparent that problems were still present. They included memory leaks and occasional browser crashes. Fast and easy prototyping of apps did not materialize as expected, developer onboarding was a significant challenge and attempts to fix problems led to new problems (such as response-time delays on mobile devices and older computers). Probably the most trouble of all was the duplication of maintaining two separate stacks. "Models needed to be represented both in Rails and in Batman, and both had to be tested," wrote Jamie Woo in the *Shopify Engineering* blog.[3]

As a consequence, a decision was made to quietly shelve batman.js and retire the Shopify 2 name. The new framework returned to a more classic architecture with some modern features: it had, among other things, server-side rendering, Turbolinks and a lightweight custom JavaScript binding system. The reboot of the project pared down the codebase dramatically, "deleting 28,000 lines of JavaScript," reported Woo.[4] It took only nine months to roll out the new version thanks to an emphasis on simplicity and developer friendliness, which allowed the work to be split over many teams.

"At Shopify, we strongly believe that any decision should be able to be questioned at any time," added Woo. "What ultimately enabled us to make the decision to switch was strong company values: open communication, a questioning nature as a core component of our culture ... instead of accepting [the] status quo or only making criticisms behind closed doors, we articulated the problems we were having and came up with a solution. We were able to move forward quickly towards this solution by openly accepting failure as a learning opportunity."[5]

SHOPIFY PAYMENTS: THE FOUNTAINHEAD

Shopify Payments was a tremendously important part of the retail operating system. Thanks to its payment processing fee ranging from 2.25% to 2.9% of merchant sales, this feature produced a fundamental change in Shopify's business model and arguably was the most significant reason why its revenues grew so fast for the rest of the 2010s. As the number of merchants and their sales grew on the platform, Shopify Payments greatly steepened the upward curve already in place.

Shopify Payments' contribution to revenue growth was not reported separately in its *Annual Reports* but the aggregate category, Merchant Solutions, was reported separately and it was driven mostly by Shopify Payments. The accounts showed that Merchant Solutions brought in 19% of Shopify's total revenues in 2012; 10 years later, it brought in 73.4% of total revenues. The graph "Growth in Components of Annual Revenues"

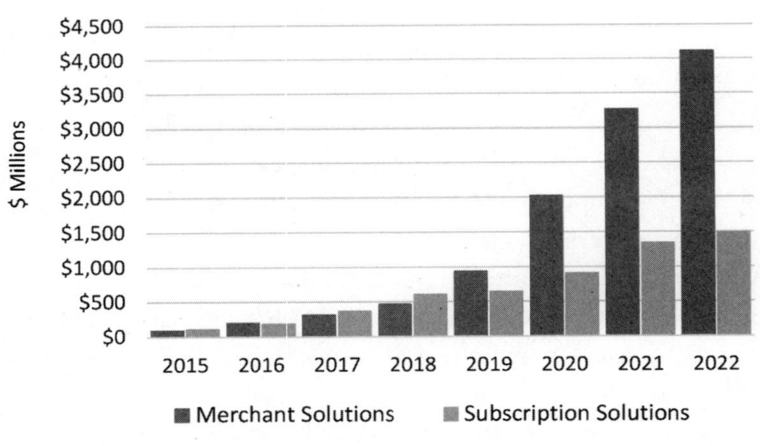

Data source: Shopify 2022 *Annual Report*

displays the trends since 2015 in Shopify's two revenue components of Merchant Solutions and Subscription Solutions.

With payments processing becoming such an important part of revenues, Shopify transitioned from a subscriptions model to largely a payments model, observed Ben Thompson, publisher of the *Stratechery* newsletter. "While Shopify started as an e-commerce platform company with a payments business tacked on, its financial results increasingly are that of a payments business with an e-commerce platform that functions first-and-foremost as a funnel to said payments business," he wrote in 2021.[1]

As Shopify became more of a payments business, it became much less susceptible to the pitfalls of subscription-based models, particularly the problem of churn. Shopify's merchants were not just paying a fixed subscription fee but also growing their sales, a percentage of which was collected by Shopify Payments. Moreover, as the merchants grew in size, they bought more merchant solutions, upgraded to higher subscription plans and signed up for a greater number of apps. In short, the merchants did not just keep paying the same fee but progressively made higher payments every year to Shopify in line with their rising sales. This is the dynamic that has more than offset revenues lost from merchants exiting Shopify.

Shopify's *Annual Reports* declare: "We consider our merchants' success to be one of the most powerful drivers of our business model . . . the strength of our business model lies in the consistent revenue growth coming from each cohort [businesses starting in different years on Shopify]." This situation is illustrated by the chart "Shopify's Annual Revenue by Cohort (2019-2022)" on page 104, which shows how growth in revenues from merchants joining in current and past years offset revenue lost from departing merchants, giving total revenues a rising tendency.

The fact that Shopify benefited from the growth of its merchants created an incentive for Shopify to help them become more successful — hence the quality of service provided in the 2010s by its client-support team, development of a plethora of tools and the loading of its website with guides, tutorials and blogs on starting and running online businesses. As a result, Shopify became a go-to authority on e-commerce for entrepreneurs.

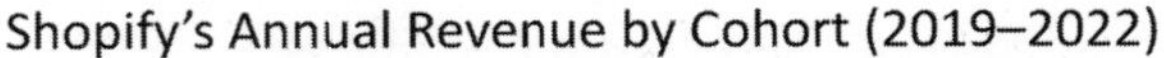

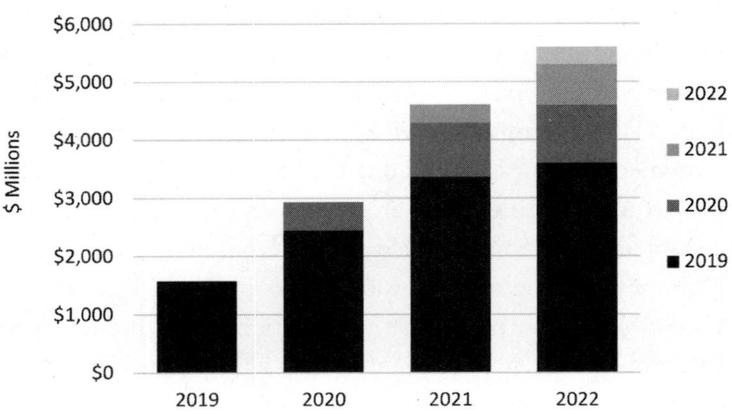

Data source: Shopify 2022 *Annual Report*

Two years after adding Shopify Payments to the platform, Shopify listed shares for trading on the stock market. Some amateur investors talk about a stock "going to the moon"; for several years, shares in Shopify were one of the best imitations of such a trajectory — thanks in large part to Shopify Payments.

CEO of the Year

By late 2014, Shopify was in the early phases of its prodigious advance. Taking notice were the business journalists at the *Globe and Mail*, Canada's most widely read newspaper. They proclaimed Lütke their CEO of the Year in 2014. By this point, Shopify had 500 employees supporting 120,000 stores with $5 billion in sales.

The newspaper's *Report on Business* magazine published a profile of Lütke when the accolade was bestowed. The profile contained the following passage:

> [Tobi Lütke] insists, "I'm actually not as important to the whole story as it might seem." . . . But ask anyone associated with Shopify and they will tell you Lütke is a visionary, that his talents have led directly to Shopify's explosive growth.[1]

What was it about Lütke that enabled him to have such success? Although computer games may have helped in several ways as he claims, there were other aspects to consider as well.

LÜTKE'S MODUS OPERANDI

The *Report on Business* magazine mentioned two traits. The first was a lack of inhibition in calling out bad ideas (like his mentor, Starr). As Shannan told journalist Trevor Cole:

> Be prepared to be crushed. . . . You need a thick skin. It's not that Tobi shouts or treats people meanly. He's simply direct, unfiltered. When he looks at the fruits of someone's labour, he says what he thinks, even if it is: "This is shit." [In later years, Lütke learned to get his point across with phrasing like: "Is this really the best way we can do this?"][1]

The second was high expectations. Shannan said (likely with a bit of humor for effect):

> He often talks about, "Your work here needs to make an impact like a crater." So it's not like just good work, it's not excellence; it's like massive, cosmic impact. It needs to be visible from outer space.[2]

These traits came naturally to Lütke, especially the forthrightness: his Enneagram identified him as a challenger. He liked to understand what inputs were used to come to a conclusion and would ask employees a series of questions that deconstructed their position down to its axioms and assumptions. That was the level where disagreements often originated and clearing them up could lead to a consensus. Nonetheless, his interlocutors could sometimes end up deflated or defensive. Also, as a way to sound out concepts, Lütke at times took a contrary viewpoint even when he agreed with a person; some of them switched to his viewpoint even though he was playing devil's advocate.

Getting more positive and productive responses from people was one reason why Lütke became a fan of the "blueprint," an idea borrowed from Levesque, his friend and a Fresh Founders alumnus. A blueprint was a write-up of someone's modus operandi, which was given by a manager to new hires when they started working with them (it was also posted on the Shopify internal wiki). The idea was to speed up the process of learning how someone operates. One thing mentioned in Lütke's blueprint was that when he went into challenger mode, people shouldn't think he was out to get them, or that he necessarily disagreed with them.

THE ART OF DECISION-MAKING

Decision-making was a key part of the CEO position and Lütke took a studied, systematic approach to it. To begin with, if a decision was reversible, he usually moved quickly. If the decision was irreversible and fundamental to the company, he went deep into gathering information. Aside from reading and consulting people, his research was "extremely" data-driven: "We do a lot of experiments and see what works. A/B testing applied to running a company happens a lot," he has said.[1] However, time constraints and complexity required making decisions with imperfect knowledge: "Once you understand a problem to about 70%, I think it's time to make a choice."[2]

Lütke further believed that if "your job was to make decisions, it should be treated like any other kind of thing to get better at."[3] One way he cultivated this skill was to keep a logbook to jot down a paragraph on the reasons taken for a major decision. He revisited the log every six months to see how his choices were faring. The logbook has provided him with valuable experience in reinforcing the importance of letting the data determine the outcome rather than letting a viewpoint shape what data was collected.

THE BIG PICTURE

The CEO's job also took him into the realm of "big picture" issues. He took a week off every quarter to step back from the day-to-day routine and gain broader perspectives by reading up on business and technology topics. He also read a lot throughout the year. He liked biographies of businesspersons because they gave him guidance and inspiration for dealing with business situations he encountered. Podcasts were a great resource too — very much so, in fact. As he told Sriram Krishnan from *The Observer Effect* in 2020: "Well, my current opinion is that one of the best things that happened in the last 10 years are podcasts. Now, I can listen to experts talking amongst each other and be a fly on the wall to the most interesting conversations ever. Of all the things I could tell my sixteen year old self about the future, I think that would be the most exciting and mind blowing development."[1]

For choosing what products to develop, Lütke had two main approaches (besides customer feedback). The first was extrapolating trend lines forward. "For example, in 2009 we knew that almost all traffic to Shopify would be coming from mobile phones by just looking at the data and connecting two points and drawing it forward," he told Ferriss.[2] The second approach was based on the tendency of technological progress to be more advanced in some regions or industries than others. "The future is already here — it's just not evenly distributed," goes the epigram attributed to science-fiction author William Gibson. At one time, Silicon Valley was the best place for spotting leading-edge technology but in the case of e-commerce, it shifted several years ago to China. "A lot of innovation is now coming from China . . . it's appreciatively more futuristic than anywhere else," Lütke informed Ferriss in 2019. "It's delivering ideas like fully automated supermarkets . . . and a post credit-card world." As for finding signposts in industries, "you have to look around for the competitive fields and see what tools the winners have figured out." A prime example was the video-game industry.

There was a caveat. Although Lütke knew his job was to focus on the big picture and set high-level priorities, he personally needed to sometimes be involved at the micro level. Once a programmer, always a programmer. As he told Ferriss during a podcast:

> I really do like going and putting my chair in some place with the engineers working on some important performance details and so on. It teaches me something about the company and it allows me to access this mastery that I once built up as a programmer. You can't spend all your time just working on things that are going to finish two or three years from now. . . . So, the thing that I optimize away [delegate] is everything in between the top and bottom levels.[3]

HANDS ON

Lütke's thinking on management style appeared to evolve as COVID-19 dragged on. While he had previously expressed openness to hiring the smartest people and getting out of their way, he was not so keen by 2022. The laissez-faire approach might be okay in some industries or during periods of stability, but he believed the constant state of upheaval in the technology industry called for a more hands-on approach.

Lütke felt that developing world-class products was all about the details, so when an environment had little margin for error or time available, he needed to "have a team of people who are okay to go into all the details" with him. That is, Lütke had come to believe from his years of experience at Shopify that feedback loops needed to be tight. He liked to work with project teams to "make key decisions where everyone brings their perspective."[1] Many of the issues had been seen by him before, so he could bring that perspective as well to help the team.

FIRST-PRINCIPLES THINKING

One of the more prominent aspects of Lütke's approach was "first-principles thinking." Many people take a course of action based on what worked before (convention) or what worked elsewhere (analogy). Lütke instead preferred delving into the subject to understand what made sense. The process often involved disaggregating theses to make sure individual propositions and assumptions were valid, which then could be reassembled to a plausible conclusion.

For example, a tool company may think that people wanted a better quarter-inch drill bit. But as Harvard marketing professor Theodore Levitt regularly told his classes: "People don't want a quarter-inch drill bit. They want a quarter-inch hole." In other words, companies focused on perfecting drill bits may discover someday that their customers don't want drill bits anymore because it is cheaper or faster to cut holes with waterjets or lasers.

One of Lütke's favourite illustrations of first-principles thinking was to be found in the book *The Box: How the Shipping Container Made the World Smaller and the World Economy Bigger*, by Marc Levinson. Back in the 1950s, long-haul truckers had to wait nearly a whole day for workers to transfer their cargo to a ship or train (and vice versa). During one such episode, trucker Malcom McLean had an epiphany: intermodal shipments would be a lot quicker and cheaper if the loaded trailer on trucks could be lifted by a crane onto a ship or a train. He designed a suitable shipping container, added tanker ships to his trucking business, and cut many hours off transportation times while slashing the cost of transferring cargo by more than 90%. Nowadays intermodal shipping containers are ubiquitous within the transportation industry. What customers ultimately wanted was the quickest and least expensive way to transport goods. Faster trucks, ships and trains were only means to the latter, not ends in themselves.

Lütke attributes much of Shopify's growth to first-principles thinking. In the early years, there were other providers of platforms for online stores. They thought their raison d'être was to give entrepreneurs a better software tool to build online stores. But did people really care about such a tool per se? No, such things were a means to achieve what they really cared about, which was reaching for goals like independence, success and earning a living. This line of thought led Shopify to its mission of making commerce easier by relieving pain points and friction confronting entrepreneurs. For example, when merchants had problems synchronizing their online and offline stores, Shopify built a point-of-sale feature called Shopify POS that recorded in-store sales and merged them with online sales.

For a company, it's tempting after successfully finding market acceptance for a product to go all in on maximizing the profits. But Shopify was also guided by its mission. On the *Escape Velocity Show*, Lütke remarked: "What sucks about starting online businesses? My answer to that is the next thing that we should be working on."[1]

Tied into Lütke's first-principles approach was "systems thinking," which engineers are well acquainted with. A system is made up of a set of parts that are interdependent. Because of this interconnectedness, making a change in one area may fail to deliver a desired solution, or may unleash unintended effects in other areas. The effective solution may not be the obvious one but instead lay deeper within the system. For example, someone may think that a way to cure public companies of their short-term focus is to educate executives about the benefits of a long-term focus — but a more effective solution may be to simply dispense with quarterly earnings reports. They are the variable that loops into and reinforces a short-term focus. It's this kind of systems thinking that Lütke believes will lead to better companies.

Under Lütke's leadership, Shopify was gaining momentum and emerging as an e-commerce darling. Much more vigorous growth was on the way, especially after Shopify listed its shares on the stock exchanges and became a public company in 2015. As we shall see, the listing was an important source of fuel for a powerful upward thrust in its growth dynamic.

Listing on the Stock Market

In the midst of the rollout of the retail operating system, Shopify went public. It did an Initial Public Offering (IPO) of its shares May 21, 2015, on the Toronto Stock Exchange and New York Stock Exchange. As the prospectus detailed, 7.7 million Class A shares were to be sold by six investment banks to investors at a price of $17 each (unadjusted for the stock split in 2022).[1] It was well received upon arrival. Strong demand enabled the banks to issue 15% more shares, bringing the total outstanding to over 8.85 million, for aggregate gross proceeds of $150.5 million. On the first day of trading, the stock soared to $28.

The Shopify IPO also created 66.7 million Class B shares by converting the private shares issued to venture capitalists, executives and staff in the years before the IPO. The Class B had 10 votes each and were not listed for trading on the exchanges but could be converted one-for-one into single-vote Class A shares and then sold. The venture capitalists held about two-thirds of the Class B shares, followed by Lütke (14.5%), Lütke's father-in-law (5.7%), co-founder Lake (5.6%), Phillips through Klister Credit Corp. (3.7%), co-founder Weinand (2.5%) and smaller stakes by other executives and staff.

THE IPO AND SUBSEQUENT ISSUES OF SHARES

Not long after the IPO, most of the venture capitalists cashed out by converting their Class B to Class A shares and selling them. Angel investor Phillips unloaded some pieces of his position in the years to come but held on to most of it and by the early 2020s, his investment of under a million dollars was worth about $2 billion. The Shopify team sold varying amounts of their holdings over the years. Along with their Class A shares, Phillips and Lütke ended up holding just over 50% of the votes for much of the period after the venture capitalists had cleared out.

In the weeks before the listing, Lütke and Finkelstein joined the IPO roadshow in the United States, where the lead underwriter, Wall Street's Morgan Stanley, and two other U.S. banks were selling the majority of the offering.[1] Finkelstein was revelling in the promotional campaign but Lütke wasn't too keen about spending time away from his focus on product development, as he told Krishnan from *The Observer Effect*:

> During meetings, I would say, "Hey, I'm here, and we've been doing this roadshow, but I actually spend a lot of my time on the product." This was to set expectations because I knew I wasn't going to attend very many investor conferences. Fundamentally, my attention belonged to the product, not to the sales and marketing of it.[2]

Finkelstein told Nik Sharma and Moiz Ali during a *Limited Supply* podcast that when Lütke started the three-week IPO tour, he told Morgan Stanley that he wanted to fly back home to Ottawa on the weekends to be with his family. Morgan Stanley apparently were rather surprised: "Morgan Stanley said no one ever had asked them to do that before," Finkelstein revealed.[3] But Lütke was never one to do something just because that was the way it had always been done. Besides, his wife was also close to giving birth to their third child at the time.

Few U.S. investors had heard of the Canadian e-commerce upstart; Lütke and Finkelstein had to explain that Shopify operated behind the scenes providing support to merchants so they could promote their own brands and develop direct relationships with customers. But make no mistake, Shopify was a force to be reckoned with: there were so many online Shopify businesses that "if you bought something on the Internet and it wasn't on Amazon but the experience was good, it was a Shopify store," declared Lütke.[4]

The Shopify executives were asked about the size of their company's total addressable market, and the pair had to explain that it wasn't just the number of small- and medium-sized businesses counted up from a survey or census. It was much larger because technological advances had made it easy and inexpensive for wage and salary earners to become full- or part-time online entrepreneurs. Mom or Dad might decide to have a go at commercializing their hobbies, or a young adult might start a side hustle outside of office hours. And so on.

Also helping put Shopify over the top was the articulate Finkelstein and some informative props at the presentations. The power extrovert was doing what he loved doing; his enthusiasm was infectious. The documentary-style video profiling Shopify was a very polished production, with Hollywood-grade lighting, camera angles, background music and other techniques.[5]

There was also substantial content in the slide deck. One chart showed revenues more than doubling annually from $23.7 million in 2012 to $105.0 million in 2014. Monthly recurring revenues from subscriptions bounded steadily higher from $1.1 million in the first quarter of 2012 to $7.4 million in the first quarter of 2015. GMV (i.e. merchant sales) blasted upwards from $0.7 billion in 2012 to $3.8 billion in 2014. Yet another chart showed how the revenue lost from merchants leaving the platform was more than offset by the remaining merchants upgrading plans, purchasing apps, and selling more on the platform.

About four months after the IPO, there was a big jump in the stock price on news that Amazon had abandoned Amazon Webstore, its platform for online stores similar to Shopify's. Additionally, Amazon advised the 80,000-plus merchants on the website to migrate to Shopify — in return for some concessions from Shopify, such as paying $1 million and allowing Shopify merchants to use Amazon Pay. Amazon dropped Webstore because it believed the addressable market was not going to be significant to its bottom line. Moreover, the website was underperforming. Nonetheless, handing over Amazon Webstore to Shopify appeared to be "a rare strategic mistake that's likely to go down in the annals of corporate blunders," claimed business journalist Brad Stone.[6]

As the quarters and years went by more and more investors piled into the stock and bid the price higher, creating a pronounced uptrend occasionally interrupted by temporary reversals. The temptation for employees to check the stock's progress must have been overwhelming but there was an office rule that anyone caught in the act had to go to Tim Hortons and buy Timbits for their team. Periodically, a box of the tasty treats would appear and do the rounds on desks on a floor. Even Lütke had to buy a box once.

One might assume that the amount of money raised by Shopify was the sum collected from the venture capitalists and IPO, or $120 million + $130 million = $250 million. But there was more. A lot more. Shopify's stock gained more than 5,000% from the IPO to the peak in November 2021; as the stock soared, it reinforced investors' love affair with the e-commerce upstart and made them eager to buy more. Shopify obliged: it floated several more issues from its treasury of Class A stock to the public, as follows (according to company *Annual Reports*):

- Third quarter of 2016: 6,125,000 shares for proceeds of $240 million
- Second quarter of 2017: 6,325,000 shares for proceeds of $575,575,000
- First quarter of 2018: 4,800,000 shares for proceeds of $657,600,000
- Fourth quarter of 2018: 2,600,000 shares for proceeds of $400,400,000
- Third quarter of 2019: 2,185,000 shares for proceeds of $693,737,500
- Second quarter of 2020: 2,127,500 shares for proceeds of $1,489,250,000
- Third quarter of 2020: convertible senior notes worth $920,000,000
- Third quarter of 2020: 1,265,000 shares for proceeds of $1,138,500,000
- First quarter of 2021: 1,180,000 shares for proceeds of $1,551,700,000

Add up the proceeds from these treasury shares, and the sum is more than $7 billion; if venture capital and the IPO are included, the grand total is nearly $8 billion in financing (not adjusted for rounding errors or broker fees). That's a humungous reservoir of fuel for powering a journey through the e-commerce universe.

THE ATTACK OF THE SHORT SELLER

On October 3, 2017, Shopify's stock closed down 12% on the NYSE, its biggest one-day drop since going public in May 2015. The cause was the release of a report by Citron Research's Andrew Left, in which it was revealed he was selling the stock short.[1] Left was a noted short seller with several prescient calls to his credit; in 2015, for example, a Citron Research report uncovered some practices that led to a downward spiral in the shares of Quebec-based Valeant Pharmaceuticals.

Left claimed Shopify was a multi-level marketing scheme that drew in customers with fanciful claims of getting rich — a deceptive practice that was against U.S. Federal Trade Commission (FTC) rules and should be investigated. Colin Sebastian, an analyst at Robert W. Baird & Co., rebutted that his survey of Shopify clients found that more than 90% said they had not seen a Shopify ad mentioning they could become millionaires.[2] True, there was a large online community offering advice on how to succeed on Shopify, but it was not part of the company — they were mostly the third-party designers, web builders and affiliates who were seeking to generate income by providing services to Shopify merchants. During the earnings report for the third quarter of 2017, Finkelstein took issue with the view that Shopify was operating a pyramid-like, multi-level marketing scheme, saying: "It is also important to note that our partners do not get paid to recruit other affiliates or partners nor do they get paid for anything other affiliates or partners do."[3] The FTC did not lay charges.

Nearly six months later, when Shopify's stock was up by approximately 25%, Left took another run at the company, and again knocked its shares down by 12% in a day. This time Left claimed that the FTC investigation into Cambridge Analytica's use of the personal data of Facebook users (for Donald Trump's 2016 presidential campaign and other situations) likely meant impending restrictions on accessing such data by anyone other than Facebook itself, which, in turn, would prevent Shopify's stores from using such data to target their ads.

Lütke responded by pointing out Shopify merchants sell in many places: their own websites, retail stores, marketplaces (like eBay and Amazon) and social channels (like Facebook and Pinterest). "The power of our platform is that we offer one interface for merchants to sell anywhere and everywhere," he added.[4] In a March 28, 2018, post on X, Lütke argued that any restrictions on Facebook data should have little effect because "our 600,000+ entrepreneurs can sell on any channel they want to. If their customers want to buy via carrier pigeon, we'll build a channel for that too. The health of any individual channel has little effect on the overall platform. Demand migrates."

Just over a year later, after Shopify's shares had nearly doubled, Left took one more stab at the stock that would not die. This time his concerns were about rising competition from Instagram and other sources; inroads by rivals could chop Shopify's stock in half, he predicted. His position wasn't based so much on a belief Shopify had a weak business model, aggressive accounting or anything fundamental wrong — in fact, Left was on record for saying Shopify was best in class for its sector. His concern was that the stock had a valuation a lot higher than peer companies. Notably, the ratio of its stock price to sales per share was two to five times higher than comparable companies. Left was so sure of an impending crash in the stock that he committed to donating $200,000 to charity if Shopify was trading above its then current price within 12 months.[5]

Shortly after his pronouncement, Shopify released its first-quarter results and again, analysts' estimates were blown away — this time with a 50% leap in revenues. Ensuing quarters told a similar tale, and by the end of Left's 12-month forecast period, the stock had more than doubled. Finally, Left gave up — at least no more bearish reports could be found. In fact, he announced in January of 2021 — after getting caught in a short squeeze on GameStop — that he was going to switch to buy recommendations. Did Left donate $200,000 to charity? No indication could be found after an extensive search; an email inquiry went unanswered.

Notwithstanding Left's campaign, Shopify staff still did very well by their holdings of Shopify stock and options. The stock went on to gain several thousand percentage points after the first short-sale call, and hundreds of millions of dollars were cashed out along the way.

WHAT THEY DID WITH THEIR WEALTH

Scrooge McDuck, the Walt Disney character who has graced comic books and TV cartoons since the late 1940s, struck it rich in the Klondike Gold Rush of 1897 and was worth "one multiplujillion, nine obsquatumatillion, six hundred twenty-three dollars and sixty-two cents." He kept his wealth in a deep vault filled with gold coins and spent a lot of time diving into it and rolling around. Thank goodness those who found their motherlode in Shopify stock weren't like Mr. McDuck. Sure, they were able to live a more affluent lifestyle, but they certainly didn't hoard it. Much of it was donated to charitable causes or invested in other companies.

Several Shopify people did indeed become quite wealthy thanks to their holdings of Shopify's shares. Lütke's stake turned him into a billionaire; some senior executives had fortunes worth hundreds of millions of dollars and other senior staff were up six to eight figures. Staff below the executive level also came into greater affluence: just before Shopify's IPO, more than 450 employees were given options to acquire 8.6 million shares at an average price of $1.57 each. "The disposition of these options is unknown but had the employees sold at roughly the same time and price as did senior executives . . . the group would have grossed close to $700 million," noted *Ottawa Citizen* journalist James Bagnall in 2018.[1] The venture capitalists, some employees and departing staff sold their stakes early: they still did well but missed out on a lot of the upward sweep in Shopify's stock.

"As residents have seen so many times before — at Mitel in the 1970s, Newbridge, Corel and Cognos in the 1980s and 1990s, and Nortel and JDS Uniphase during the 2000 tech bubble — the new money at first finds its way into luxury cars and real estate, then into charities and new startups," added Bagnall. Some executives bought properties in Ottawa's leafy enclave of Rockcliffe Village, which was filled with mansions inhabited by diplomats, old money and tech tycoons. Fauser's fine accommodations were acquired in 2017 within an exclusive neighbourhood of Vancouver. Other executives and high-level employees hired top-notch architects to design abodes on prime land fronting the Ottawa River.

The new money also went to charities through direct donations or via private foundations. The Thistledown Foundation was created by Lütke and his wife to promote decarbonization, but it switched to fighting the COVID-19 pandemic in 2020, gifting $26 million to children's hospitals in Canada, as well as funding fast grants to researchers. Miller and his wife set up the Vohra Miller Foundation "to improve the health of the planet and its people." One of its grants established First Exposure, a partnership with the University of Toronto for research on protecting children from the risks of medications, pollutants and other substances during pregnancy and lactation. The Northpine Foundation was launched by Phillips and his wife; it takes an entrepreneurial approach to a variety of social issues, such as recidivism and racism. Waverley House Foundation was established by Bruce McKean to support basic research into the identification and treatment of mental illnesses.

Not surprisingly, a good number of former Shopify employees have founded and invested in their own startups or become angel investors. Their conspicuous presence in the startup community was such that they earned the sobriquet "Shopify Mafia," which was a riff on the "PayPal Mafia" epithet assigned to the former PayPal employees that started and invested in companies like Tesla, LinkedIn and YouTube.

In the spring of 2021, *Business Insider* interviewed nearly three dozen members of the "Shopify Mafia" for the article "Meet 35 Members of the Shopify Mafia."[2] One of them was Harry Brundage, who had joined Shopify as an intern in 2011 and rose to become a director of engineering before leaving in 2017. With co-worker Mohammad Hashemi, he co-founded a startup called Gadget, which offers tools that make it easier for software developers to build e-commerce apps. It has several blue-ribbon backers, including Sequoia Capital, Bessemer Venture Partners and Shopify's Fauser.

Erin Chan worked as a product manager in Shopify's point-of-sale group and spent her spare time working with her husband on Rhenti, a platform founded in 2017 to make it easier for property owners and renters to connect. It obtained financing from a number of rental companies and was working with over 1,000 landlords.

Inspired by a trip to Italy, Greg Macdonald started Bathorium to sell bath bombs, soaks and other bath products. When it reached $5 million in annual revenue in 2021, he left his Shopify merchant-manager job. "Shopify is the only company in the world where you can have a million-dollar side hustle and still work your day job," Macdonald told *Business Insider*.[3]

Other Shopify alumni have formed angel investing funds. For example, a former VP of product, Adam McNamara, and his colleague Joshua Tessier are the driving force behind Ramen Ventures, an angel fund. Another case is Fahd Ananta, a Shopify product lead: in 2021, he started Roach Capital to invest in "hard to kill" early-stage software companies. Financial backers included former Shopify executive Satish Kanwar. Another branch of the Shopify Mafia was the Backbone Angels, a collection of current and past female Shopify employees interested in financing startups launched by women. Forsyth is a member. In 2021, the Backbone Angels funded over 40 startups.

The senior managers are the most prolific group of angel investors from the company. One of the leaders, according to Crunchbase, was Lütke. He had more than two dozen angel investments to his credit as of late 2022.

Finkelstein was named Canadian Angel Investor of the Year at the 2017 Canadian Startup Awards gala and did a stint as one of the judges on CBC's *Next Gen Den* (the online version of CBC's *Dragons' Den*, aimed at young entrepreneurs). He had nine angel investments in place as of the fall of 2022, according to Crunchbase.

Miller was also an active angel investor. He selected those startups that he believed could have a big social impact through fighting climate change or empowering entrepreneurs. Miller also met with the startups and passed on what he has learned from his experience at Shopify.

For a long time, the most active angel investor at Shopify was Phillip's Klister Credit Corp. After he retired in 2023, Crunchbase gave that status to Farhan Thawar, a VP and head of engineering. His more than three dozen holdings included Parallelz (a platform that rapidly transforms native mobile apps into native web apps), Hookdeck (a webhook infrastructure for ingestion and error handling), Shakepay (makes it easy to buy and earn bitcoin) and Outpoint (data modelling platform that improves marketing budget allocation).

Shopify executives were not business barons like Mr. Monopoly, wearing top hats and pinstriped trousers in their private clubs with glasses of brandy and cigars in hand. Quite the opposite. They had social consciences and a concern for the plight of others and the environment, as highlighted by the charitable foundations they set up and the donations of millions of dollars to various causes. They also invested in dozens of startup companies, some of which would become sources of jobs and new technologies.

Retail Operating System II

The rollout of the retail operating system continued after the IPO, adding more tools to the Shopify platform and further increasing its value to merchants. Shopify's reward was that the number of subscribers kept climbing and merchants on the platform kept growing their businesses and sales.

SHOPIFY PLUS: THE BIG PLAYERS

Shopify catered mainly to small- and medium-sized companies during its early years but another growth engine was strapped on when Shopify Plus was birthed in 2014 to service large companies. Within five or six years of its launch, it was contributing more than a third of the platform's revenues.

When Loren Padelford saw an ad in 2014 on LinkedIn for Vice President of Sales at Shopify, he was confused because Shopify was gaining notoriety as a fast-growing technology unicorn headed for an IPO, so it should have been an easy matter for them to pick up the phone and headhunt talent at other software firms. Padelford had no connection to anyone in Shopify he could speak to about the job; nonetheless, he still applied — even though it would have been an exercise in futility where he had previously worked because high-level jobs were mostly filled via personal or business networks.

In his college days, the six-foot, four-inch, 275-pound Padelford played football as an offensive lineman at the University of Guelph, and nearly ended up in the professional leagues when he was selected by the

B.C. Lions in the fourth round of the Canadian Football League's entry draft of 2000.[1] That scenario was not to unfold, and Padelford returned to the University of Guelph to graduate with a BA in psychology, followed by an MBA in marketing at the University of Liverpool. He went on to land a job in marketing and worked his way up within a Toronto-based software company to managing sales teams that put together nine-figure deals for clients in the government and corporate sectors. His employer was acquired by another company, as were the next two companies he worked at, leaving him looking for work in 2014.

After he answered Shopify's ad, Padelford was not expecting much to come of it. "I just figured no one's ever going to call back because they must have their pick of whoever they like," he told Zubin Mowlavi, host of the *Coffee & Commerce* podcast. But he did get a response, although it took a long time: "Nothing happened for nine weeks and then I got a call and they were, like: 'Hey, you want to come talk to us?' That started a 16-week interview process."[2]

The weeks of interviews for Padelford were a "fascinating journey into the psychology of Shopify and what they were thinking." Lütke, Finkelstein and Miller were confounded by their most successful and largest merchants thinking they had to leave Shopify and buy enterprise software from other companies. They thought it was a false stratification of the market and merchants would be better off staying with Shopify if they wanted a comparable level of service at a much lower pricing point. "'That's crazy, let's stop that,'" Padelford recalled them saying. "And so, they're like, saying to me: 'Do that — figure out how to stop that from happening.'"[3]

Padelford was somewhat puzzled. It seemed to be a different job than the one he applied for. "I was, like, 'Sorry, what? Is that a job? I'm not sure I follow — you didn't actually say . . . what do you want me to do? You want me . . .' and they're, like, saying: 'Stop this problem from happening. . . . We have this nascent thing that we're not quite sure what it is and we're not quite sure how to scale it up and we don't really have a ton of experience with the, you know, quote-unquote enterprise level — so, see what you can do with it.'"[4] And that is how Padelford became general manager of Shopify Plus in 2014.

Lütke wanted Shopify to be a platform where companies could scale up without having to go somewhere else. He also felt there could be a growth opportunity in signing up more companies already at the enterprise level: indeed, some had already done so, including Anheuser-Busch and Nestlé. But he didn't want to launch an all-out effort to go upmarket until there was a stronger signal. He had seen how many companies had run aground when they tried moving upmarket too soon and too fast. His thinking seemed to be: let's get it up and running to retain some of Shopify's larger merchants and see where it goes from there. In the meantime, he was going to have it "walled off" separately from the rest of Shopify, in an office by itself in another city. It seemed as if Shopify Plus was an experiment that needed to be conducted in a secret lab far away from the rest of Shopify.

Shopify executives informed Padelford that the Shopify Plus team was to be located "anywhere in the world as long as it's in southern Ontario and it's not Toronto and it's not Ottawa." It seemed obvious to Padelford that Shopify Plus should then be located in the Kitchener-Waterloo area, near the tech hub and the University of Waterloo — with Wilfrid Laurier University and the University of Guelph close by. They would be able "to feed off that ecosystem and hire great people." So, in January of 2015, office space was rented in Kitchener-Waterloo and the first five sales reps were hired to complement a small crew already chipping away at the project. The subscription fee for Shopify Plus would be much higher than Shopify's regular plans but still far less than what a higher-end e-commerce platform or IT team would charge.

The trouble was, Padelford did not have "any real idea of what" he was actually doing. "It was kind of like the executives were saying, 'Hey, we have this thing that might be another thing and you should try that.'" But this was Shopify, and "when someone offers you a seat on the rocket ship you don't ask which one you should take." Padelford began by hiring five sales reps straight out of university with no sales experience and "no idea what we were doing."

Padelford didn't mislead the new hires about the state of affairs and warned them they were kind of like test pilots for an aircraft still not yet built. "I scared them as much as I could about the job and I was, like, this will suck; we don't know what we're doing and you shouldn't take this job because you're probably gonna get fired in eight months and we're all gonna get buried."[5] That was more or less how the interviews were conducted.

"I mean what I really found fascinating is that for some people, the more you tried to scare them, the more excited they got and so, like, the people who were left at the end were the ones prepared for this amazing death-like experience," he added. Later, some of them told Padelford that they thought he was scaring them on purpose because he was looking for people who didn't care what they did on the job — they just wanted to be at Shopify no matter what.[6]

The space rented in the Kitchener-Waterloo area was a "crappy little office," in stark contrast to the tony settings in Ottawa and Toronto. Padelford told his staff it was intentional: his unit wouldn't get a nice office until they proved themselves. "What I was saying is we've not done anything yet. Ottawa and Toronto deserve their big offices because they have been around for a while and have hundreds of thousands of customers whereas we have nothing done. So, it was also a goal; I wanted the team to own it and to feel, like, if we did this thing they could look back and say, 'I did that right,' which creates a different emotional state for people."[7]

On the first day of work, Padelford told the new hires: "I really don't know anything; I have no sales training for you, so what I'd like you to do is, like, pick up the phone and call people and then come back and tell me how it worked out." They first targeted existing Shopify customers who were getting big and thus at risk of jumping ship. The new hires were told to ask them: "'Like, hey, do you want to upgrade to Shopify Plus?' They just were calling people cold and learning, and we were developing the scripts on the fly and trying to figure out what worked and what didn't. It was a ton of fun," disclosed Padelford.[8]

Over the next six months, many of the larger Shopify merchants signed on. Calls had also started coming in from non-Shopify merchants asking what this Shopify Plus was all about. Padelford was at first confused by the calls because he thought Shopify or some other company was already serving the mid-level market, but when he looked over what was available, he just saw a "wasteland of garbage, just a sea of terrible platforms." Going after that underserved segment became the next focus of the Shopify Plus staff.

The enterprise-level companies not on Shopify's platform frequently had an online e-commerce presence built by in-house IT staff or an IT consulting firm, but what Lütke and fellow executives saw happening was this: staff in the marketing departments of these large corporations were having problems getting their promotional ideas implemented in a timely manner by their IT departments — so they approached Shopify and used their personal credit cards to get a website up in a day or so to run their campaign or a trial of a concept. The chief information officer would usually complain to the CEO about the unauthorized maneuver, but once the CEO got involved and saw how quick and cheap it was to go online, he or she usually sided with the marketing people.

Why might IT departments in enterprise companies be unresponsive or slow in their dealings? For one thing, as organizations got larger, a certain amount of bureaucracy crept in. For another, their software systems were not the greatest. As Lütke told Jason Del Rey at the Code Commerce conference on September 17, 2018: "No one thinks about it this way but it's absolutely true that the higher you go in any software market the worse the quality of a software gets because the people who buy the software are not the people who actually have to use it."[9]

The first test case was Red Bull, the energy drink company. The "sessions were hilarious," recalled Padelford. "They were, like: 'Who are you? What is this Shopify thing? We're Red Bull — you can't possibly do this.'"[10] So Shopify proceeded to show them what could be done, and the Red Bull brass switched to saying the demos couldn't be true. It didn't seem possible according to "'our e-commerce software provider who is charging us millions of dollars and took years to implement,'" reported Padelford. Finally, Red Bull agreed to give it a try and Shopify Plus "crushed it." The iconic Red Bull brand became the first proof of concept, and other larger consumer companies began to take a look at Shopify Plus, and they started to come on board.

SOCIAL COMMERCE

Multichannel Shopify set up sales channels connecting merchants to social media websites. One of the first integrations was with Pinterest in 2015. Later that year, a second integration was implemented with Facebook to sell products in the Shop section on Facebook Pages. A third channel allowed merchants to sell on X with "Buy Now" buttons. These early partnerships were followed with many more. They included:

- integration with Facebook Messenger for conversational commerce (2016)
- integration with Amazon to allow Shopify stores to sell on Amazon (2017)
- channel set up for Shopify merchants to sell products on eBay (2017)
- channel created to feature products of Shopify merchants on Buzzfeed (2017)
- channel on Instagram made available (2017)
- merchants can list products for free on Google Shopping tab (2020)
- launch of Walmart channel to sell on walmart.com (2020)
- partnership with Alipay to support merchants with cross-border payments (2020)
- launch of TikTok channel for selling Shopify merchandise (2020)
- Facebook Shops allows storefronts for shopping (2020)
- launch of Spotify channel so artists can connect to their Shopify store (2021)
- TikTok Shopping link to Shopify store checkouts (2021)
- partnership with YouTube to scale the creator economy (2022)
- X sales channel app for Shopify merchants via its app store (2022)

The venture into social commerce was expected to be a big growth driver for Shopify. Amazon might have a marketplace with many visitors dropping by every day, but Shopify would have a presence in the places where many people spent most of their time online — it was kind of like in the old days, when a merchant had a store in the town square where the townsfolk congregated.

The room for growth seemed considerable in North America, given how far social commerce had advanced in China: social commerce sales in 2023 accounted for 16% of total e-commerce retail sales in China compared to 5% in the United States, according to the publication "Comprehensive Guide to Social Commerce in China."[1]

ARK Investment Management, founded and managed by Catherine Wood, had a major holding in Shopify because of its exposure to the growth potential of social commerce. A researcher at the company, Nicholas Grous, wrote:

> Implemented correctly, social commerce combines the convenience of online shopping with the network effects of social media, resulting in a powerful growth driver. . . . Based on ARK's research, as more platforms transition from pureplay to social, the [U.S.] e-commerce market could scale 50% at a compound annual rate.[2]

Lütke was asked at Startupfest's annual conference in 2016 if social media really needed Shopify's help with e-commerce: they already had users' names, personal profiles and credit card numbers, so wouldn't it be easy for them to set it up themselves? He replied that social media sites needed Shopify because e-commerce was not a core expertise for them whereas Shopify had been doing it for years. The front-end of e-commerce — getting the transaction and the money transferred — was the just the easy first 10% of the entire operation; the hard part was the back-end. As Lütke said:

> These orders need to be processed . . . there is a workflow behind this — you need to coordinate with people on inventory, go to your dropshippers, charge for shipping right. . . . The back office is surprisingly complex because it's not really a technology play but more like using technology to implement something humans have been doing

> for a long time — therefore, it's messy and that's the component [they] don't want their engineers to get into, like implementing esoteric tax laws into their codebase.[3]

Partnerships between social media and e-commerce platforms were therefore welcomed in the mid- to late 2010s. These early joint ventures had Shopify merchants advertising on social media websites, and when someone clicked on their ad or buy button, they were referred back to the merchant's shop to submit their order and payments. Shopify benefited from receiving processing fees of up to 2.9% on the payments from consumers on social media; the benefit to social media sites was the revenues received from merchants' advertisements.

But how stable would these partnerships be? Writing in the *New York Times*, Yiren Lu was one observer wondering if Shopify's partnership ethos could continue to work in the social media sphere: "Facebook and Shopify currently present a united front, but it's hard to imagine, given how important commerce is to the monetization of Facebook's platforms, that Facebook won't eventually try to cut Shopify out of the equation."[4]

E-commerce analysts, however, did not seem too worried about Facebook, TikTok and other social media sites dumping Shopify. "There is really no precedent for a social media e-commerce site to threaten one of the major e-commerce platforms, and I don't expect it to happen," Rick Watson, an e-commerce consultant at RMW Commerce Consulting told *Business Insider*.[5] While some Shopify merchants may set up separate stores on social media sites, they would still likely continue to operate a Shopify store because Multichannel Shopify allows them to sell to dozens of social media places and marketplaces from one spot on their dashboards. Shopify's expertise in back-end functions was also hard to duplicate.

THE BANK OF SHOPIFY

Solmaz Shahalizadeh, the daughter of two professors, built a bank for Shopify. It launched in 2016 under the name Shopify Capital to provide financing to Shopify merchants in support of their growth. As VP of

Data Science & Engineering at Shopify, she led the team that developed the machine-learning models used for predicting a merchant's likelihood of repaying the money loaned to them.

Before joining Shopify in 2013, she had gone to Shopify headquarters to attend a charity hackathon called Random Hacks of Kindness, where tech companies and individuals gathered to help solve technology problems for non-profit organizations. After it was over, someone at Shopify asked her to come back for a talk. When she did, they chatted about her projects and work experience, at the end of which it became more apparent she was in a job interview, because she got an offer to become the firm's first financial data analyst.

"I never actually submitted a resume," she said during a *Data Driven NYC* conference in 2019. "I think that's one of the strengths of Shopify's hiring: we don't go into conventional methods — we just try to get to know people and find out about their experiences and what exciting problems they have worked on."[1] Shahalizadeh's resume, by the way, would have shown that she had completed a bachelor and two master's degrees in the fields of computer science and bioinformatics, after which she published research in peer-reviewed journals and developed financial statistics for Morgan Stanley.

There are many reasons why a business might wish to borrow money. It may need the funds to purchase a large amount of inventory to meet an expected surge in demand resulting from media coverage or an influencer's recommendation on social media. It may need funds to finance a marketing campaign that clears out an inventory overhang, meet payroll during a cash crunch, develop a new product, sustain operations during seasonal lulls, acquire more equipment to expand production and so on.

Shopify Capital was launched first in the United States in 2016 and then the U.K. and Canada in 2020, followed by other countries. Shopify was well suited to extend financing to its merchants thanks to the ability to view their transactions in the back-end of its e-commerce platform. From this data, Shahalizadeh and her team could quickly develop an idea of what stores were good credit risks — for example, a company with a lot of regular sales every month would likely pay back its loan. It could receive a loan relatively quickly, without all the usual paperwork and qualification process to be endured at the banks.

Notices could be sent out by Shopify to the qualifying stores to let them know they were eligible for cash advances ranging from $200 to $2 million. The advances could be accepted with a few clicks of the mouse; a few days later, the funds would be deposited in the merchant's account — without the requirements for credit checks, posting collateral or giving up equity. Repayment would be a simple matter of deducting a small percentage from the merchants' daily revenues. Short-term loans of less than a year were also available. Stores with few or irregular sales would not likely be eligible for the credits.

But wasn't there a risk Shopify could end up taking a financial hit if delinquent loans piled up on its books? What if a merchant's sales suddenly plunged? Certainly, this could happen, but Shopify had protection. A few months after Shopify Capital launched in the United States, a partnership was formed with the Export Development Corporation (EDC), a Government of Canada agency that insures the credit extended by Canadian companies to foreign buyers (and sometimes domestic ones, depending on conditions). If a company were to default on the cash advances provided by Shopify, it would be insured by the EDC.

A July 21, 2021, Shopify blog post by John Sime reported on a study undertaken to assess the efficacy of the Shopify Capital initiative: Did it actually help stores grow? Comparing the merchants who had accepted early rounds of funding to a control group of merchants with similar characteristics but who had not borrowed, the study found the group receiving funds "experienced 36% higher sales in the following six months."[2] The three most common ways the money was applied: financing inventory, expansion of production and marketing campaigns.

Yet when Shahalizadeh and her team first began working on developing Shopify Capital, it was not a foregone conclusion that the money-lending initiative would be adopted. To ensure the machine-learning models could be trusted, it was first essential to make sure the databases were clean. Consistent data definitions and solid data pipelines had to be put in place.

Next, to win support within the company, a pilot phase of the project took a portion of the database and developed machine-learning models that were easy to explain and demonstrate to the product managers and treasury staff responsible for administering the lending program. A key milestone was when they became comfortable enough with the process for Shahalizadeh's team to proceed with developing models for the whole database. But what really contributed to its acceptance was her team sitting down with the administrators for the first six or nine months of full production and showing them "why this offer is going out and why this money is going to be loaned out . . . so that we gain their trust," Shahalizadeh said.[3]

After the Shopify Capital project, Shahalizadeh's division also took on a number of other new projects, leading off with a major initiative to develop machine-learning models that would help merchants detect fraud when dealing with customers and their orders. She was also rewarded with a promotion to the position of Vice President and Head of Data, which put her in charge of a team of more than 500 data scientists, engineers and product managers. Shopify Capital was a major enhancement of the Shopify platform and her chef-d'oeuvre — by mid-2022, its machine-learning models had advanced nearly $4 billion in loans to merchants.

As the amount of capital committed to merchant loans got quite large, Shopify moved to sell portions of the loans in the summer of 2023 to HCG Fund Management LP, a speciality finance company in the prvate-credit space.[4] In return for handing over the interest payments to HCG Fund, Shopify got a large infusion of capital that could be used to continue pursuing its mission.

The Heroism of the Engineers

As platform features were added, upgraded and re-engineered over the years, the codebase underlying Shopify's platform became elephantine (the Ruby on Rails component was one of the largest installations of its kind in the world). Behind the scenes, Shopify's engineers toiled to put it together and keep it going. There were lots of late nights, infinite dedication and yes . . . acts of heroism and bravery.

SHOPIFY DODGES THE BLACKBERRY CURSE

Shopify's transition to mobile e-commerce appeared to be getting off on the right foot with the launch of Shopify Mobile and Shopify POS. But several months after Shopify's IPO in 2015, Lütke dashed off an urgent message to staff. A crucial passage went:

> There is no way to sugar coat it. Shopify doesn't get mobile yet. I've been doing a lot of pushing on mobile, but I just can't seem to make enough of a difference due to the magnitude of the change needed. . . . There is no way for me to overstate this. If we want to avoid being yet another BlackBerry/Nortel, we have to build mobile into our DNA.[1]

Shopify had earlier decided to become a mobile-first company because usage rates for smartphones and tablets were soaring in the years after the introduction of the iPhone and other brands. This was becoming evident in the data collected by Shopify's platform. For example, the number of persons using mobile devices to buy products on Shopify more than doubled during 2012, from 10% to 22%; by the middle of 2014, half of the traffic to Shopify stores originated from a mobile source.

But more work still had to be done on mobile. The small screens of smartphones struggled with the complexity of displaying the Shopify platform. The quality of images was not the greatest and functionality was limited. Also, separate teams had developed the Apple and Android versions of Shopify Mobile, so there were three versions of the Shopify platform and only the desktop version could fully accommodate customer needs. Moreover, the user experience was not too friendly — for example, users of mobile phones had to type in the entire address of a website whenever they wanted to visit it.

One glaring omission was the lack of a sign-up button to start a store from a smartphone. When the Shopify app was opened, users were asked for their login and password but that was it. There was no way to become a merchant. "We didn't support that. No one thought about it," Lütke complained. "We were as unhelpful as humanly possible by not even acknowledging they might want to start something right there."[2]

In the earlier days of Shopify, a problem could be presented to the company and "a hero" often emerged from such calls to action, thanks to the entrepreneurial culture and close-knit relationships. But when the crisis with mobile devices unfolded, Shopify had been through several waves of expansion and was up to 1,750 employees. Staff assumed others would take care of the mobile challenge, and then went back to the projects they were already working on.

Shopify was still doing well at the time, growing fast and earning recognition as a rising star. Yet, as Lütke watched the data reports come in on mobile traffic, he grew increasingly worried about complacency in the ranks. Half of the research and development budget was going to wireless projects but the period of exploration and discovery was dragging on.

Meanwhile, countries in Asia were bypassing desktop computers and going directly to using smartphones. Lütke was learning that if he wanted to peek into the future to see where technology trends could go, the harbinger was China — and now the country was demonstrating that mobile devices were indeed the next technology wave. Yet Shopify's product teams at the time were developing new merchant services without thinking about how they scaled on mobile devices. When product managers presented mock-ups of new applications, Lütke would ask, "Hey, so what does it look like on mobile?"

After the August 2015 memo from Lütke came out, the company's Hack Days were used to work on mobile-related issues. And as requested, employees began using their smartphones more often, or using the company-installed mobile testing stations, to become more familiar with mobile capabilities and attuned to what needed to be done. Lütke also met with a team of senior staff from various departments to formulate a plan for fixing the company's mobile apps.

It was a critical challenge that was assigned to the assembled group of programmers and product managers. As the work progressed, there were some false starts and revisions, such as switching to different programming languages and redoing the work of previous months. Meanwhile, user ratings were tumbling and had reached alarming lows for the Apple and Android versions of Shopify Mobile. The Android version seemed most at risk, as its rating spiralled down to 3.1 out of 5 stars by May of 2016.

Miller, still CMO at the time, was becoming uneasy with the company's response to Lütke's call to arms. While a lot of good groundwork was getting done, it was beginning to look like the finished product was going to come too late to keep up with rival platforms. Miller then approached Lütke and said he and Shopify's director of product, Christopher Lobay, wanted to create a team to "start solving these problems and change the direction in the company." Lütke agreed with their proposal. Some time afterwards, Lütke told Sean Silcoff at the *Globe and Mail*: "He was completely right. It seems silly that I didn't spot that myself."[3] In other words, someone needed to have sole accountability; Miller and Lobay took it on.

The team set a goal to have the app ready by September 2016, in time for the peak shopping periods of Black Friday and Cyber Monday. As the deadline got closer, it seemed a new version could be released on time, but only if some of the planned features were left out and added in subsequent upgrades. The function to start a store, so dear to Lütke's heart, was on the list of deferred capabilities. But engineering director Tom Burns dug deep and logged the hours to implement it. "There was some clear heroism at the end," Lütke noted. The app was uploaded to Apple and Google app stores in late September, just in time for the upcoming shopping rush. It was a huge success and worries about a setback evaporated.

In February of 2017, Lütke appointed Miller to the position of CPO. For Lütke to hand over the reins to Miller on product development was a huge deal because Lütke was very passionate about product development and liked calling the shots on that front. Lütke's passion for product development was like "a father's love for his children," Miller said.[4]

The appointment appeared to be a reward for Miller's efforts on the mobile fix, but there was more to it. For years, Miller and Lütke had talked about Shopify's product development. And working out of Toronto, Miller was able to run trials on some product ideas that Lütke came to appreciate. "So I think he had a lot of respect for my thinking and he knew that I cared about it deeply," Miller noted.[5]

KEEPERS OF THE CODE

Jean-Michel Lemieux was Shopify's CTO in charge of several thousand programmers from 2016 to 2021. Lemieux was one of Shopify's key executives, yet, as a teenager and young adult, he never imagined he would be a manager. He thought managers had to be extroverts and by his own admission, he was an introvert. "If I spend eight hours a day with other humans, I will self-destruct," he told an interviewer.[1]

In his final year at an Ottawa high school, Lemieux took music, fine arts and math courses to prepare for the somewhat solitary pursuits of musician or painter. But one night, he logged into a computer that his dad had given him and put together a soundtrack for a musical that his school was staging. "The power that the computer could bring to whatever you wanted to build just blew me away," Lemieux recalled.[2]

After high school, he enrolled in the computer science department of the University of Ottawa. He nearly dropped out because he was so far behind the other students in coding skills; they had done a lot more in high school than just putting together a soundtrack for a musical. But he stuck it out and "got hooked" after discovering painting and coding were similar flow processes. "I just went from painting to programming as a very natural evolution," he said.[3]

Following graduation from university in the mid-1990s, Lemieux developed software for telephone networks and developer tools. Someone gifted him a book on managers that made him think he could be a manager. He accepted an offer to manage software teams at the Ottawa branch of IBM, and from there, went to Australia to grow the R&D function at Atlassian to more than 500 staff while building "a kick-ass marketplace and platform."[4]

Afterward, he joined Shopify and found himself assigned, among other things, to a multiyear redesign of the codebase. Set up without an architectural plan, the codebase had defaulted to a monolithic design, that is, "a software system in which functionally distinguishable aspects are all interwoven together, rather than contained in architecturally separate components."[5] Processing payments, adding products, managing third-party apps, arranging shipments of goods and a vast range of other functions were all built into the same structure with no boundaries between them. In the early years, this monolithic architecture was useful: it was the easiest to implement, allowed developers to get features out quickly to customers, and simplified database queries, among other things.

However, as the platform grew in size and reached a certain scale, it led to greater connections and interdependencies between the different functions, so when changes were made in one area it sometimes produced unexpected changes in others. Adding new code could inadvertently trigger "a cascade of unrelated test failures."[6] A tweak to the code calculating tax rates, for example, could affect shipping rate calculations in a way that would be hard to diagnose because of unknown linkages. The coupling also made it difficult to onboard new developers: instead of just learning the business logic of the area they joined, they would need to understand many more other areas because of how everything was interdependent.

It was clear that the linkages between different domains needed to be minimized. The solution was to modularize the monolith so that the coupling could be reduced by erecting boundaries between the different components. New developers could then focus just on learning the area they had been assigned to, greatly speeding up the orientation phase. Also, testing could be run just on the affected area, rendering the testing process faster and more reliable. It was a huge, multiyear task.

BATTLING THE BOTS

Lemieux and his team were kept busy fixing and fine-tuning other features on the platform, such as: 1) improving images on Shopify websites to provide more of a WYSIWYG experience, 2) incorporating 3D imagery and the ability to digitally position products in virtual settings, 3) adding payment-by-installments for costly items and 4) currency conversions and language translations. About halfway through his sojourn as CTO at Shopify, one job produced some sleepless nights and concerns for his safety.

At first, everything was quiet and peaceful. Lemieux asked Lütke if Shopify could give him $100,000 to buy a truckload of sneakers. "Cool," Lütke replied.[1] When they were delivered, Lemieux put them up for sale on the Shopify platform. They sold out within minutes. No, it didn't make him rich (the payments were donated to charity). There was another motive: Lemieux wanted to test the robustness of a new checkout process his team had built, so he needed a product that would draw a sudden avalanche of orders.

He knew celebrity-branded sneakers would fit the bill because of his previous encounters with sneaker bots. They used automation software to buy up whole inventories of sneakers in a matter of minutes. Lemieux was first alerted to the bots in 2018, when a sneaker drop caused visitor traffic to spike through the roof and crash his servers.

Shopify put some anti-bot and throttling measures in place. They seemed to work; Lemieux posted on X a graph showing that regular shoppers were able to get through to buy a good portion of the inventory for a product listed for sale. The graph had the unintended effect of "poking the dragon." The botters fired off a barrage of posts that trolled

Lemieux up, down and sideways. People at work told him to watch out and stay away from the botters because "they're . . . going to find where your house is."

So, he went quiet for a while. However, after a time, Lemieux decided the best strategy was to engage the botters on X. "I think that's where the love-hate relationship started," Lemieux said. "I was saying, listen, I'm just doing my job and I'm gonna have to work with you guys so why don't we get to know each other; I'm a friendly Canadian and it's hard for me to be too much of a badass."[2]

Nonetheless, the botters found workarounds to Shopify's anti-bot and throttling measures, so Lemieux doubled down and hired people with specialized knowledge to develop more substantive solutions. The techniques included raffles, domain swaps, puzzles, trivia questions and blocking transactions that follow the shortcuts used by bots. A degree of success was attained. Many Shopify merchants were happy to use the anti-bot tools Shopify made available.

Other merchants chose not to use them and let the bots have free rein. They didn't mind having their inventory sell out so quickly. In fact, some commentators wondered if the panic buying may have been part of a clever marketing scheme. As the *New York Times* noted, the bots created an "artificial scarcity that makes a sneaker valuable and . . . a brand seem cool."

The sneakers subject to buying frenzies had vibrant resale markets. Those in mint condition could be resold on sites like StockX and GOAT at great markups. As the *New York Times* observed: "When the pandemic hit, sneaker resales reached a frenzy. . . . The sale price for a new pair of vintage 'Chicago OG' Air Jordans . . . went from $3,000 in 2017 to $7,500 in May 2020 to $19,000 in February 2021."[3]

In March of 2021, Lemieux put up on X a video of the botters lamenting the difficulties of cracking Shopify's bot protections. By then, the dialogue on X between Lemieux and the botters had taken on more of a tone of mutual respect. The *New York Times* interviewed Lemieux and quoted him saying: "I know more about bots than maybe anyone on this planet because I had to reverse engineer them to understand how they work."[4] But there was a lot more out there on the platform to be concerned about; Shopify and its engineers had more battles to fight.

TROLLS, FRAUDSTERS AND HACKERS

The botters were not the only troublemakers on Shopify's platform. It was often under attack by a variety of trolls, fraudsters, and black-hat hackers. The guardians of the code had to defend against them in order to ensure Shopify's platform serviced subscribers without interruptions.

DDOS trolls: In its early years Shopify was hit with denial-of-service (DOS) and distributed denial-of-service (DDOS) attacks, whereby Shopify was flooded with waves of frivolous traffic from single or multiple sources seeking to overload the platform and prevent it from responding to legitimate inquiries. This was addressed in due course but for a time, Lütke was at a loss on what to do and sought some answers on *Hacker News*, posting March 24, 2009: "How do people protect themselves against extortion and malicious ddos attacks? What software/hardware protects the bigger sites on the net?"[1]

Payment fraudsters: Another problem that emerged was payment fraud, which was addressed by developing a Shopify tool called Fraud Protect for Shopify Payments, birthed in October of 2018. Fraudulent payments commonly happened when someone used another person's credit card to make a purchase without the cardholder's consent. When the real cardholder notices the unauthorized charge, they will usually request a chargeback from the bank that issued the card; it will often respond by taking the purchase amount from the merchant's account and returning it to the credit cardholder. Thus, the merchant ends up without a payment for a product that was shipped.

To develop Fraud Protect for Shopify Payments, Shopify's vast databases of merchant transactions were analyzed to spot characteristics of fraudulent orders. For example, it was found that purchase orders using different billing and shipping addresses were more likely to be fraudulent. The various signals were then combined into algorithms used to screen incoming orders for fraud. If the merchant saw that an order was flagged as high risk, they could either reject it or delve into the details and make their own judgment call.

Black-hat hackers: Hackers frequently probed for gaps in Shopify's software to access private databases. By 2018, Shopify's security team had several dozen personnel dedicated to mitigating the risks. Shopify also approached HackerOne to hire some white-hat hackers to participate in a "bug bounty" program, which paid them for the bugs they found in its codebase. To lure white-hat hackers, the Shopify payouts were made one of the richest on HackerOne. By 2018, the bug bounty program had uncovered more than 750 bugs and paid $850,000 in bounties to over 300 programmers.

"Until you have a robust set of eyes on your stuff, it's really hard to know what you're missing," said Andrew Dunbar, Chief Information Security Officer at Shopify.[2] A variety of vulnerabilities were uncovered, such as the one that would have allowed unauthorized access to merchant invoices. However, a computer-science student had the honour of receiving one of the largest payments — $50,000 — for discovering that an application created by a Shopify developer inadvertently provided a pathway to the token for accessing the GitHub account, which led to Shopify's source code repositories.

DMCA trolls: The Digital Millennium Copyright Act (DMCA) in the United States enabled a website owner to have material removed from another website if it was infringing on their copyright, or even to shut the offending website down for recurring violations. Shopify received thousands of DMCA notices every month and forwarded them to the targeted merchants. Shopify was often compelled to remove product displays, or, in the case of unresolved violations, to close the store. The affected store owner could file a counter notice to have the copyright-infringement claim investigated; if false evidence was found, Shopify could restore the removed items and/or shuttered store after 14 days, a length of time specified in the DMCA. However, a disruption that long can result in a significant loss of revenue for a shop.

This DMCA process was open to abuse. Knowing that merely filing a DMCA could compel Shopify to strip or close one of its stores for at least two weeks if not permanently, some DMCA trolls submitted nuisance claims against other stores. Such patently spurious DMCAs that crippled or shut down stores were very upsetting experiences for honest Shopify merchants.

One instance in the fall of 2023 involved an individual who filed more than 70 DMCA takedown demands against Shopify shops selling perfume products. With the number of nuisance claims on the rise in 2023, this one appeared to be the last straw, and Shopify decided to clamp down. A system was put in place to scan DMCA notices for bad-faith claims. If they were found to be groundless, Shopify would take legal action against the claimants. By December, lawsuits had been filed against several DMCA claimants to cover damages and legal costs, as well as to obtain an injunction to halt further fake DMCA notices. It was hoped that the litigation would not only reveal the identities of the DMCA trolls through the disclosure process but also have a deterrent effect on sending out false DMCAs.

Escape Velocity

Shopify was emerging as a leading supplier of e-commerce services but there were still so many more growth opportunities. Shopify's dazzling track record and the resources at its disposal bestowed the confidence to go after them. Toward the end of the 2010s, Shopify looked to: 1) go upmarket and add more enterprise companies to its roll, 2) spread out more into international markets and 3) tap into new industries such as cryptocurrencies and cannabis. It also decided to pursue a conventional marketing campaign and begin building a fulfillment network to ship products for merchants.

MOVING UPMARKET

Shopify Plus was originally set up to give merchants a reason to stay on Shopify as they grew in size and needed more services. After the win with Red Bull, Shopify Plus switched to actively seeking new customers among the strata of large companies ($20 million to $125 million in annual sales) and enterprise companies (greater than $125 million in annual sales).

The Shopify platform already had a number of features that could appeal to these whales. One, in particular, was the ability to handle high volume sales. "The platform is built for flash sales. This is actually one of the main reasons why established brands switch over to us!" Lütke posted in an online forum.[1]

But Shopify was not content to rely on just the existing features of its platform to attract new customers from the high-end niche. Additional salespeople were hired for Shopify Plus, trade shows were added to the schedule, and a team of Technology Partners was drafted to handle customizations more complex than what could be addressed by existing and new apps on the API. The Shopify Global ERP Program also enabled Shopify's merchants to be integrated into the Enterprise Resource Planning solutions offered by Microsoft, Oracle and other companies.

To further address the needs of the whales, new features and tools were added to the platform. They included: Shopify Flow (automation of repetitive processes such as ordering inventory), Scripts (for customizing checkouts), Launchpad (for automating flash sales, product launches, etc.) and Augmented Reality (rotating and placement of 3D images).

When Shopify Plus got an assignment from a client, it often was for only part of their operations. These small assignments were viewed by Shopify as "land and expand opportunities," chances to demonstrate what it could do and hopefully win more business. Still, some prospective clients had to be turned away because even with the Technology Partners team, the job would be too challenging or protracted. These cases tended to have legacy systems that posed severe integration challenges and made it difficult to improve performance. "Oftentimes, they do come back to us and say, okay, well, we actually have rethought this, and we're not going to bring all these integrations with us," Finkelstein disclosed.[2]

By the time Padelford left Shopify Plus in the summer of 2021, it had expanded to 1,500 employees and signed up 14,000 subscribers. The client list was a varied one. Even Amazon had a website on Shopify Plus — for its Whole Foods subsidiary. There were traditional consumer-packaged-goods (CPG) companies (such as Hasbro, Unilever, Procter & Gamble, Levi's, Lysol, Clearasil and Frito-Lay); industrial and commercial products companies (such as Muffler Express, Cummins Engine and Ford); brands that had grown large on Shopify (such as Allbirds, Soylent and Gymshark); and various other brands (including Polaroid, Visa, Jones New York, Canadian Tire, *New York Times*, De Beers, Netflix and Budweiser).

There were plenty of celebrities who were Shopify Plus clients too, including: Kim Kardashian, Adele, Lady Gaga, Victoria Beckham, David Beckham, Taylor Swift, Cristiano Ronaldo, Tom Brady, Arnold Schwarzenegger, LeBron James, Drake, Ellen DeGeneres, Justin

Timberlake, Beyoncé and Justin Bieber. "The celebrity brand vertical is really heating up," Finkelstein remarked during Shopify's earnings call for the fourth quarter of 2018. A clever move by Finkelstein was to interview several of the celebrity merchants and post the clips on YouTube and other social media. Their celebrity status would attract a good number of viewers and help promote both the celeb's business and Shopify's platform.

GOING INTERNATIONAL

Towards the end of the 2010s, Shopify directed more attention toward international expansion. It had merchants based in dozens of countries but in most cases, it was not a huge presence outside of English-speaking countries. Shopify had held back from international expansion because it wanted to make sure it was doing well in the United States first. Nonetheless, in the first quarter earnings call of 2018, Finkelstein declared that Shopify was "embarking on a multiyear journey towards making Shopify as simple and effective globally as it is in our core geographies." One of the first steps in this journey was to transition to a global cloud service provider (Google Cloud). Next, steps were taken to make Shopify's platform multilingual and tailor features such as payments, shipping and capital lending to other countries' customs.

For the first round of international expansion, priority was given to Germany, France, Japan and Singapore. Shopify felt they would be the easiest countries to achieve some early successes in since its platform had the closest product fit in those places. Germany was of particular interest to Lütke because his parents and other relatives "keep telling me about how poorly Shopify works every time I'm in Germany," he quipped at a Bloomberg Live event in 2019.[1] Still, it was not going to be a simple matter of translating the platform into another language and adding a multi-currency capability. A good understanding of the cultural differences in how people shop in those countries would be needed in order to adapt payment methods and other features of the platform.

In the second quarter of 2018, Shopify Payments was launched in Germany after it was "localized" to allow features unique to German credit cards. By the end of 2018, the Shopify platform had been translated into seven languages, and multi-currency status was added. Along with additions to the global partner ecosystem, these undertakings helped raise the portion of international business from 21% in 2017 to 24% of total merchants in 2018.

A leap forward came in September of 2021 with the release of Shopify Markets, "a centralized hub with all the tools needed for engaging in global commerce all from a single Shopify store."[2] A partnership was announced in January 2022 with the Chinese online marketplace JD.com (its GMV was just behind Amazon in world rankings) to enable U.S. Shopify merchants to sell into China. To further accelerate and simplify international expansion, this was followed by the launch, in September 2022, of Shopify Translate & Adapt and Shopify Markets Pro (powered by Shopify's partnership with Global-e).

While Shopify was looking to expand internationally, e-commerce firms from other countries were looking to expand into North America. Two from China, Shein and Temu, were enjoying a fair amount of success. Shein had become America's largest fast-fashion seller while Temu was thriving by selling a diverse assortment of products. Sometimes the quality was not the greatest, but the pair offered the lowest prices on many products, with generous refund policies. Shein and Temu shaved costs by shipping directly from China to U.S. customers, thus avoiding import duties on orders less than $800 and deleting the cost of maintaining large inventories in U.S. warehouses.[3] They may also have sold items at a loss in order to gain market share. Their deliveries could take more than a week but American consumers were still happy to purchase from them due to the low prices.

CRYPTOCURRENCY AND CANNABIS

Technological advances and legislative changes in the 2010s created new industries and products. Since Shopify's mission was to make commerce better for everyone, it added tools that entrepreneurs could use in the new sectors.

The rise of cryptocurrencies in the 2010s was significant. Cryptocurrencies use blockchains that record financial transactions on decentralized, peer-to-peer computer networks, enabling people to transact outside of government-sanctioned financial systems. On February 14, 2018, Shopify partnered with the leading North American cryptocurrency exchange, Coinbase Global, to add its payment gateway, Coinbase Commerce, to the Shopify platform. This enabled merchants to accept payment in several cryptocurrencies, such as Bitcoin, Ethereum and Litecoin. There were other partnerships on a smaller scale, including the installation in 2022 of Crypto.com (which accepted 20 kinds of cryptocurrencies, including Ether, Dogecoin, Litecoin and stablecoins). Shopify first integrated crypto payments into its platform in 2013 via the BitPay gateway for accepting Bitcoin.

Cryptocurrencies are a controversial topic. There are many critics; there are many supporters. The critics, such as Berkshire Hathaway chairperson Warren Buffett, have said cryptocurrencies fluctuate in value too much to be useful as a medium of exchange and encourage speculative behaviour; they are also said to facilitate money laundering, tax evasion and the financing of terrorist activities.[1] Supporters, such as venture capitalist Marc Andreessen, believe the bad actors can still be traced by authorities despite the popular view that Bitcoin and other cryptocurrencies permit anonymous transactions. In addition, they can displace credit card payments and thus eliminate credit card fees for online transactions (and end credit card fraud), allow the unbanked to perform transactions and permit micropayments as small as a fraction of a cent so gaming, media and other businesses can replace subscription- and advertising-based revenue models with pay-per-item or pay-per-article models.[2]

A concern for Shopify was that its merchants could lose sales if consumers switched to other e-commerce platforms that accepted crypto payments. Shopify's commitment to its merchants was paramount, so it added cryptocurrency gateways. As Finkelstein explained: "Our job as the retail operating system for brands all over the world is no matter what a merchant wants to do on Shopify, we have to make that available."[3] By mid-2022, companies like Microsoft, Whole Foods, Starbucks, Twitch and Home Depot were accepting digital currencies.[4]

Shopify embraced crypto even though its potential to replace credit card payments threatened one of Shopify's major sources of revenue. But eliminating such payment fees would be in the interests of merchants and promote higher levels of e-commerce, so Shopify needed to get in front of the disruption and prepare its transition, if and when required. Early adoption on its part could give Shopify an edge in processing cryptocurrency transactions and set it up as a go-to destination for shoppers if digital currencies became more mainstream. To further recoup any loss of revenues from the transition to crypto, Shopify could also develop other services for merchants; an example would be a rewards and loyalty program for the merchants' customers.[5]

In 2021, Shopify gave its merchants the ability to sell non-fungible tokens, or NFTs (digital content that cannot be accessed without permission of the creator). An example of an application was the artist who wanted to restrict access to their digital art so it could be sold and owned exclusively by the buyer. For example, lifestyle guru Martha Stewart converted some of her favourite photographs to NFTs and put them up for sale on one of her websites; once someone purchased one of her photos, it could be enjoyed or re-sold only by them. In June of 2022, Shopify introduced a "tokengated" feature that merchants could use to reward loyal customers by allowing them to connect their crypto wallets to the merchant's store and deploy NFTs to unlock benefits, such as early access to product drops and limited-edition merchandise.

Another new industry emerged when recreational use of cannabis was legalized in Canada on October 17, 2018. Shopify had already been the preferred platform for licensed producers of medical cannabis for many years, so it was not too much of a transition to enter the recreational segment. Shopify became the place to buy recreational cannabis online in Canada, winning supply contracts with the retail outlets of the larger provincial governments and becoming the point-of-sale channel for some of the largest licensed producers, including Canopy Growth, Aurora Cannabis and Hexo.

Cannabis sales on the opening day had a clean launch on the Shopify platform. The Ontario Cannabis Store alone attracted 1.3 million unique visits in the first 24 hours. In Shopify's earnings call for the fourth quarter of 2018, Finkelstein pointed out: "The provinces that didn't use Shopify, did have some problems and the ones that did use Shopify had no problems whatsoever, so we're quite proud of that." Shopify didn't always toot its horn so overtly but its push into recreational cannabis was not just about gaining a foothold in the Canadian market but also about letting other countries know that it could handle recreational cannabis sales if and when they legalized it.

FUELLING THE SHOPIFY BRAND

While funds may have been scarce in the early days for Shopify to pursue a conventional marketing campaign, there was now several billion dollars sitting on the balance sheet. After Miller left the CMO position in 2018, Shopify found a new CMO, Jeff Weiser, to lead a more conventional approach to marketing and branding.

The first stage was initiated under the "Let's Make You a Business" banner, and consisted of TV, video, billboard, radio and social advertising in a dozen key markets within North America. By doing so, Shopify was hoping to make people more aware of the entrepreneur option, and to become the name that came to mind when thoughts turned to starting a business. "Our brand is all about using commerce to help people pursue independence," Weiser told *Strategy Online*. "There's a lot of people caught in a corporate wheel, but when they start a business with Shopify and act on their dreams it's a freeing experience for them."[1]

The TV spot featured real Shopify merchants in settings furnished entirely with items from Shopify merchants — all tagged with the names of their shops to create an impressive visual display of the immense variety of businesses on Shopify. The digital-video component featured an impassioned plea from Finkelstein to join the entrepreneurial tribe at Shopify.[2]

The billboard segment let people know that Shopify was available to help entrepreneurs build their businesses. With a hat tip to Finkelstein's T-shirt business from his younger days, one proclaimed: "No partner will take your funny T-shirt more seriously." Not to leave Lütke's sock side hustle out, another proclaimed: "That sock business you're thinking about could be a sock empire. Let's make you an empire." Other slogans included: "Let's make what you do for fun, what you do for a living" and "Let's make your mom's 'famous' recipe actually famous."

Another initiative was to launch Shopify Studios and produce TV, film and digital content about entrepreneurs.[3] In 2019, the studio released four dozen short videos on YouTube under the "My Shopify Business Story" heading, dealing with "the highs and lows of the entrepreneurship journey as told by Shopify business owners around the world."[4]

A company report concluded that Shopify's first branding campaign had produced "a marked increase in the number of small- and mid-sized businesses saying they will definitely try Shopify." Yet Weiser was let go in February of 2020. It seemed there were some internal issues: *BetaKit* reported "that operations may not have been running smoothly within the marketing division, with issues around culture. . . . The division has reportedly faced some recent turnover with its senior [staff]."[5]

With the CMO's exit, the marketing function was restructured again. Part of it was merged back into the product division to resume product tweaks that would expand the size of market by removing more friction. The other part, made up of branding, communications, creative work and Shopify Studios, went to Finkelstein's division, where it was assigned to Amy Hufft, who had joined the marketing team in 2018 after spending 15 years marketing brands in the fashion industries and some time prior getting an MBA from Columbia University.

The campaigns of the year before were continued. For example, Shopify Studios produced a network TV series called *I Quit*, about people leaving their day jobs to follow their entrepreneurial ambitions. It premiered on the Discovery Channel in August of 2020. Another production was a documentary that came out March 12, 2021, on Disney Plus under the title *Own the Room*. It followed five students competing in the Global Student Entrepreneur Awards in Macau, China.

Hufft and others on the marketing team had been challenged to take risks and hack traditional branding methods to come up with innovative approaches, like an entrepreneur would. She remembers Lütke saying: "You don't get in trouble for taking risks at Shopify. You get in trouble for not taking risks."[6] One risky move she took was to hire the three funniest people in Shopify to go on company social channels and try as hard as they could to get fired (only constraint was to check the legal and financial implications with her first). One of the posts featured a person giving a big wink of the eye under the caption "Amazon: I won't make a knock-off of your product."

"It was ridiculous stuff and the executives would ask the next morning, 'What's happening with our social media team?' But it was making people laugh and reminding them not to take things so seriously," remarked Hufft in her presentation for *The Gathering* forum.[7] A lot of the readers got "what Shopify was trying to do and some became brand ambassadors, reposting the off-the-wall stuff to their followers. Once we let go of the concept of strategy and got truly bold, we saw a massive engagement," Hufft added. Indeed, the analytics showed that traffic to Shopify's X account more than tripled after the change in approach in early 2021. Hufft was to be involved in several other unconventional branding exercises after that, but then left Shopify in June of 2022 to take a job with Zoom as Head of Brand and Communications.

THE SHOPIFY FULFILLMENT NETWORK

No doubt, Lütke's successful track record during the 2010s had left him more seasoned and confident not only in his skill set but also his company's capacity to execute. Why not go after bigger game? There was indeed bigger game: the giant pain point for merchants of shipping orders. Building a new fulfillment network could take care of that.

The launch, which took place at the *Shopify Unite* conference in Toronto on June 24, 2019, was recorded and posted on YouTube.[1] The video begins with a cheerful woman walking onto the stage, her shoulder-length black hair glistening under the ceiling lights. Reaching the center of the stage, she turned her gaze to the dimly lit auditorium filled with programmers and website designers. Smiling, she spoke a few introductory words. Then she introduced the featured speaker: "Many of you know him and he's been absolutely pivotal in the development of Shopify and the retail operating system. Please join me in giving a very warm welcome to our Chief Product Officer, Craig Miller!"

Loud applause broke out, strobe lights spun and upbeat music played as the tall, lean frame of Miller climbed the stairs onto the stage. He began talking about the problems Shopify merchants faced when shipping products to their customers, like delays and high costs. "Merchants then go looking for third-party logistics providers and what they discover terrifies them." As he spoke, Miller paced leisurely back and forth across the broad stage, bare of any object except for stage lights and a ceiling-to-floor screen on the wall behind him.

About 20 minutes in, he turned and faced the audience squarely, to proclaim: "Today I'm excited to announce the Shopify Fulfillment Network!" Loud cheering and clapping erupted; the huge dark screen behind Miller turned a bright emerald green as if clouds had parted. Emblazoned on it were the words: Shopify Fulfillment Network.

As the CPO at Shopify, the job of introducing the Shopify Fulfillment Network (SFN) fell to Miller. On the screen, it was shown as a network of mostly third-party warehouses and shippers stretching across the United States to ensure faster and more reliable deliveries. The projected cost would be $1 billion over five years. "Once enabled, a merchant on SFN doesn't need to think about picking, packing, shipping or fulfillment ever again," said Miller with a grin. Again, the loud applause.

Shopify was not pitching the SFN as a challenge to Amazon's fulfillment network. It was simply following its mission to make commerce better by taking the pain points out of logistics for its merchants. The latter would be able to click on an icon and have Shopify do fulfillment with a pledge to their customers — called Shop Promise — to deliver within two days to 90% of the U.S. population. While it was no match for the one-day promise offered by Amazon Prime, Shopify's delivery commitment would still boost sales for merchants, its studies showed.

What tied the SFN together was a Shopify software system that connected warehouses and other nodes in the fulfillment network for the purpose of tracking and directing shipments. The incentive for partner warehouses and transportation services to sign up and adhere to service standards was the huge amount of steady business they would enjoy as a result of having hundreds of thousands of Shopify merchants sent their way.

In September, four months after Miller's presentation, Shopify acquired 6 River Systems for $450 million. Its trolley-like Chuck robots roamed warehouse floors to help workers pick and retrieve shipments. The company was co-founded in 2015 by two former executives of Kiva Systems, a warehouse pioneer that Amazon acquired in 2012 to get its fulfillment network going.

Shopify was also approaching logistics and transportation firms to add them into the SFN. With the ability to send massive shipments their way, Shopify was able to negotiate deep discounts to pass along to its merchants. Programmers at Shopify and 6 River Systems also got to work on the software that would knit the SFN together. An R&D center was opened in Ottawa to test new robotics and fulfillment technologies.

A lot more work was to come. It was going to be a big job. But Shopify itself was now a big company. Indeed, it had recently joined the big leagues of North American e-commerce.

Entering the Big Leagues

Shopify's rapid growth over the 2010s brought it into the orbit of U.S. e-commerce titans. By 2019, Finkelstein was able to report that Shopify had emerged as "the second largest e-commerce retailer in the United States," based on GMV (the value of sales generated by its merchants). Of course, Amazon was the largest by far. This ranking was corroborated by market-research firm eMarketer, which found that Amazon was overwhelmingly in first place with a 41% share of U.S. retail e-commerce sales in 2021, followed by Shopify (10.3%), Walmart (6.6%), eBay (4.2%) and Apple (4.0%).[1]

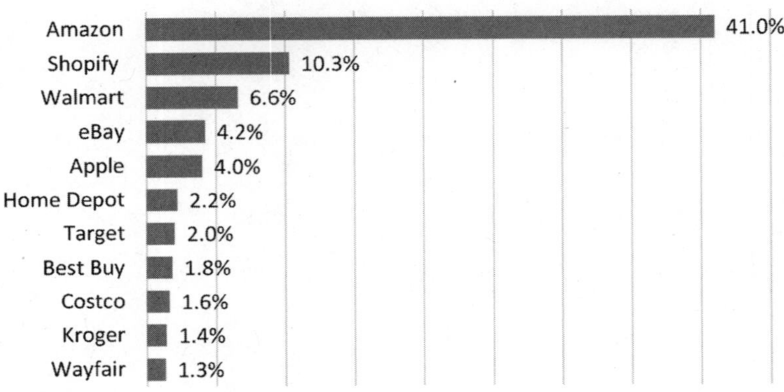

Data source: eMarketer, cited in *Shopify Investor Overview Deck — Q2 2022*

THE EMPIRE VERSUS THE REBELS

Given the way Shopify was growing and its opportunity set, some observers thought it could end up challenging Amazon despite the latter's gargantuan size. New York University marketing professor Scott Galloway told *BetaKit* in 2019 that if any company could breach the impenetrable fortress known as Amazon, it would be Shopify.[1] Journalist David George-Cosh interviewed Catherine Wood of ARK Investment Management in 2021 and reported in a BNN Bloomberg article that "Wood believes [Shopify] can still grow as big as Amazon, given the long-term opportunities in the social e-commerce space."[2] Andrew Button's article for the Motley Fool website concluded that although Shopify was not likely going to be the next Amazon, it was capable of delivering Amazon-like returns.[3]

At times, it looked like Shopify and Amazon were becoming fierce rivals. In an "Ask Me Anything" session in 2019, Lütke used a *Star Wars* metaphor to characterize the relationship between the two companies, saying Amazon was trying to build an empire and Shopify was trying to arm the rebels.[4] Around the same time, Amazon had quietly formed an internal project team, Project Santos, to brainstorm ways to compete with Shopify.

Yet, Lütke downplayed the notion that Shopify and Amazon were locked into a zero-sum battle to the finish. The opportunity in the e-commerce space was just so large that it could support the growth of many participants well into the foreseeable future. If anything, Shopify and Amazon were more like frenemies. That's the way it usually was with tech companies operating in expanding markets. Frenemies were rivals but they were also friendly and co-operated: since 2015, for example, Shopify had let its merchants use Amazon Pay and Amazon had let Shopify's merchants sell on its website (when a consumer buys from Amazon, sometimes they are actually buying from a Shopify merchant).

Moreover, Amazon and Shopify were not actually competing directly against each other. They were operating in separate market segments, where the customers had different needs. Amazon was a marketplace offering a wide range of goods to consumers at low prices and unmatched fulfillment. Even Lütke was impressed: "You really want the lowest price and fastest delivery on these kind of things," he told a Startupfest conference. "I shop on Amazon too, its search engine is amazing."[5] By contrast, Shopify was providing a service to entrepreneurs, making it easy and inexpensive for them to conduct commerce.

It was Shopify's merchants that were selling directly to consumers, in Amazon's domain. Shopify's merchants were able to compete against Amazon because, as Lütke described it, Amazon offered "products with barcodes" while Shopify's merchants offered mostly "products without barcodes."[6] Products with barcodes tended to be standardized goods, like toothpaste and detergent, so low pricing was a key consideration for consumers. Products without barcodes tended to be differentiated in some way, such as by craftsmanship, customization, unique designs and so on — the result was a degree of immunity from price competition.

While the degree of immunity varied, many of the differentiated products had good sales and pricing power over long periods of time. A prime example is Starbucks coffee (not sold on Shopify). At one time, North Americans didn't pay much for a cup of coffee, but then Starbucks ramped up the quality and in-store experience to be able to consistently charge a high price. Sometimes products without barcodes have good sales and pricing power over shorter periods; take, for example, merchants that jump early on a fad or meme, such as the Shopify jeweller that came out with a line of Pokémon Go jewelry during the Pokémon Go craze.

Bombas is a longer-running example from the Shopify platform of a product differentiated by craftsmanship and design. Prior to launch in 2015, its founders spent a great deal of time trying different materials, designs and other aspects to see if socks could be made more comfortable, durable and noticeably better than what was available. Once they were satisfied with their results, Bombas went to market and have since successfully delivered enough value to sell their socks at higher prices than the standard issue. They also differentiated their brand by becoming a "buy-one-give-one" company — that is, for every pair of socks purchased, they donated a pair to the homeless (the idea for Bombas was sparked by one of the co-founders discovering that the most needed item at homeless shelters was socks).

Aside from usually having the best prices on standardized goods, Amazon enjoyed a competitive edge thanks to its unparalleled fulfillment and inventory capabilities. Many third-party merchants chose to set up on it because they obtained access to this advantage. Another reason they chose Amazon was because of high levels of consumer traffic: a survey published by Wunderman Thompson Commerce found more than 60% of online shoppers in the United States and Europe start their product search on Amazon versus a search engine.[7]

Nonetheless, many merchants still preferred Shopify because they had more freedom to conduct their business, create a relationship with their own customers and build their brand. For example, they could access their sales data to do analytics, ship in boxes with their own logo, sell at lower price points, set higher margins and perform various other tasks that independent businesspersons can do. Moreover, many of them felt they might end up ranked low in the search function on Amazon, or they simply did not need help finding customers — they already had an audience or knew how to get one through marketing.

Take Ralph and Michelle Montemurro of Toronto. After furnishing their son's nursery in 2015, they decided to start a business making and selling a line of furniture with design simplicity and exceptional comfort. They considered selling on Amazon but it didn't feel right for their high-end furniture. "On Amazon, all the product listings are in the same cluttered format, with the same low-quality photographs," they told journalist David H. Freedman.[8] Sure, hordes of shoppers went to Amazon, but the Montemurros felt uncertain that its search function would fetch them enough traffic. Nor would they be able to get much data on their customers to fine-tune their marketing campaigns and build customer relationships. And given that Amazon could see if their sales were taking off, they worried that the e-commerce giant would start producing knock-offs of their products. So the couple set up their business, Monte Design, on the Shopify platform.

There is, in fact, a history of Amazon merchants complaining about Amazon practices such as creating white-label versions of successful products sold by its third-party merchants. It got to the point where a U.S. congressional committee investigated. In 2020, its findings were published in *Investigation of Competition in Digital Markets*,[9] which concluded that Amazon "has monopoly power over its third-party sellers, bullies its retail partners and improperly uses third-party data to inform its strategy for selling self-made private-label products on its e-marketplace."[10] Also, in 2022, Amazon settled two European Union antitrust cases (without a fine) by agreeing to abstain from producing cheaper knock-offs of the most popular products of its independent merchants.

Then there was the cost to merchants of selling on marketplaces like Amazon. Writing in the *New York Times*, Yiren Lu provided some specifics in the case of Amazon during 2020:

> Today, if a business lists an article of clothing on Amazon for $50, Amazon gets $8.50 in commission; if the seller opts to advertise on the site, Amazon likely gets at least another $6.50. And if Fulfillment by Amazon is used, Amazon's total cut gets closer to 40%. Amazon ships F.B.A. products in its own envelopes or brown boxes, highlights competing vendors on the site and charges extra for things like early reviews and dedicated account managers.[11]

After a lengthy investigation, the U.S. Federal Trade Commission and 17 states charged Amazon in September of 2023 with violation of U.S. antitrust laws. A great deal of the lawsuit zeroed in on how the success of third-party merchants on Amazon was made contingent on spending as much as 50% of their revenue on advertising, fulfillment and other services from Amazon. This not only seriously squeezed their margins but pressured them to charge higher prices in order to offset some of the squeeze.

The antitrust lawsuit could lead to severe penalties for Amazon. However, such lawsuits usually take years before a ruling is handed down, and even then, acquittals are obtained or some modest concessions can lead to an out-of-court solution. In the meantime, Amazon will continue to be an empire with many disparate and moving parts, all backed by deep pockets: in 2021, it had $50 billion cash on its balance sheet, nearly 10 times as much as Shopify's balances. Amazon also has the opportunity to cross-subsidize between different product lines, that is, if a product line is facing competition, Amazon can pour earnings from stronger product lines into its weaker line to neutralize or eliminate the competition. Amazon is the 800-pound gorilla — but for now, it is a frenemy to Shopify.

TO PATENT OR NOT TO PATENT

Shopify may have morphed into one of the big players in e-commerce but it still resembled more the startup when it came to patents. By 2019, it had secured less than 175 patents on its intellectual property (IP). Other large firms in the e-commerce space were much further ahead at the time: Alibaba had more than 45,000, Amazon had at least 25,000, eBay close to 8,000 and Walmart over 5,500.[1] It wasn't for lack of innovation that Shopify lagged so far behind. The reason was that Lütke had not been a fan of patents. "An idea is worth exactly one good bottle of scotch," he once said. "I think it's a farce that patents can be granted for anything, anywhere, in the tech industry."[2]

Other tech titans seemed to share Lütke's view of patents. Microsoft co-founder Bill Gates once declared that patents have the shelf life of a banana; Elon Musk, CEO of Tesla, made company patents available without a licensing requirement to anyone. Yet Microsoft became one of the biggest patent holders in the United States. And what Musk gave away to the public were said to be the lower-valued patents, released on condition they were not used against Tesla — all of which can be seen as "part of a clever strategy to increase global demand for electric vehicles," according to Jim Hinton, an IP lawyer.[3]

Patent lawyers at times issued warnings that Shopify risked having its growth impaired by the theft of its IP. However, Shopify's *Annual Reports* indicated it was pursuing an alternative to patents in the form of copyright, trade secrets, trade dress, domain names, trademarks and other rights. There were also confidentiality, assignment and license agreements with employees and third parties to limit the use of Shopify's IP.

"Factors such as the skills and ingenuity of our employees, as well as the functionality and frequent enhancements to our platform, make our intellectual property difficult to replicate," added the *Annual Reports*. Other software companies also seemed to be moving toward competing on product rather than IP. "They argue that rather than worrying about protecting an invention, it's more material to spend your energy turning that invention into the best product as quickly as you can," noted University of Toronto professor Shiri Breznitz during a seminar hosted by the Munk School of Global Affairs & Public Policy.[4]

But there was another side to the patent issue. As Shopify grew, so did the number of lawsuits launched against it by companies claiming Shopify was infringing on their patents. A number of court cases Shopify won. One it lost in late 2022, resulting in an order to pay $40 million in damages.

By the spring of 2023, Shopify had enough of what it believed were unfounded claims. Many of the lawsuits were coming from what Shopify called patent trolls, that is, entities funded by anonymous investors to purchase patents for the purpose of suing other companies for infringement. After Lower48 IP LLC sued Shopify for patent infringement in 2023, Shopify filed a motion in a Texas district court requesting disclosure of the identities of the investors behind the lawsuit. It was unsuccessful but there were encouraging signs in other states, where court judgments appeared to open the door to greater disclosure. Shopify also announced its intention to pursue the issue via continued litigation and lobbying for appropriate legislation.

COVID-19 at Warp Speed

On January 30, 2020, the World Health Organization declared that the COVID-19 virus was a public health emergency of international concern (PHEIC), its highest level of alarm. Over the coming weeks, populations fled public venues and workplaces to shelter in their homes. National health-care systems were increasingly overwhelmed and the death toll mounted. The global economy ground to a halt and major stock-market indexes in North America plunged by a third for most of February and early March in 2020. Shopify's stock tanked by 25%.

"THE PANDEMIC JUST TURBOCHARGED THEM"

Then, just as with the financial and economic crisis of 2008 and 2009, Shopify's fortunes turned around in the midst of calamity. People switched from in-person to online shopping, dramatically boosting the sales of Shopify's merchants. People waiting out the pandemic at home also had leisure time to start online businesses. CFO Amy Shapero (who had replaced Jones in 2018) was the bearer of an abundance of good news during Shopify's earnings calls. By the end of 2020, revenues had soared to $2.9 billion, an 86% increase from 2019; the next year, in 2021, revenues leaped again, rising by 58% to $4.6 billion. After bottoming out in March of 2020, Shopify's stock soared, rising by nearly fivefold to the peak in November of 2021. "The pandemic just turbocharged them. It's ridiculous," Watson at RMW Commerce Consulting was quoted as saying.[1]

The way Shopify responded so quickly to the needs of its merchants also fuelled the enormous uptick in its business. Since the company's mission was to make commerce better for entrepreneurs, the most pressing thing was to provide solutions that could help merchants deal immediately with the disruption of COVID-19. Lütke had Shopify quickly pivot away from more than half of its current workload to take up projects that would help merchants cope as soon as possible. "The most important thing is to keep the most important thing the most important thing," Lütke said in response to a question raised during a 2022 *Knowledge Project* interview about how to lead a company through troubled times.[2]

Shopify equipped merchant websites with curbside pickup and local delivery options to help its subscribers stay in business. It increased by $200 million the funds that could be advanced through Shopify Capital and further expanded the program to the U.K. and Canada. It also made gift cards available so merchants could sell them to raise cash against future sales, gave would-be entrepreneurs a break by increasing the free trial period to 90 days, made Shopify Email free so merchants could stay in touch with customers and provided online resources to support merchants with securing government funding and finding community forums, live webinars, online meetups and tutorials. "We pulled a lot of features forward in time because they are helpful right now," Lütke said on X, April 28, 2020. "Pardon the dust, we had to lower the acceptable quality bar in some places to pull it off."

For small businesses, Shopify was a lifesaver. Take, for example, the craft brewery Great Lakes Brewing in Toronto. When COVID-19 first stunned the world in early 2020, half of its business disappeared overnight when most of its buyers in the bar and restaurant industries shut down. The brewery's owner, Peter Bulut, had to close his own restaurant and store too, laying off a quarter of his more than 50 employees. On top of that, he had hundreds of thousands of gallons of beer sloshing around in tanks and barrels, with nowhere to go. "I didn't sleep for two weeks after that," Bulut told journalist David H. Freedman.[3] Realizing his only hope was to try to sell his beer online and do home deliveries, he had an employee contact Shopify. Within days, Great Lakes was a thriving e-commerce operation. Hundreds of orders were streaming in daily. Instead of having to lay off his sales staff, they were kept busy delivering beer to customers' homes. In a matter of weeks, sales volumes actually rose above levels that existed prior to the pandemic, enabling Bulut to rehire staff that had been laid off.

COVID-19 also accelerated the adoption of the direct-to-consumer model among enterprise-level companies. One of the first to go this route was Heinz, which for over 150 years had distributed a wide range of condiments to consumers through grocery stores and other retail outlets. Seeing in March of 2020 that people were unable to get out to the stores, Heinz's e-commerce consultants contacted Shopify Plus because its out-of-the-box solution would be quick to implement while still providing a sufficient degree of customization. A week after signing up, Heinz's online store went live in the U.K. on April 9, 2020.

SHOPIFY SHOP

A smartphone app under development, called Shopify Shop, was rushed into service in April of 2020 as part of Shopify's goal to do whatever it could to help merchants deal with the empty aisles in their stores. Billed as a "shopping assistant," the app allowed smartphone users to search for local Shopify merchants and find those that supported delivery, pick-up or in-store purchases. Other features were included. Of note was Shop Pay, which facilitated checkout with pre-filling of credit card and shipping information, one-click purchases and extensions such as installment payments, loyalty programs, handling of gift cards and upsell opportunities. Another feature was personalized shopping recommendations based on brands that a user had already shown interest in through their purchases or follow lists.

The app pulled Shopify further into the limelight of a consumer-facing brand — not so much on purpose, but for the sake of its merchants. Developmental work had begun in 2018 after Shopify noticed that smartphone users were increasingly downloading native apps to access websites, rather than relying on web browsers to navigate to them.[1]

This meant that individual Shopify stores could end up receiving less traffic from mobile devices since consumers were unlikely to download shopping apps from each individual store. In fact, it would be impossible to install individual apps for all Shopify merchants since there were close to a million of them in 2019. To solve this problem, Shopify acquired Tictail, a Swedish startup with expertise in native mobile apps. Its several dozen staff were put to work in a nearly autonomous unit within Shopify to produce Shopify Shop.

Ariel Michaeli of Appfigures thought the launch of the Shopify Shop app in 2020 was "one of the most clever in the shopping industry."[2] Normally, it takes new apps some time to gain traction, but Shopify Shop came roaring out of the gate, shooting immediately into the top three of downloads for its category in the United States. The way Shopify did this, as Michaeli described it, was to bundle Shopify Shop with Arrive, an app released by Shopify in 2017 to track packages delivered from Shopify stores and most major online stores. It already had 15 million installations, and as shopping shifted online with the onset of COVID-19, daily downloads doubled to 100,000. At that point, it was merged with Shopify Shop, and this feature helped the app land in the App Store with 70,000 daily downloads.

The impressive features and launch had Michaeli and other reviewers excited about the prospects for Shopify Shop. They speculated that if Shopify Shop's search function was extended to allow shoppers to browse all Shopify stores and products, it would effectively create a marketplace that could compete with Amazon. "Although Shop isn't yet a direct shopping app, Shopify has the power to turn that on at any moment," Michaeli wrote.[3] "When they do, Shop will not just have a diverse product selection but also the downloads and popularity to take on incumbent Amazon."

Adoption of the Shop app spread quickly after its launch and became one of the "most downloaded and installed shopping apps" in the United States, as reported by Marketplace Pulse's Juozas Kaziukėnas.[4] Debate emerged internally over what to do with the app. If it became a full-fledged marketplace, Shopify merchants would likely benefit from much greater traffic flows. However, Shopify would then be in a similar position with its merchants as Amazon was with its third-party merchants. For example, the search function would have to rank and list merchants in search findings. Many merchants had avoided Amazon because of such features, and they could end up unhappy if Shopify were to become a marketplace as well. Moreover, such a conversion would put Shopify in direct competition with Amazon and could turn their frenemy into an enemy. As of 2022, Shopify Shop's search function had not been extended to search across all stores.

CODE RED!

Some fundamental issues arose with the checkout function in 2020. They were serious enough that Lütke issued a code red, which is a directive to make resolving the problem a top priority. If the lead on the checkout project asked anyone in the company for help, they had to respond right away.

Lütke called on Glen Coates to be the lead. He joined Shopify in 2019 as a product manager when Shopify acquired his startup Handshake, a commerce platform for wholesalers. He spent his first year at Shopify running the Handshake team within Shopify and then moved over in 2020 to address Shopify's checkout issues.

One main concern was the increasing "spikiness" of traffic on the Internet. The sudden rushes of shoppers to merchants' websites caused by influencers' referrals, flash sales, product launches, media interviews and so forth were becoming more frequent and intense due to the shift to online shopping during the pandemic. The surge in business was good for merchants, but now their checkouts and websites were more vulnerable to crashing, leaving them empty-handed. Shopify already had the "highest throughput checkout on the Internet"[1] but more was now needed to handle the sudden surges.

The checkout problem may have originated with what techies call Conway's Law or "org chart shipping," which basically postulates that the development of products tends to reflect the nature of a company's organization more than the needs of its customers. At the time, Shopify was organized into about a dozen divisions based on different product lines — and each had its own full stack of functions for dealing with their product line. As Coates noted: "One of the reasons that the checkout got into so much trouble was that a lot of the fundamental problems required many of these divisions to collaborate because the checkout bridges everything in Shopify and so when you have this org that's set up on all these different product lines, it gets really hard to coordinate solutions that need to bridge the lines."[2]

By mid-2021, Coates was able to report that throughput at the checkout was now "seven times higher"[3] and Shopify merchants did not have to worry as much about crashes caused by sudden tidal waves of orders. To head off other code reds before they surfaced again, eight or so of the core product divisions were combined into one unit and given to Coates to run, under the title of VP of Core Product.

The first thing Coates did was to reinstate the separate product divisions and assign managers to each one. His Shopify division had over 2,000 staff and hundreds of projects, so it would be overwhelming if they all reported directly to Coates. But he was not reverting back to the status quo with its lack of alignment and work being held up. Instead of reporting directly to Lütke like before, the product divisions in the core group would be reporting to Coates and his managers, who would have the advantage of being a dedicated resource with the time and focus to resolve misalignments between the divisions.

To avoid wasted time and misdirected work, Coates also believed that it would be better for product managers to spot problems at an early stage. Teams that were beginning projects needed to sketch out a plan on what they wanted to achieve and give updates on progress. In the past, differences in opinion on what and when to build had arisen due to unexamined assumptions and principles, so it was important to discuss these to head off misalignments. A key Shopify principle is that the interests of merchants are paramount, so a developmental plan that optimized results on that basis should be the one that goes forward. Other constituencies such as developers are important too, but secondary to merchants.

BUY-OUTS AND IPOS

By 2021, venture capital and buy-out firms began to take an interest in businesses on Shopify. They sifted through more than a million of them, looking for operations in which they could take an equity stake or buy outright on the belief they could be upgraded. Before 2021, the venture capital and buy-out firms had focused on Amazon merchants, but the latter didn't have access to a lot of their sales data, so it wasn't easy to assess their potential. Furthermore, the Amazon marketplace did such a good job on inventory and fulfillment that there were fewer opportunities to improve performance on that front.

Buy-out firm OpenStore raised more than $100 million and acquired 40 Shopify businesses in its first year of operation, making it the largest operator of Shopify stores. Its process for acquiring stores was very streamlined: a Shopify store was invited to link to the OpenStore website, transmit its financial and other data, and then answer a few questions. OpenStore ran algorithms on the data, and if everything checked out, an offer to buy was sent within a few days. If the store owner liked the offer, they could click on the accept button and receive payment up front in cash within two weeks. Another buy-out aggregator, Everstores, stepped into this space with an initial fund-raise in the fall of 2022.

Serial entrepreneur Miguel Facussé was one of the merchants who received a buy-out offer. He had sold street snacks in Costa Rica, built houses in Honduras and run a sushi restaurant in Miami before launching menswear brand Jack Archer on Shopify in April 2021 — then selling it within a year to OpenStore for nearly $1 million. Before the sale, Facussé had ramped up Jack Archer's sales by researching pain points for menswear. Then he experimented with copywriting to find ads that worked well enough on Facebook and Instagram. One particularly effective slogan was: "Pants shouldn't be a pain in the butt."[1] Reassured by his testing, he contacted a manufacturer and placed a large order for men's clothes to hold as inventory while he went to market.

Within a year of acquiring Jack Archer, OpenStore grew revenues from $1 million to $10 million, reported Andrew Silard, OpenStore's

Head of Consumer Growth.[2] To optimize paid search on Google, Facebook and Instagram, OpenStore took dynamic ads to the next level by running at scale the video ads found to be the most effective during their testing process. They also launched a VIP program via SMS, giving customers early access to product drops, an in-SMS checkout (which increased revenue 10 times versus the status quo), and an AI sizing recommendation tool that increased orders by 200% and reduced returns. They also ran pricing tests and found that lower prices could increase revenues (the increase in quantities bought more than offset the drop in price).

There were also marketplaces, like Flippa, which allowed individuals to participate in the buying and selling of online businesses. Take, for example, John Chen, who left a position as an investment analyst at a hedge fund to buy and sell Shopify businesses on Flippa.[3] His first acquisition was a home run: he bought a jewellery business for about $7,500 and within two years sold it for $500,000 — after boosting annual sales to $1 million mainly by advertising on Facebook but also by using email, SMS and influencer marketing. Afterward, he bought a wedding gift business for $20,000 and resold it for $40,000. He also paid $60,000 for an apparel store catering to plus-size women, then increased sales nearly tenfold by applying his marketing know-how.

Alternatively, Shopify merchants that have grown to a large size have the option of doing an IPO. Several have done this already, including Oatly Group (oat-based milk with a texture like dairy milk), FIGS (specially designed apparel and products for health care professionals), Vita Coco (coconut-water beverage), Allbirds (quality footwear), Warby Parker (quality eyewear), Flow Beverage (naturally alkaline water from artesian springs, bottled in eco-friendly packaging). They mostly listed on the stock exchange in 2021 when it was near a peak during COVID-19, so when the pandemic eased and in-person shopping picked up again, their stock prices trended downward from their lofty valuations. Nonetheless, the IPOs provided large infusions of cash for their coffers.

The cash infusions from buy-outs and IPOs enabled many Shopify stores to dramatically boost sales. Their expansion generated a lot of revenue for Shopify too, via payments processing and other channels.

While much of the world economy had ground to a halt during COVID-19, online companies like Shopify and its merchants were flourishing. Business was in fact booming. Still, the world was in the grip of a terrible pandemic; there were changes and upheavals to deal with.

Thriving on Change

When COVID-19 broke out in early 2020, Shopify's office employees were sent home to wait out the pandemic. About two months later, in May of 2020, Lütke made this measure permanent; from then on, staff would be working remotely. Thereafter, the company's press releases gave Shopify's location as "Internet, Everywhere" instead of the customary "Ottawa, Canada." Shopify's regular newswire service refused to allow this amendment, so Shopify switched to a more accommodating newswire service.

DIGITAL BY DESIGN

Many staff were not happy with the switch to remote working. Shopify offices were nicely designed with many cool perks and an employee-friendly environment. The skeptics preferred the atmosphere on the office floor and feared in-person collaboration would suffer. "I was into the humans and the people I worked with at Shopify," Miller said. "I remember thinking that it felt like a giant loss."[1]

Proponents thought it would be a good way to attract talent from around the world: successful job candidates would not need to move to Ottawa or a branch office but could stay in California, New Delhi, Edinburgh or wherever they lived. Even for workers living in the same cities as Shopify's offices, remote working could be appealing: just avoiding a daily commute of one to two hours could lower stress and yield greater opportunities to get more things done.

Many jobs easily lend themselves to working remotely. Indeed, Shopify's customer support team of several thousand individuals had already worked remotely for years. In many ways, the support team was the blueprint for going fully "digital by design." The years of remote working in Shannan's division had provided useful insights, so taking the whole company to remote mode would not be such a huge leap into the unknown.

Another job amenable to remote work was programming. Lütke had looked back fondly on his early years in Canada when he participated in the Ruby on Rails open-source community online and built many useful programs co-operatively with other programmers from their various locations around the world. In Shopify's early years, Lütke and Weinand were trying to replicate this kind of open-source environment within the office so that new ideas could surface easily and set off chain reactions of more new ideas. "The closest relation to any organizational system we had is actually from the open-source community," Lütke told the *Masters of Scale* podcast in 2020.[2] In this kind of environment, participants worked independently but also collaborated.

It would be a mistake to assume everyone at Shopify was sitting alone in their basement or home office all the time. Shopify was just moving away from "office centricity," as Finkelstein described it. Employees didn't have to stay home to work. They could go to a café or some other place where they did their best work. Teams were still encouraged to spend time meeting periodically in person at a co-working place or other places such as one of Shopify's ports (Shopify offices refurbished into meeting places). If they were working on something difficult with a tight deadline, it might be resolved faster if everyone got together to work it out face to face. Workers were also free to meet up informally in smaller groups.

Recognizing that in-person experiences still mattered, Shopify instituted get-togethers called "bursts." These were team meetings of 10 to 20 people scheduled a few times a year for several days at places within Canada or around the world in France, Ireland, Laguna Beach or elsewhere. Shopify staff had smartphone apps they could use to book the arrangements.[3] Once the trip details of where, when and who were supplied via the app to the logistics team, they took care of the nitty-gritty details of booking flights, hotels, food and other requirements.

No one had to pay anything or worry about expense receipts going back and forth.

A related perk was the Destination90 program. For up to 90 days per year, it lets employees travel and be digital nomads exploring the world, backpacking their laptops from one place to another to perform their programming, customer service and other assignments. And, of course, they had to stay in touch with their team and stay current with what was going on.

Internal communication, culture and connectivity were also promoted via in-house electronic channels. Shopify could still do virtual town hall meetings, emails, texts and Zoom meetings. There was also asynchronous video, where team leaders could record and send a message to team members. As Finkelstein put it: "I'll hit record on my QuickTime button and I'll say, 'Hey everyone, give me 30 seconds of your time; there's something important I want you to listen to and I'll invite you all to direct message me or I'll be on our Zoom later so you can do an AMA or a town hall or some sort of round table.'"[4]

LOGISTICS: THE FIVE STAGES OF GRIEF

During COVID-19, Shopify worked with its SFN partners to comply with guidelines issued by the Centers for Disease Control and Prevention agency. They included "following social distancing rules, deep cleaning of warehouses . . . and closure of a warehouse for a period of time as advised by local public health authorities in the event a worker becomes ill."

Throughout 2020, Shopify's quarterly financial reports regularly mentioned that it was continuing "to build the product-market fit of the Shopify Fulfillment Network." Translation: Shopify was in the midst of a period of testing and experimenting to ensure users were happy with their SFN experience before ramping it up. Enrolment of merchants was being "managed" to build at a pace consistent with ensuring quality standards.

In 2021, Shopify's quarterly financial reports gave much briefer updates on SFN. The word "fulfillment" was mentioned only two or three times in each quarterly report, as opposed to an average of 10 times in quarters the year before. In early 2022, some media outlets, notably *Business Insider*, began publishing news of SFN setbacks and problems, as disclosed by unnamed individuals who had worked on the network. First, in January, it was reported that many "of the original strategists left in 2021."[1] Also reported in January: Shopify terminated or reduced the scope of contracts with several warehouse and fulfillment partners.

It appeared the product-fit period was turning into a merchant-fit period. Merchants were being told that the SFN could cope with only selected classes of merchants: for example, the list of eligible merchants was narrowed down to those that shipped 10 to 10,000 orders a day, made no special requests, were okay with shipping without their logo on the box, did no wholesaling, and did not leave marketing materials inside shipments.

In February, *Business Insider* reported another problem. Shopify was "stumbling where it usually excels — in software." A former lead on the SFN project disclosed that "the work to build and integrate the central warehouse management software is still in progress." Two fulfillment partners added that the "software also doesn't have the functionality required to offer complicated fulfillment services."[2] Also, during the February earnings report, CFO Shapero outlined a new timeline and cost for SFN: Shopify was now expecting the cost to be $2 billion, double the original projection. This was due to a switch to leasing and operating more of the warehouses on its own.

Then came the huge announcement from Shopify in May 2022 of the acquisition for $2.1 billion of Deliverr, a company which connected independent, third-party warehouses together via a common software to create a nationwide fulfillment capability. Shopify had planned to deliver this kind of software itself but the task was proving to be more difficult than expected. Deliverr had an asset-light infrastructure capable of providing two-day delivery across multiple channels (it was the first fulfillment company to support Walmart's Two-Day Shipping badge for its marketplace sellers). Shopify hoped that the acquisition of Deliverr could leapfrog the software problems and speed up the rollout of the SFN.

Over the remainder of 2022, the Shop Promise badge was made available to selected merchants on SFN to display on their storefronts, which studies showed boosted conversion rates at checkouts by up to 25%. As 2022 ended, Shopify was still in the process of building out the SFN. Analysts' concerns lingered. Commenting in January of 2023, RMW Commerce's Watson noted: "I kept waiting for Harish Abbott to take over fulfillment, but it was somewhat telling he took the cash instead of the shares. . . . Who else could they find to execute the Deliverr vision . . . than the founder of Deliverr?"[3]

"Logistics is hard," Lütke had remarked at a meeting with analysts. One thing that Shopify found particularly challenging was the problems that arise when different computer systems are not talking to each other: "A lot of friction exists in different systems not talking to each other," Lütke declared. "A lot of our work goes into bridging legacy systems."[4] During *The Network State Podcast*, he added: "One of the most surprising and consistent themes [in e-commerce] is just how much more complicated atoms are than bytes. It's like, there's five stages of grief that everyone's going through at Shopify whenever we get into the realm of logistics."[5]

SHOPIFY IS A TEAM NOT A FAMILY

Electronic communication channels within the company, such as Slack, saw a rise in keyboard-warrior behaviour and rants on political and racial issues in the midst of the pandemic. Many people were not using their own photo in their Slack accounts, and the anonymity encouraged some heated discussions that likely would not have otherwise surfaced. A few forums, in fact, had to be shut down because the discussions were becoming distracting. Lütke would also use Slack to provide frank feedback to selected employees for subpar work. "Slack exacerbated things," Miller said. "In a company with thousands of people, they can all see Tobi laying into someone."[1]

Measures were introduced to discourage negative and off-topic conversations, beginning with recruiting volunteers to be "channel champions," tasked with establishing ground rules and reporting incidences of bad behaviour and intolerance. By the summer of 2020, Lütke had reached his breaking point with the "endless Slack trolling, victimhood thinking, us-vs.-them divisiveness, and zero-sum thinking." He sent out an email to managers saying that such behaviours "must be seen for the threat they are: they break teams." Managers should "stay focused on Shopify's mission of empowering online commerce. . . . Shopify is a team, not a family. . . . Shopify is also not the government. We cannot solve every societal problem here." This memo was later leaked to the press.[2]

In a September 29, 2020, letter to company staff, Lütke announced a major shake-up at the executive level. To start with, Miller was leaving Shopify.[3] As Miller later revealed, he and Lütke were having differences of opinion on where product development should go. "Effectively there can only be one Chief Product Officer," said Miller later in a podcast interview.[4] Nonetheless, Lütke praised the departing Miller for his contribution: "It's been one of the privileges of my career to work alongside Craig for the last 9 years. He first helped us find product & market fit as head of marketing, and over the last few years he built our world class product team as CPO. Craig played a critical role in getting Shopify to where it is today."[5] The letter went on to say Lütke would take over Miller's responsibilities on product development.

Next, Finkelstein was going to move from COO to President so that he could focus on telling Shopify's story. The vacant COO position would be filled by Shannan; in announcing his appointment, Lütke said, "He has created and scaled one of the secret ingredients of Shopify: our Support team. In a lot of ways, Support is the blueprint for the future of Shopify — fully digital and globally distributed. . . . [Shannan] will bring his experience and ability to the rest of the company now, helping us scale our team structure to support our ambitions and remain merchant obsessed." Forsyth and Frasca would report to Shannan.

"Yes, that's a lot of change," Lütke wrote. "But Shopify comes with a warning label on the box: 'thrive on change' is our most important cultural value in 2020. Thriving on change means we strive to be antifragile. The best systems and organizations in the world aren't just robust, they actively embrace disruption because it makes them better. This is what we trained for. This is how we rise to the next challenge."[6]

TELLING SHOPIFY'S STORY

Finkelstein's promotion came at a good time for him. After becoming COO in 2016, he had continued to function like a "Swiss army knife" executive, taking on a variety of tasks while heading a team of over 6,000 people. He was spread thin and getting a feeling similar to being a jack of all trades, master of none. "I never kind of settled in to say where do I actually want to fit in, like, what is my craft here?" he told Steve Bartlett, host of *The Diary of a CEO* podcast.[1] The isolation created by COVID-19 was also hard for the outgoing Finkelstein to deal with.

Fortunately, Lütke brought to his attention the role of President, where he could focus more on what he loved doing, which was to represent Shopify in the public domain, liaise with stakeholders, increase awareness of Shopify as the entrepreneurship company and invite more people to become entrepreneurs. The head count on his team would be lower but, freed of a lot of the COO tasks, he could go deep and hone his craft as Shopify's "chief storyteller."

A key area where Finkelstein represented Shopify was in interviews in the mass and social media. There were regular appearances presenting and discussing Shopify's quarterly financial reports, special events like Black Friday and Cyber Monday sales, company developments and e-commerce in general. One of his highest media profiles was frequent appearances on the U.S. business channel CNBC, where his information-gathering and articulation skills came in handy for delivering skillful updates on Shopify's quarterly financial results and answering questions from hosts such as Jim Cramer. No doubt the exposure on CNBC was a factor in attracting investors to Shopify.

Finkelstein was often complimented on how well he handled interviews and presentations, but the truth was that it was a lot of hard work. For those interviews on CNBC, he "put in five hours of work memorizing those data points," he disclosed to Bartlett. Finkelstein also told Bartlett: "I put a lot of time into preparing for my conversation with you today, a lot of time. I've watched all your interviews . . . what I do have is a really good work ethic. . . . I was never the smartest kid in any of my classes. . . . I just outworked everybody else and I think if anyone out there wants to emulate anything that I've done, emulate my work ethic."[2] In another interview, during *The Danny Miranda Podcast*, he said: "I work really hard on storytelling. It is my craft. I'm constantly trying to tweak things. I re-watch everything. I will re-watch the video of this podcast three times to figure out if I said too much or went on any tangents or too many rants. . . . I work really hard at it. It does not come easy."[3]

December 5, 2023: Harley Finkelstein at Shopify's Investor Day at the NYSE.

Lütke also raised the profile of Shopify through a passion project of his. In early 2022, Shopify launched an esports organization, Shopify Rebellion,[4] to field teams of professional gamers that compete in tournaments — starting with a *StarCraft II* team whose members included the 2016 world champion, Byun Hyun-woo, and the first woman to win a major esports tournament, Sasha Hostyn. Since then, Shopify Rebellion has put teams together for other esports. Shopify Rebellion may have been a fun project for Lütke but it also served the purpose of raising Shopify's profile in the esports community: many esports teams would like to sell merchandise online and so they might be interested in a platform like Shopify; when esports players outgrow competitive gaming, they sometimes can be recruited as programmers or e-commerce entrepreneurs.

DEPARTURES AND REMINISCENCES

By early 2023, Shopify's executive ranks had experienced a lot of turnover. Fauser was the first to leave, in 2016. He was followed by Weinand (2017), Jones (2018), Weiser (2020), Miller (2020), Forsyth (2021), Frasca (2021), Lemieux (2021), Shapero (2022) and Shannan (2022). Allan Leinwand, who had been hired from Slack to replace Lemieux as CTO in 2021, left in March of 2023 (citing personal reasons).

Some media outlets speculated that Lütke's demanding management style was a factor contributing to the churn. True, he had his standards — indeed, around the time Shannan conveyed his intention to retire, he reportedly told Lütke: "'Hey Tobi, one of the biggest differences between you and me is you have an extremely high opinion in people's ability and therefore you're constantly disappointed."[1] Nonetheless, Shannan had made a major contribution to Shopify and in announcing his exit from the COO role, Lütke praised him, saying: "I would also like to thank Toby [Shannan] for his invaluable leadership and commitment to Shopify over the last decade."[2]

Were Lütke's standards too high? Perhaps, but then again, it is hard to argue with the success that Shopify captured during its first two decades. High standards can be a good thing if a company is to excel. Moreover, whether due to disagreements, disappointments or a desire to leave the pressure cooker behind, turnover in staff is to be expected in the normal course of events, never mind the stresses and strains imposed by a pandemic. And in the case of Shopify, leaving was made a lot easier by the windfalls that employees enjoyed on their restricted stock units (RSUs) and stock options during the upward trend in Shopify's shares from 2015 to 2021.

In an April 27, 2021, interview with Chu, Miller reminisced about his Shopify journey from 2011 to 2020. The session provided an interesting view from the inside of what it was like to work at Shopify.[3] Miller remembered opening up the Toronto office in 2011 and working with his first hire in a co-working office. The two of them were sitting next to the kitchen and when the microwave was turned on, their Internet connection stopped working; Skype meetings with Ottawa staff were at risk of abruptly terminating. The Internet problems quickly passed as a tidal wave of growth hit, causing the workplace to relocate about a half dozen times up to 2020 to progressively larger (and better equipped) offices within Toronto.

Like some other Shopify executives, Miller never aspired to be a manager leading large teams. He thought he was just "going to be like that guy who sits in front of a computer all day and never interacts with humans." During his years at Shopify, however, he went from feeling good when he built something to feeling great when he shepherded teams toward a goal. "I love working with really smart people and seeing them succeed — nothing makes me happier," he revealed.[4]

When he first started supervising, Miller was a micromanager, telling programmers how to write their code almost down to the line. It drove them "absolutely bonkers." What ended up working for him was investing the time and effort to "find some people who are able to inspire the team, figure out what the problem is to be solved, and build it in the right way to get it out as fast as possible." As it turned out, most of these special individuals were brought onboard by recruiting founders of startups or people otherwise experienced in developing products and bringing them to market.

Miller didn't write out 15-page roadmaps for product managers and teams to follow. His main role was to "make sure that at least at the highest level we were all aligned on the right goal." The execution was more up to the product managers and their teams. But it was not easy, especially in a hypergrowth environment. Miller was asked what the hardest thing was about being an executive. After a moment, he said: "Smiling." There were so many pressures and struggles at work, or some days when "you wake up on the wrong side of the bed in a bad mood."

But when meeting with a team, all that has to be compartmentalized so that "you can be positive and show excitement for the project," because teams usually take their cue from the leader.

"I wanted to give everyone a bit of a mental safe space so that they could do their best work and not have to worry that someone was immediately judging or pressuring them."[5] In other words, the objective was "to encourage and get the best out of everyone" — but creating that kind of culture is tricky when there are time constraints and competing interests. So, as the CPO, Miller had to find a way to make sure everyone was in a good spot and pushing forward, while sometimes providing air cover for them while they got projects back on track.

"I often kind of thought that I was like those people just spinning plates on those sticks [like in the clips from the 1960s *Ed Sullivan Show*] and one is starting to wobble so you run over and start spinning that one again and then another one's starting to wobble and you run to that one," Miller said. As if it wasn't hard enough keeping the plates spinning in his own department, Miller was the kind of person who had to help out where he could. If he heard of a problem elsewhere in Shopify or even in the partner ecosystem or merchant community, he often went to see what could be done. So, as Shopify scaled up, it felt like he had gone from 2 plates to 30 plates spinning and wobbling in the air. "Sometimes I felt like I'm not really giving proper attention to my family, then realizing as more effort was put into the family, work starts to slide so you run back there . . . it feels like it's a losing game for a very long time."

Because Shopify then relied more on culture and heroes than on structure, rules and procedures, the workplace was at times chaotic. Not to be overlooked was the fact that staffing levels were more than doubling most years and the procedures put in place one year became quickly redundant, so managers had to play catch-up.

"I would have loved for the environment to be less chaotic, but there were some . . . great products that came out," reminisced Miller.[6] "If I had to choose between having a good product-management discipline and having a good product, I'm going to choose having a good product. We often have to just say we know it's chaotic but we can all agree that getting this feature out to merchants is the most important thing, full stop. That was the thing that helped rally the team and to just accept the chaos and to recognize underlying it there's some organizational trust between each other and that we care about each other."

Miller struggled with knowing his unit was not a "well-oiled machine." But he felt if he changed one thing, it would be hard to tell what the downstream effects would be. He knew there were some things standing in the team's way but there were some things that were part of the magic. Miller concluded: "I didn't know which things needed to change and which things to keep; if you accidentally throw away the good stuff and keep the bad stuff, this company's going to disappear fast."

He used to get comfort from an excerpt he found in a book, *How Google Works* (2017), written by Eric Schmidt and Jonathan Rosenberg (former senior executives at Google):

> The steady state of a successful Internet Century venture is chaos. When things are running perfectly smoothly, with people and boxes on charts enjoying a 1-to-1 relationship, then the processes and infrastructure have caught up to the business. This is a bad thing. When Eric was CEO at Novell, the company was running like a well-oiled machine. The only problem was that the new-great-product cupboard was bare. If everything seems under control, you're just not going fast enough. . . . The business should always be outrunning the processes, so chaos is right where you want to be. And when you're there, the only way to get things done is through relationships. Take the time to know and care about people.

Another fun read was *I'm Feeling Lucky: Confessions of Google Employee Number 59* (2011), by Douglas Edwards, Google's first director of marketing and brand management. The following passage particularly resonated with Miller:

> Dennis Hwang spent the day before the launch coming up with ideas for a logo and trying to make it work in

> conjunction with the clown-colored Google brand. . . . Even after four years at Google, I found it astounding that one twenty-something guy was sitting alone at his desk, sipping tea and developing the main branding element for a product to be used by millions of people — the night before it was scheduled to launch.

"I ran into so many situations like this during my career," Miller noted March 2, 2022, on X. "The trick is to make sure the chaos never seeps outside your walls."

It was sad to see the departure of Miller and so many other individuals who contributed to Shopify's success. They had spent many good years on what felt for most like a journey with friends, solving problems. But Shopify appeared to be evolving in several respects, giving up some of the friendly, free-wheeling environment of a startup for some of the businesslike environment characteristic of large companies. And now that Shopify was digital by design, it could cast its recruitment net much further and wider to hire executives capable of picking up where the old guard had left off.

Staying Alive

As COVID-19 wound down and the world returned to normal, there were plenty of new faces on the executive team and board of directors.

Senior executive positions filled with new faces were: CFO (Jeff Hoffmeister, the Morgan Stanley investment banker who led Shopify's IPO), COO (Kaz Nejatian, previously Shopify vice president in charge of payments processing, lending, cash-management and related tools for merchants), General Counsel (Jess Hertz, previously deputy assistant to President Joe Biden and legal counsel at Facebook), Chief Human Resources Officer (Tia Silas, previously VP of Human Resources at Wells Fargo) and CTO (position retired and duties farmed out to Farhan Thawar, Shopify's VP of Engineering, and Lütke).[1] The CMO position also appeared to have been retired after Weiser's departure. Senior executive staff were Finkelstein as President and Lütke in the CEO, CPO, and Chairman positions.

Other key roles were filled with new faces too, including: VP of Core Product (Glen Coates, previously at Handshake), Chief Revenue Officer (Bobby Morrison, previously at Intuit), Chief Information Security Officer (Andrew Dunbar, formerly Shopify VP and Director of Security Engineering), Chief Growth Officer (Luc Levesque, previously at Facebook), VP of Product (Daniel Debow, previously at Salesforce) and Head of Marketing (Anne-Marie Goulet, previously at Salesforce). A vacancy on the board of directors was filled by Bret Taylor, previously Salesforce co-CEO and Google product manager (Google Maps).

A DIFFERENT KIND OF COMPANY

Some observers may have been concerned with the amount of turnover. But Finkelstein liked the new team. He posted on LinkedIn: "Without a doubt, today we have the best team ever."[1] The switch to remote working made it possible to attract executive talent from around the world, mainly from U.S. tech companies and other parts of corporate America. One could hence argue that the new faces elevated the talent level in the executive ranks and prepared Shopify for becoming a different company, one more like a large U.S.-style e-commerce company focused on priorities such as fintech products and the high-end of retailers.

Of course, the new executives did not need to move to Canada. They worked remotely from the places where they had already put down roots, which was mostly in the United States — one of the exceptions being Nejatian, who was based in Old Fort Bay, Bahamas (the award for best work location goes to him). The switch to remote working also made it possible for many long-time Shopify staff to move to places outside of Ottawa. This went all the way to the top: in the summer of 2023, Finkelstein and his family moved back to his hometown of Montreal, where his aging parents, sister and wife's family were located. Lütke and his family moved to Toronto in the summer of 2023, to be near family and Shopify's engineering team headed by Thawar.

With Finkelstein's and Lütke's departure from Ottawa, there were not many executives left in Shopify's hometown. In fact, about the only one still in Ottawa was Chief Information Security Officer Andrew Dunbar. It was sad for some Ottawa residents to see such an exciting and energetic presence gone; the city felt different after its departure. But Shopify was growing up and had bigger fields to roam. Indeed, in the fall of 2023, the company signed a lease for space on the eighth floor of a building near Manhattan's Chelsea Market and the High Line area, where several other large technology companies have offices, including Google. It seemed this new location was a beachhead for establishing closer relationships with key players in the U.S. technology sector, including members of the FAANG group (Facebook, Amazon, Apple, Netflix, and Google).

The promotion of Nejatian was perhaps the major development in the transition to a new team, if only because of the importance of the COO position in the Shopify org chart. Who was Nejatian? He immigrated to Canada with his family from Iran after he was arrested at the age of 11 by the Gasht-e-Ershad (morality police) for expressing opposition to Iran's theocratic government. His mother had also told the religious police that "if they thought her hijab was immodest, they should avert their eyes," wrote Nejatian in his July 1, 2017, article, "My Canada," published on medium.com.

In Canada, he adapted well, graduating from the Queen's University School of Business and the University of Toronto Faculty of Law. Before joining Shopify in 2019, he worked as a lawyer, founded mobile-payments company Kash and served as Product Lead for Payments and Billing at Facebook. Nejatian had also written a book in 2017 entitled *A Payment History of the United States*. With his book and stints in payments at Kash, Facebook and Shopify, it looked like Nejatian's main focus in his new position was going to be on Shopify's most important money maker: payments processing and related fintech innovations.

Nejatian's appointment may also have had something to do with his management style. According to a straw poll in June of 2023 by *Business Insider*, current and former Shopify employees viewed Nejatian as intense, focused on efficiency and "frequently dropping F-bombs in meetings."[2] One employee said Nejatian brought Silicon Valley work practices to Shopify, implementing stricter planning cycles and "more structure to Shopify's previously 'easygoing' culture." The employee added: "He gets things done. He's very assertive in a work sense."

Some people thought Shopify was "starting to resemble an American tech giant — less soul, more cutthroat," reported Tim Kiladze in the October 28, 2022, *Globe and Mail*.[3] One piece of evidence marshalled in support of this view was an X post by Nejatian. When he heard the Ontario Liberal Party was pitching a four-day work week, he expressed his disapproval, saying that China's growth was fuelled, in part, by company employees working from nine a.m. to nine p.m. six days a week and that the Protestant work ethic was key to the development of the West.[4]

A former employee interviewed by *Business Insider* commented on the post, saying: "Shopify always felt to me like a company that cared about its humans and the humans that worked there cared about each other — this felt very different from that. . . . It's another example that they are not the same company as they used to be and that their internal and external values have shifted."[5] In subsequent exchanges, Nejatian clarified that he was not endorsing work habits in China or the Protestant work ethic, only saying that work should be valued and celebrated.

Reporting to Nejatian was Chief Revenue Officer (CRO) Morrison, onboarded in August 2022, with 25 years of prior work experience, including positions as Chief Sales Officer at Intuit, vice president at Microsoft and a manager at Verizon. He had a fresh perspective and interesting take on the gales of change buffeting Shopify.

Shopify was the first founder-led company for which Morrison had worked, and he found it a very different experience. For the first few months, what he saw was "things that seemed broken — a lack of systems, lack of organization, lack of structures." By his sixth month, however, his thinking had changed: "What initially appeared chaotic, was actually intentional. Orchestrated. . . . Fast. Bold. Operating outside of bounds, without fear of failure. Iterating, iterating, iterating."[6]

Morrison noted that most companies growing to a large size tended to become bureaucratic, risk-averse and enmeshed in "a cultural 'wax' that builds up over time to slow them down." But Shopify could be the exception because it did not accept convention for its own sake. Even so-called best practices for companies were to be avoided if they did not stand up to first-principles thinking.

It appeared that one of Morrison's roles at Shopify was to help usher in operating discipline. At the six-month milestone of his employment, he was "now starting to see shadows of this but not the hard lines." In his opinion, Shopify could benefit from more organizational structure but also from retaining much of its unique culture. He was impressed by still seeing "people working at lightning speed, doing a million things . . . and an organization . . . that was intensely passionate about our mission." Furthermore, as he added: "The culture here is the opposite of wax. It's like rocket fuel. It's like something I saw recently on TV about escape velocity. . . . At Shopify, we achieve this through something called GSD, or Get $h!t Done. And . . . we GSD at a speed I've never experienced."[7]

December 5, 2023: The Shopify executive team at Shopify's Investor Day at the NYSE. From left to right: Glen Coates, Bobby Morrison, ———, ———, Kaz Nejatian, ———, Jeff Hoffmeister, Tia Silas, ———, ———, Jess Hertz, ———, Harley Finkelstein and ——— (many of the unidentified persons are from Shopify's Investor Relations team; absent: Tobi Lütke).

THE COMPENSATION CRISIS

As COVID-19 stopped being so much of a threat in 2022, people around the world rejoiced and began to emerge from their cocoons. However, in-person shopping revived and moderated Shopify's growth, triggering a collapse in its richly valued stock. Media coverage, once glowing and bullish, turned gloomy and bearish. Some of the coverage even wondered if this was Shopify's denouement.

All of this was enough of a trial for Shopify executives, but there was more: the plunge in Shopify's stock dragged down the value of employees' shareholdings and stock options. As these equity holdings had become a big part of employee compensation, their tumble predictably spurred grumbling within the ranks. Some employees were even leaving to work at other companies with higher base salaries.

Management moved to stabilize the situation at an April 2022 town hall meeting. Employees were told that an overhaul of the compensation system was coming. Called Flex Comp, it let employees determine how their compensation would be split between salary and equity, and how the equity would be split between RSUs and options.[1] Moreover, equity grants would vest immediately, in equal monthly installments, instead of after the "cliff" of a year. Lütke himself had made a choice between salary and equity a few years before, selecting a salary of $1 and the rest of his remuneration in stock options (this gave him a strong incentive to create shareholder value).

Having more choice in how to receive compensation allowed employees to achieve a better fit for their preferences. It would also allow employees in countries with different tax laws to optimize their mix within those locations. Finally, it ended the practice of tying equity returns to the state of the stock market at the end of the "cliff" period. Having such cliff periods in the compensation formula had injected outcomes not tied to the company's actual performance; it made employee lifetime earnings dependent on random external factors, particularly investor sentiment in the stock market.

The process of choosing one's compensation mix was automated by creating a new software tool accessible on employee computer screens. There was a slider to select the proportions for cash and equity, and another to select the mix between RSUs and stock options. To encourage selection of the equity component, Shopify added a 5% bonus based on the amount of equity compensation selected. After an employee made their choices, a summary table was displayed to make it less confusing and time-consuming to determine exactly what their compensation was. However, employees with unsatisfactory performance ratings would not get Flex Comp until their contribution to the company was back on track.

Creating the software tool may have been a factor in delaying the arrival of Flex Comp until September of 2022. A group of developers had been recruited from all over Shopify to work on the project, which was of a size that normally would have taken a year or two to complete. They got it done in a few months, although at the end it required a "two-week coding sprint" that included dozens of developers, including Lütke himself, doing pairs programming in a war room late into the night. The tempest over compensation passed. There was also talk the new tool could be licensed to customers outside of Shopify. The result was not only a more effective human resources solution but also a commercial opportunity to license it to other companies.

In early 2023, Shopify's compensation system was tweaked again, to deal with another issue. Historically, an employee at the top of their pay scale in a technical position would have to become a manager to get a higher salary. But they often did not enjoy being a manager or were not as good a manager. Hence, Shopify opened up higher salary levels to technical staff. The good ones could get paid as much as managers without becoming a manager.

THE CORPORATE GOVERNANCE CRISIS

About the time the furor over compensation erupted, a simmering issue involving corporate governance boiled over into the public realm and drew vigorous opposition from several quarters. In April 2023, Shopify announced that the annual meeting in early June would vote on granting Lütke a "founder's share" with a variable number of votes that when combined with his Class B shares would bestow 40% voting control of the company.[1]

The founder's share would be non-transferable and guarantee 40% voting control regardless of how many new shares were issued, as long as Lütke's holdings of Class A and Class B shares remained above 1.1% of the total (he held approximately 6% at the end of 2021). The founder's share could be cancelled if Lütke was not an executive officer, board member or consultant whose primary job was with the company.

The founder's share was introduced because Lütke was at risk of losing his influence over Shopify's direction. Over the years, the venture capitalists and some Shopify executives had liquidated all, or part, of their positions by converting their non-trading, multiple-vote Class B shares into single-vote Class A shares and selling the latter into the market. Class A shares were also issued by the company to finance acquisitions, operations, and annual obligations under the employee Stock Option Plan and Long-Term Incentive Plan.

Lütke and Phillips for years held a controlling bloc of votes thanks to their relatively large positions in the Class A and B shares (after the venture capitalists had cashed out). But with so many Class A shares issued and trading, their margin was getting thin and Phillips, now in his early 70s, wanted to retire. In short, Lütke was facing the prospect of not having enough voting power to determine Shopify's direction.

The proposed governance changes were issued by a committee of independent directors at Shopify. They believed it was necessary to ensure Lütke kept control so Shopify could continue prioritizing long-term over short-term growth. However, several proxy advisory firms — notably Institutional Shareholder Services; Glass, Lewis & Co.; and Egan-Jones Ratings — advised shareholders not to vote for the founder's share. They were concerned that the concentration of power could come at the expense of minority shareholders.

One feature was welcomed. Whereas many dual-class share structures allowed control of the company to pass to the CEO's heirs, Shopify's founder share had a sunset clause that prevented this transfer once he stopped being involved with the company or didn't hold the required number of shares. Moreover, if the sunset clause was triggered, his Class B shares had to be converted into Class A shares, ending the dual-class, multi-voting arrangement in place.

At the Annual Meeting in early June 2023, the vote on creating a founder's share went through. The proposed 10-for-1 stock split easily passed (it was unusual to see such a stock split after a large price drop, but Shopify explained that since employees don't get partial shares in compensation packages, the split made it easier to add stock to their pay packages).

THE "BUY WITH PRIME" CRISIS

At times, it appeared Shopify and Amazon were not frenemies but enemies. Such was the case over the second half of 2022 and into 2023, when Amazon launched and promoted its "Buy with Prime" button that non-Amazon merchants could install on their sites to give their customers access to the speedy shipping and other perks of Amazon Prime. If it was used by a Shopify merchant, sales could be siphoned away from Shopify Payments; analysts estimated that losing the payment processing fees of up to 2.9% could be a substantial setback for Shopify. Moreover, the transactional data generated by Amazon Pay would not show up on the admin dashboards of Shopify merchants, so they would not get a full picture of their business from Shopify's analytics, and/or develop full relationships with their customers.

Shopify held off approving an integration with its platform and entered into negotiations with Amazon to secure terms acceptable to both. In the meantime, its merchants were free to add the button to their own website, but as the negotiations with Amazon dragged on, Shopify's Terms of Service document was amended to permit only Shopify's designated checkouts on its platform; any attempts by a merchant to independently add the Amazon script to their store site triggered a pop-up message that warned: "You have a code snippet on your storefront that violates Shopify's Terms of Service. This script removes Shopify's ability to protect your store against fraudulent orders, could steal customer data and may cause customers to be charged the wrong amount." The warning did not go over well with Amazon. It rebuked Shopify in a statement to CNBC: "We use Amazon Pay to process payments for Buy with Prime orders. Amazon Pay is backed by the fraud protection technology used on Amazon.com. . . . Merchants have complete control over the prices customers are charged."[1]

Nonetheless, late in the summer of 2023, Amazon and Shopify reached an agreement. The pact allowed Amazon to integrate its button with the Shopify platform by placing an app on Shopify's API so that Shopify merchants already using Amazon's fulfillment network could add the "Buy with Prime" button to their checkout. In return for this concession to Amazon, Shopify Payments would process the transactions and take the payment-processing fees; Shopify merchants would have access to the data on their customers' transactions. Amazon would collect fulfillment fees from Shopify merchants for orders routed through "Buy with Prime." The stock market showed its approval for Shopify by bidding up its stock nearly 10% on the day the news broke.

INSOMNIA

During the pandemic, Lütke worked long hours, seven days a week. Talk about stress: turnover was high among the executives, grousing on Slack channels was getting loud and corporate crises came in waves. Then COVID-19 waned and online shopping pulled back, inflation soared and interest rates climbed: Shopify's stock took a deep dive, spreading disillusionment within the investment community and media. It also drastically reduced Lütke's personal wealth held as shares in Shopify, by several billion dollars.

All the work pressures brought on insomnia. To keep going, he started taking sleeping pills but then became concerned about developing a dependency, and he resolved to get off the pills and fix his sleeping problem with some research and consultations. He considered some therapies but chose instead to read a couple books, get some apps for establishing a routine much like a therapist might prescribe, and began wearing an Oura Ring for tracking sleep cycles.

He was prepared to take a month off work but by the third day of his regime, he was sleeping well again. While the steps he took helped, essentially what turned it around was more of a mental process: "There is no need to train for sleep. It is like hunger, your body will tell you when you are hungry and it will tell you when you are sleepy," he said in a November 2022 interview. "Go to the bedroom at a regular time and have a chair beside the bed to sit and read until you feel sleepy. If you wake up in the middle of the night, go to the chair and read until [the eyelids are drooping and head is nodding off.]"[1]

20

Rebooting the Engine

From mid-2022 to the end of 2023, the clouds parted for Shopify. Its stock began climbing again, rising by 150% over the 18 months to the end of 2023 (a doubling in price from this plateau would bring the stock back to its all-time high reached in late 2021). Shopify's rebound got a boost from cost cuts, higher subscription prices, a large divestiture, and revenues from Shopify POS when in-person shopping revived as COVID-19 eased (although long-term growth in the point-of-sales niche may not be spectacular for Shopify due to low margins and established competitors, such as Square). There was also a plethora of company initiatives aimed at ongoing market opportunities in e-commerce.

LAYOFFS, PRICE HIKES AND CUTBACKS

In July of 2022, Shopify slashed costs by laying off 1,000 staff, or 10% of its workforce.[1] The axe fell heavily on the customer-service team, which had taken on hundreds of new hires during the pandemic to cope with the spike in store openings. Afterward, an email to employees mentioned that Shopify was going to revise how it evaluated the performance of customer-service staff; this was followed by the posting of a Code Yellow "for urgent and immediate attention" to improve customer-service levels that had deteriorated below acceptable levels. There were also reports from employees of an uptick in the number of third-party contractors hired from the Philippines to do client-services work.

Another initiative was to hike prices by more than 30% for the first three tiers of subscriptions; client defections were expected to be minimal because the price increases were the first in 12 years. There was no fee increase for Shopify Plus clients — the company was hoping to stoke company growth by expanding further into the higher end of the market. But service levels were cut for Shopify Plus merchants with annual sales less than $10 million; the cut curtailed their access to merchant success managers.

A TIGHTER SHIP

Shopify also began to run a tighter ship. Coming back to work after the December break to start the new year in 2023, employees found that a "Chaos Monkey" was on the loose. This was a procedure in software engineering that involved radical experimentation and simulations to test the robustness of systems. Meetings of three or more people were cancelled (except on Thursdays) and a tool was created for estimating the opportunity cost of meetings; the majority of Slack channels were cancelled and replaced with channels from Meta Platforms' Workplace.

Dropping the Slack channels was not popular. But Nejatian said that they had to go because Slack had become "bloated, noisy and distracting." It was full of endless updates, broad announcements and trivial discussions about what kind of food to order in. If the changes under "Chaos Monkey" felt chaotic, that's "kind of the point," he added.[1] In his email, Lütke chimed in with the same message he had conveyed since the beginning of Shopify: "What I'm trying to create is an environment where almost everyone around me feels uncomfortable all the time, because I'm dragging them into the next box."

On May 4, 2023, the earnings report from Shopify for the first quarter was due. Just before it came out, Shopify dropped a bombshell. It was divesting the SFN project to logistics company Flexport, which would take over the completion of the project and be Shopify's preferred fulfillment channel. In return for handing over the SFN, Shopify got a 13% equity interest in Flexport to add to its existing 6% stake. At the same time, Shopify announced a further 20% reduction in its global workforce.

That day and the next, Shopify's stock exploded 34% higher mainly because of the elimination of SFN's drag on finances and reduction in payroll. And Shopify Promise could continue being phased in through partner Flexport. One might also expect that there was some potential for Shopify's equity interest in Flexport to appreciate over time.

HIGH RATE OF INNOVATION

While Shopify worked on improving its cost structure and productivity, its high rate of product development continued unabated. In the spring of 2022, a semi-annual publication, *Shopify Editions*, was introduced and listed more than 100 product releases from the previous six months. Each issue since then has listed 100-plus new products from the previous six months. *Shopify Editions* serves as a catalogue for merchants to browse and acquire new tools that will help them grow; it is also a marketing instrument, showcasing Shopify's utilities to participants in the e-commerce sector. The smaller-scale tools included: Shop Mini (software development kit for creating apps on Shopify Shop), Shopify Credit (credit card for Shopify merchants, based on their sales not credit history), Shopify Collective (for cross-selling brands from other Shopify merchants) and Checkout Apps (more than a dozen new apps to allow customization of the checkout function). Although it may have looked like a small-scale release, Shop Cash had the potential to be significant. It was a rewards and loyalty program for shoppers using Shop Pay to check out on Shopify Shop. It gave them 1% back on purchases made through Shop Pay. Rewards and loyalty programs are known for being effective at retention of customers and contributing to sales.

Several major product announcements were also made in 2022 and 2023. They included: Sidekick, Commerce Components and other tools for larger companies, and Shopify Collabs.

Sidekick

OpenAI's launch of a new generation of ChatGPT in November 2022 was a wake-up call for the world. It was a chatbot with the artificial intelligence (AI) to simulate conversation between a human and a digital device: in response to questions and requests, the chatbot would scan immense databases and provide a fulsome response in sentence-paragraph form, then respond to follow-up questions to refine its response. In Lütke's words,

> We are at the dawn of the AI era and the new capabilities that are unlocked by that are unprecedented. Shopify has the privilege of being amongst the companies with the best chances of using AI to help our customers. A copilot for entrepreneurship is now possible. Our main quest demands from us to build the best thing that is now possible, and that has just changed entirely.[1]

Shopify's work on AI had already ramped up behind the scenes, before OpenAI's announcement. The finishing touches had been put on Shopify Magic, which used a ChatGPT-like technology to quickly write product descriptions for merchants once a few keywords or features were inputted. Another Shopify development was integrating with Google's Bard offering. It was aimed at helping enterprises mitigate "search abandonment," a situation where a customer searches for a product on a retailer's website but leaves when they cannot find it (a Google-commissioned survey found that the cost of global search abandonment to retailers was more than $2 trillion a year).

The plan to launch a copilot for entrepreneurship, as announced by Lütke after the fall launch of ChatGPT's latest iteration, was a particularly significant event for Shopify. In July of 2023, Lütke posted in his X account a 2.5-minute video with the headline: "I've got something very exciting to announce." It was the Sidekick AI copilot. Lütke went on to declare: "I've been part of the technology industry since the mid-1990s. . . .

I have never seen anything like AI. This will be an unbelievable boon to entrepreneurship."[2]

The video showed a demo of how Sidekick can save merchants a great deal of work and time. First, Lütke typed in a question asking why sales were down for his snowboards. Sidekick answered it is due to "minimal snow" and some other factors, adding a chart showing the trend in sales. "Put everything on sale," Lütke then typed. Using a default setting of 10% for discounts, Sidekick marked down all the snowboard prices and added tags to show they were on sale. Sidekick was next told to put the surfboard collection on the home page, take down the snowboards on sale and convert the website to a surfer theme. Done. The demo of Sidekick querying and transitioning the website took less than two minutes.

Tools for Larger Companies

From the spring of 2022 and throughout 2023, Shopify Plus pushed further into the high end of the e-commerce market. It also came out with a cluster of new platform features to win over more whales (large and enterprise-level companies). In so doing, it was facing off against some of the largest software companies in the world, notably Adobe, Oracle, and Salesforce.

The batch of product releases announced in the *Spring '22 Shopify Edition* included Hydrogen, the stack for headless commerce whereby the front-end (store front) was decoupled from the back-end so it could be customized without affecting the back-end. Also released was Oxygen, a host for Hydrogen, and Functions, which allowed developers to amend back-end logic to produce tailored commerce solutions.

Shopify Audiences was introduced to Shopify Plus merchants mid-2022, and further enhanced in early 2023. Shopify Audiences used machine learning on Shopify's merchant databases to find groups of customers most likely to buy a certain product. This information could then be used by merchants to send digital ads to those groups most receptive to their products. Shopify Audiences was developed to plug the gap left behind by Apple effectively banning cookies tracking users' online activity (which could be used to target ads to the people most likely to buy their products).

In the first half of 2023, Commerce Components was launched. It gave enterprise-level retailers the ability to customize their stacks by integrating separate Shopify components within their own systems. The launch customer was Mattel, the toy maker with the iconic Barbie brand in its portfolio of products. Months before, Finkelstein had visited Mattel and toured its headquarters with President and COO Richard Dickson. Finkelstein asked him what Mattel needed: "He said he needed incredible speed, endless flexibility, and the ability to pick and choose the parts of Shopify infrastructure they needed."[3] That's how Mattel ended up as the launch customer for Commerce Components.

Shopify Pay was made available to enterprises through Commerce Components, even if they were not on the Shopify platform. Shopify thought this feature would be a big winner because a Boston Consulting Group study had found that accelerated payment methods like Shop Pay were the best at reducing cart abandonment,[4] and a top consulting firm had found Shop Pay was the best of this elite group.[5] An estimated $260 billion was lost over the past decade through cart abandonment, so enterprise companies, which tended to have custom tech stacks and their own payment systems, could elevate conversions of shoppers by switching to Shop Pay.

Some large clients also wanted to sell at the wholesale level, so Shopify built a B2B channel into the dashboard. An early user was Brooklinen, a supplier of bed sheets, pillows and related items; it was taking bulk orders from hotels, and the B2B channel enabled it to replace the "time-consuming, manual process of phone orders." Morrison also believed B2B was going to be one of its biggest growth opportunities in 2024 and beyond, with projections calling for growth of 18% annually until 2030.[6] That's why Shopify added more than three dozen B2B features to Shopify Plus in 2023.

Shopify Collabs

YouTubers, bloggers and other creators of online content have established a large and growing presence online. They are aware that their audiences present opportunities to merchandise but they lack the time or appetite for business, so a collaboration with an entrepreneur may be welcomed. To facilitate the linkups, Shopify launched Shopify Collabs in August of 2022 (after it acquired startup Dovetail and brought founder Mike Schmidt and his team into Shopify). The Shopify Collabs tool essentially made it easier for creators and entrepreneurs to find good matches for partnering. Merchants on Shopify could download the app for free to search a list of creators; vice versa, creators could search a list of merchants. Two examples of collabs were Shopify's own partnerships with MrBeast and Drake.

Collabs with MrBeast

An illustration of how collaboration between a merchant and a creator might unfold is illustrated by the one between Shopify and MrBeast, a YouTube superstar whose videos of expensive stunts, competitions and giveaways have attracted more than 200 million subscribers. MrBeast and Lütke first met in 2019, when MrBeast, whose real name is Jimmy Donaldson, launched the Team Trees project to raise $20 million to plant 20 million trees. Lütke donated $1,000,001 to become the biggest donor, one-upping Tesla CEO Elon Musk's contribution of $1,000,000. This donation opened the doors to chats between Lütke, Finkelstein and MrBeast, which culminated in MrBeast opening two stores on Shopify.

His first shop was ShopMrBeast.com, a merch store selling his hoodies and other branded clothing; the second was Feastables.com, which sold MrBeast chocolate bars and other branded snacks. Both sites have done very well, thanks to his massive following and innovative marketing approach, where his products are blended in with his videos as part of the narrative. In addition, the products were made to his specifications because he wanted to offer something different or better than what was on the market.

"We got a chance to meet him and help him with his stores as much as we possibly could," Finkelstein said on *The Danny Miranda Podcast*. "He would ask for something and we would over-deliver and after a while he just became a fan of Shopify's. . . . We were already fans of his and we started talking about collaborating on different videos together."[7]

This was how Shopify began to show up in MrBeast's videos. Many collaborations between creators and entrepreneurs will be transactional, where the creator or influencer simply receives a monetary payment. Shopify liked to instead have a more personal relationship with the creator. "With MrBeast, you can't just throw money at him," said Finkelstein. "He gets to choose who he works with and so we first met him . . . and then he launched his merch store on Shopify . . . If you go back to the early days of Shopify and think about Tim Ferriss or Daymond John or Seth Godin or Marie Forleo or Tina Eisenberg, these are not people that you can simply just say I want you to be a part of our community: you actually need to build real relationships and so we've always done that."[8]

Collab with Drake

In July 2023, rapper and singer Drake had his Shopify store, Drake Related, revamped using Hydrogen, Shopify's headless commerce framework that was unveiled in 2022. It became one of the first websites to test and use the Shopify Collective tool for cross-selling products from other merchants. Drake Related now lets visitors go on a virtual tour through Drake's studio, lounge, bedroom, closet, court, garage and other rooms — to browse and purchase a range of limited-edition items offered by him and other merchants.

Two months after his store had been revamped, Drake went on tour in North America. Before departure, he and Shopify created a bat-like signal that could be beamed outside his concert venues when his fans exited after the show; the signal would have a 10-foot by 10-foot QR code that the fans could scan into the Shopify Shop app on their phones to get freebies, including unreleased Nike sneakers — as well as go on the virtual tour through Drake's rooms.[9]

Collabs with Micro-influencers

For small- to medium-sized businesses with limited budgets, an alternative to using big-name promotions is enlisting the help of micro-influencers, suggests Finkelstein. He himself has used micro-influencers to build his side gig of a tea business called Firebelly. "If you . . . want to find a great influencer, rather than look for someone with the most subscribers on YouTube, look for small channels that have great engagement. Those people are less expensive and you may see a higher return on investment."[10]

Micro-influencers can be found, as well, in places like Reddit and Pinterest forums. Podcaster Jason Stapleton related a story about a horse trainer who had an audience of only 2,000. But there were businesses that wanted to advertise on his podcast because they knew the audience would be interested in their product lines of saddle bags, horse-grooming brushes, tools for repairing hooves and so on. "Everybody in the horse industry paid attention to this podcast and he made a fortune because there was no [online] place else that sold these items," Stapleton said.[11]

FUTURE OPPORTUNITIES

Some new market opportunities loomed on the horizon and were promising fields for new product announcements in upcoming issues of *Shopify Editions*. Two of them were open banking and livestream shopping.

Open Banking

In the spring of 2023, Shopify partnered with U.K.-based Volt to offer its "Pay by Bank" solution to Shopify merchants in Europe and Brazil, so they could present customers with the option of making payments that settle instantly via direct account-to-account transfers of funds (versus the usual delays of going through a bank or other intermediary). Volt's service is part of the global trend toward "open banking," whereby digital links are established between different financial services to remove delays and manual work in the transfer of payments and sharing of financial information. For example, financial technology companies can give renters the same ability as homeowners to build their credit score if the renter's bank has set up a software connection with the credit bureau to verify monthly rental payments.

Open banking is still in its infancy and has the potential to be a major driver of growth for e-commerce firms. Aside from helping renters establish credit scores, there are several other applications. For example, there is a lot of manual and time-consuming labour to complete the paperwork and gather hardcopy documents for loan applications — but much of this burden can be avoided if there is open banking and digital sharing of information across financial firms. Another application arises when people have accounts spread across different banks, brokerages, insurers, pension plans, utilities and so on: open banking allows the accounts to be brought together in one spot for viewing them all together on a person's computer or phone.

Some applications are already in use. A few years ago, Shopify made the cash-sharing app Venmo available to its U.S. merchants; it permits U.S. citizens to make payments by transferring funds directly from their account to the account of another person.

While many countries are moving toward open banking, Canada has been a laggard. Canadian policymakers and bankers seem concerned that open banking could lead to disintermediation of financial transactions, creating uncertainties for financial stability. But other countries don't seem to be as worried and are pushing ahead.

Livestream Shopping

Livestream shopping is similar to the TV shopping channels that have been around for decades, except a mobile phone and "Buy Now" button have replaced a TV set and "Call Now" message. Surveys of livestream shopping audiences reveal that viewers like the discounts, educational aspect (learn more about products), entertainment value and opportunities for real-time interaction with hosts.

China led the way, starting livestream shopping in 2015 and has since enjoyed rapid growth: livestream shopping sales in China surpassed $500 billion in 2022, up from $18 billion in 2018. Meanwhile, livestream shopping revenue in the United States registered about $50 billion in 2022, a tenth of China's total.[1] Livestream shopping in the United States remains in a modest uptrend, and China's experience suggests there is more growth potential ahead for Western countries.

It would not be surprising to see Shopify enhance, or add to, its previous initiatives in this niche. Past initiatives included: several apps on the Shopify platform that merchants can download to create livestream sales on their store's website, such as the Now Live app. Of special note is the app that integrates the TalkShopLive video commerce platform with Shopify stores; it was launched in 2019 and is experiencing phenomenal growth. On its sales channels, the sellers and presenters include many famous people such as Oprah Winfrey, Paul McCartney, Garth Brooks, Dolly Parton, Ed Sheeran, Terry Crews, Catherine Zeta-Jones, Patti LaBelle, Tim Tebow, Paris Hilton, Tim McGraw and Jennifer Lopez.

Epilogue: Wrapping Up

There are some peripheral issues to consider regarding Shopify's dramatic track record. Let's wrap up by covering several of them, starting with the role of luck, followed by the benefits of the entrepreneur spirit, Shopify's externalities, and promoting entrepreneurship. To end, a review and summary is provided of the key factors in Shopify's growth over the past two decades.

ROLE OF LUCK

Lütke has said luck accounted for much of his and Shopify's success. Having an angel investor show up to provide the first round of financing during a cash crunch "was largely a fluke."[1] Another early bit of good fortune was the boost from the financial crisis and recession of 2008 and 2009, as well as later, from the pandemic in 2020 and 2021. Lütke confided to Ferriss that the Build a Business contest was a game of chance and that the success of Shopify was due mostly to chance.[2] In October of 2012, a reporter asked if he thought he was lucky: "I'm ridiculously lucky," he replied, with a chuckle. "Growing up, I spent my time doing useless stuff, looking at computers. It was sheer luck that what I was interested in accidentally turns out to be one of the most useful skills you can have right now."[3] The timing of Shopify's listing on the stock exchanges in 2015 was like "winning the lottery five times in a row," Lütke declared in the podcast *How I Built This*. "This is not the kind of company that could have been started two years later. . . . Luck is such a major component."[4]

What to make of this? It seems reasonable to say there are two kinds of luck. The first is the completely random kind, like winning at the casino throwing dice or feeding a slot machine. The second is the luck of a scientist when an accident in some procedure during a period of experimentation leads to a new cure or invention. For the second kind of luck, there is an interplay between human effort and the course of events. So, it's not an entirely random result; there is an element of probability linked with the amount of preparation and application. As the great scientist Louis Pasteur once said, "Chance favors the prepared mind."[5] Shopify's first financing, the one that helped stave off insolvency in 2007, may have seemed a fluke, but it was hearing about Shopify's product quality that lured angel investor Phillips to Ottawa.

Finkelstein was questioned in the podcast *Perfectly Mentored* about luck in business. "It's incredibly important," he replied. "Luck and timing certainly play a role — but so does putting yourself in a position where you can execute on that good fortune."[6] Finkelstein also told another podcaster: "I talk about my T-shirt business and little DJ business but I don't talk about the slipper company, watch company or nurse-uniform company — my past is littered with a ton of failures. Luckily for me the things that succeeded offset the stuff that didn't."[7]

Despite his many references to being lucky, Lütke was indeed aware of the role of human intervention. Appearing on *The Pylon Show* in January 2020, he observed: "Building companies is a journey and that journey is successful or unsuccessful largely due to luck, but in certain situations the thing that makes the difference is making good choices, and so your skill of making good choices ends up being a very important input into the potential of a company."[8]

An entrepreneur thus cannot expect that willpower, industriousness and ingenuity alone ensures success. But they do have a correlation with luck, so more of each raises the odds of a fortuitous outcome. And if a startup does fail, the entrepreneur can try new ventures to stay in the game and remain in a position to "execute on that good fortune."

LET'S HAVE MORE "UNTERNEHMERGEIST"

Economists have long expounded on the benefits to society of having a vibrant entrepreneurial culture. If entrepreneurs had a patron saint, it would be economist Joseph Schumpeter, a professor at Harvard University during the 1930s and 1940s. His 1942 magnum opus, *Capitalism, Socialism and Democracy*, argued that entrepreneurs were the source of innovation and the main reason why much of the world has enjoyed rising living standards over the past two centuries. In a process called "creative destruction," they took on the risk and exertion to develop new products, industrial processes and technologies that replaced existing arrangements of lesser utility.

Unternehmergeist, the German word that Schumpeter coined for "entrepreneur-spirit," was the driving force that enhanced consumer value, labour productivity, employment and national output. One illustration of the impact of entrepreneurs is how they thwarted the dismal projections of Thomas Malthus. His 1798 treatise, *An Essay on the Principle of Population*, declared that widespread poverty, famine, and mortalities were inevitable as geometric population growth raced ahead of the capacity of arable land to feed people.

Except for a few periodic and isolated regional episodes, such a gloomy scenario has failed to materialize. The reason why is because entrepreneurs developed and commercialized new technologies that boosted the productivity of farms. The improvements included new fertilizers, more efficient irrigation and higher seed yields. There was also greater mechanization. For example, in 1701, Jethro Tull perfected a horse-drawn seed drill that sowed seed in neat rows and covered them with soil to the right depth. Another key development was John Deere's invention of the steel plow in 1837. By 1900, steam engines on wheels moved under their own power to supply power to stationary threshing machines. Henry Ford as a boy saw them and got the inspiration to build automobiles. By the 1920s, tractors and combines tilled, planted and harvested farm fields.

Governments and politicians speak in favour of having more entrepreneurs, but their solution is usually to fund incentive packages, accelerators and other programs. The problem with that approach is, as Lütke states,

> they increase only the demand side . . . between the demand and eventual supply lies friction . . . we've realized that every time we take away friction and make the process of starting a business simpler, what we get is more entrepreneurs. The demand was high but the ability to overcome the friction along the way was simply not that well distributed.[1]

However, there are some barriers and sources of friction that Shopify and other e-commerce companies cannot eliminate on their own. They need to be addressed by governments. One particular recommendation Lütke offers is making licensing requirements less pervasive and onerous. Sometimes, they have been put into place for issues that no longer apply, or reflect, as economist Milton Friedman argued in *Capitalism and Freedom*, attempts by incumbent operators to create barriers to entry that protect them from competition (under the guise of protecting consumers). Lütke also believes another way to encourage entrepreneurship is to "demystify this process in schools."[2]

SHOPIFY'S EXTERNALITIES

Like most other companies, Shopify generates positive and negative externalities. Let's start with the positive externalities, which in the case of Shopify is primarily the social benefit of increasing the number of entrepreneurs. The main avenue by which Shopify produces this outcome is through reducing the frictions and barriers that block entrepreneurs. Another avenue is by providing direct support to entrepreneurs through its client-services team, and the encyclopedic collection of materials on its website and YouTube. Not to be overlooked are its outreach programs — for example, the financial support given to Operation HOPE (a charity that aims to create one million new Black-owned businesses by 2030) and joint sponsorship of the Pow Wow Pitch (a *Shark Tank*-like competition for Indigenous entrepreneurs).

It may be laudable that Shopify generates the positive externality of more entrepreneurs, but what about negative externalities — for example, emissions from the delivery trucks carrying online purchases to customers? Shopify's *Annual Reports*[1] and company news releases have reported the following actions:

- migrated data centers in 2018 to Google Cloud, which runs on renewable energy
- launched the Sustainability Fund in 2019 to invest at least $5 million annually in the most promising technologies and projects fighting climate change
- formed Frontier, an alliance with Stripe, Alphabet, Meta and McKinsey to purchase $925 million of carbon removal by the end of 2030
- as of March 2021, agreed to purchase 15,000 tonnes of permanent carbon removal — "more than any company in history"
- in June 2022, released Planet, an app that Shopify merchants can use "to zero out their shipping emissions"

PROMOTING ENTREPRENEURSHIP

More than two million entrepreneurs were active on the Shopify platform by the end of 2022. They were seeking to monetize hobbies, supplement job income or break free from the nine-to-five routine. Others were full-time entrepreneurs by necessity, like Lütke and Finkelstein in their younger days. Yet others were full-time entrepreneurs by choice because the upside potential was more exciting than a regular paycheque, or they preferred calling their own shots. There were also the large businesses that started out small on the platform and blossomed, and the ones that were already big brand-name companies, seeking to add online sales to their street stores. Within this heterogeneous mix was a great deal of flux. In any given year, new businesses were starting up and many were closing down.

Shopify liked to encourage people to become entrepreneurs. Obviously, there is some self-interest in this but it also had the positive side effect of generating more entrepreneurs in the world. Neither was entrepreneurship glorified or promoted irresponsibly. For example, a blog post on Shopify's website cautioned that anyone thinking of starting a business should be aware of the survival rate: nearly half of startups in the United States failed within five years, according to U.S. government data[1] (although the survival rate is somewhat better on the Shopify platform, Lütke claimed at the Shopify Unite 2017 conference[2]).

In their interviews, talks and articles, executives at Shopify were careful not to present entrepreneurialism as only sunshine and blue skies for founders. In reality, it can have its emotional lows. As Lütke pointed out in a 2021 interview:

> When I started Shopify, nearly every day I thought we were gonna be dead tomorrow but I also thought maybe we're gonna be unstoppable. . . . Sometimes I was a week in one state and a week in another state. It just oscillated back and forth and that's still going on — if anything, the oscillation has increased in speed, sometimes before breakfast even, it goes both ways.[3]

One way Lütke dealt with the roller-coaster ride was through perspectives found in Stoic philosophy. A book that helped him was *Meditations*, by Marcus Aurelius (Roman Emperor from 161 to 180 AD). It is a collection of notes that Aurelius wrote to himself about achieving peace of mind when buffeted by the vicissitudes of life. "If thou art pained by any external thing, it is not this that disturbs thee, but thy own judgment about it. And it is in thy power to wipe out this judgment now," he wrote. Another book on Stoicism that Lütke recommends is *A Guide to the Good Life: The Ancient Art of Stoic Joy*, by William B. Irvine.

REVIEW OF SHOPIFY'S GROWTH TRAJECTORY

1. In 2004, Lütke and Lake became entrepreneurs and launched an online store, Snowdevil, to sell snowboards. They abandoned this business after a year to launch Shopify, but Snowdevil had not been a waste of time. Since they had been entrepreneurs,

it gave them a good idea of how to design Shopify to meet the needs of other entrepreneurs.

2. In 2005, Lütke and Lake became aware of an underserved niche in the e-commerce market: entrepreneurs and small-business owners who wanted to set up online stores but lacked the coding skills or the capital to hire IT staff. Lütke and Weinand thus launched Shopify in 2006 for easily setting up and running online stores at a low cost.
3. Before the launch, early-stage marketing (admittedly unplanned) occurred when Lütke and Weinand participated in online communities and gave updates on Shopify when it was under development. Many participants in the communities became early adopters.
4. A default marketing strategy for Lütke and Weinand was to design the platform well enough so that it was capable of generating word-of-mouth advertising; when an angel investor heard the praise, he visited and provided funding/mentoring at a critical time.
5. Shopify's decision to locate its headquarters in Ottawa, Canada, turned out to be a good move. As Bessemer Venture Partners said, Lütke was able to hire the best staff available in the Ottawa area "at 60%-70% of the cost of similar talent in Silicon Valley or New York."[1] Moreover, job tenures in secondary talent markets like Ottawa were four to five times longer than the 18-month average in primary markets like Silicon Valley, so Shopify could afford to invest in developing its employees to bring them up to Silicon Valley standards.
6. When Lake left, Lütke assumed his CEO duties. This gave Shopify a technologist CEO, which venture capitalist and Internet pioneer Marc Andreessen argued were needed to steer companies through a world disrupted by new technologies[2] (take, for example, Netflix displacing Blockbuster). Moreover, Lütke's devotion to product development was unparalleled, his pursuit of continuous learning kept him informed for making decisions, his engineering approach came in handy with

structuring operations, and his management style relying on tight feedback loops and compass metrics delivered results.

7. Lütke and Fauser developed an API for which partners could build apps and themes satisfying the needs of subgroups of Shopify subscribers. The revenues generated by the apps and themes were generously shared with the partners, and helped set off the flywheel where the number of apps and merchants on the platform became self-reinforcing. "This [API] is a big competitive differentiator for Shopify," noted Bessemer Venture Partners.[3]
8. By 2010, Shopify's subscriptions were taking off and cash flow was reviving. This development and Lütke's confirmation of the viability of several growth initiatives (via trials and experiments) helped persuade venture-capital firms to offer a Series A financing. It was a good time to get funding because the growth and healthy financials gave Shopify sufficient leverage to obtain funding without giving up too much control. Series B and Series C rounds followed in 2011 and 2013, respectively.
9. Hired in 2010 to boost business development, Finkelstein was instrumental in Shopify crossing the chasm from early adopters to mainstream users. He was, among other things, a catalyst in building up Shopify's ecosystem of third-party developers and designers, and a driving force behind an affiliate program whereby bloggers, YouTubers and other online creators were rewarded for referring customers to Shopify. He was also a key contributor to the running of the annual Build a Business contest.
10. Also hired in 2010 was Shannan, who built up Shopify's client services team to become a "secret growth hack" for the company. Support staff solved not only technical problems but with many of them being entrepreneurs at one time or another, they had the expertise and empathy to help with business problems. They could also point out from the growing list of apps which ones could solve a merchant's problems (bringing in revenues to Shopify as well), and that became a critical source

of information on the needs of merchants (thus informing Shopify's priorities for product development).

11. Miller, an SEO guru, was hired in 2011 to help people find Shopify online; after that, his goal was to get more people *interested* in finding Shopify online, which he did by removing e-commerce pain points through new features, such as Shopify Email. Wherever problems arose, Miller would go to see what could be done to help: a particularly important intervention of his helped Shopify with its transition to a mobile-first platform.
12. By 2012, Weinand and Forsyth were spearheading the development of a distinctive work environment and culture. It contributed to job satisfaction and employees getting sh!t done. Employees did not have to be directed or monitored much, nor was it necessary to come up with a lot of rules and procedures. Everyone knew the direction they had to go, and there was enough trust that people would find the best way to reach the objective. In short, employees were encouraged to be self-directed in finding ways to contribute and add value to the company. The culture emphasized openness to feedback, providing a safe space to take risks, growth mindsets, continuous learning and adaptability to change.
13. Shopify executives contributed to the culture by being transparent and maintaining a high level of communication with employees through measures such as townhalls, Ask Me Anything sessions, Hack Days, internal podcasts and more — so employees felt in the loop. The executives also rejected personas in order to be their authentic selves, which often meant being open, honest and not afraid to show vulnerability to reveal a more personal side of themselves in the interests of encouraging dialogue, trust and creativity.
14. Probably one of the most important factors, however, in the formation of Shopify's culture was the recruitment process. The company hired many founders and ex-founders of startups, as well as people who exhibited a proclivity toward entrepreneurialism during the Life Story segment of the interview process. The

practice of acqui-hiring — acquiring startups primarily to recruit their founders and employees — was also quite significant. Once brought into Shopify, the startups and founders could operate in a nearly autonomous way. This factor alone likely accounts for why Shopify was able to maintain a startup culture as it scaled up.

15. By early 2013, Shopify's commitment to innovation and Lütke's first-principles thinking led to an announcement that Shopify was going to transition to a retail operating system to give entrepreneurs tools for overcoming friction and pain points wherever they were present. This decision took Shopify into a new realm of growth opportunities, which led to new tools such as Shopify POS and Shopify Payments. The latter was a huge source of growth in revenues. Shopify Plus, under Padelford, was also a smart move to retain and increase the number of enterprise-level retailers as customers; another key tool was Multichannel Shopify, which enabled its merchants to sell on many social media websites from one location.
16. Shopify latched onto a powerful financial flywheel after its IPO in 2015; with its quarterly financial reports regularly beating analysts' consensus expectations, there was a strong uptrend in the stock that enabled Shopify to float several additional issues of shares to rake in more than $7 billion by 2021. In effect, an upward spiral was playing out between corporate growth and stock issues. However, it was halted in 2022 as COVID-19 ebbed and offline shopping resurfaced, followed by various Black Swan events in the form of supply bottlenecks, soaring inflation and spiking interest rates. Nonetheless, most of the billions of dollars raised via many share offerings still remained on the balance sheet throughout COVID-19 and was available to finance growth initiatives during and after the pandemic.
17. During COVID-19, Shopify permanently adopted remote working, which proved to be an astute move in the sense that it allowed Shopify to subsequently recruit talent from anywhere in the world and so expanded the pool from which it could hire. Many seasoned executives from top U.S.

> companies joined Shopify in 2022. Although the workforce was spread out over a large geographical area, Shopify was able to maintain aspects of its culture through electronic communication channels such as Zoom.

As of 2024, Shopify is currently in the midst of a reboot to its growth engine with what appears to be an emphasis on profitability. It has trimmed costs, offloaded the financial drain of the SFN, and is actively pursuing several growth opportunities: generative AI (Sidekick, etc.), the high-end market segment, Shopify Collabs, B2B wholesale channel, open banking, livestream shopping, and a variety of fintech products for entrepreneurs. It will be interesting to see how it all plays out.

Acknowledgements

Many thanks to Jack David, co-founder of ECW Press, for green-lighting this book. It was a homecoming for me because ECW Press, many, many years ago, published my first book, for which I have always been grateful. This time around, Lesley Erickson, Emily Ferko and Sammy Chin were a great help and a pleasure to work with. Also a thank you to Karen Milner of Milner & Associates for helping me reconnect with ECW.

I was fortunate to find an abundance of information on Shopify from a multitude of sources (those cited in the book can be seen in the Notes section). However, company executives declined to be interviewed. Nonetheless, they had given dozens of refreshingly candid interviews over the years, still online in various podcasts and other social media. Those interviews turned out to be an excellent source for answering the questions I had planned to ask the executives — and then some.

It was great having family keep me company while writing the manuscript. My wife, Ann, was working from home, as were my two sons, Lawrence and Shawn, taking a break from post-secondary studies to give entrepreneurship a try by operating an online store. An added bonus was watching the boys earn an income in the six figures from their store. Even if they had not made a profit, I am sure it still would have been a valuable experience for them.

Notes

NOTE TO READER: If a link for any of the following sources is broken or missing, the content can usually be retrieved from the Internet archives via the Wayback Machine (https://web.archive.org).

INTRODUCTION

1. Staff Report, "Shopify's six-year earnings streak shatters in Q3," Digital Commerce 360, October 28, 2021, https://www.digitalcommerce360.com/2021/10/28/shopifys-six-year-earnings-streak-shatters-in-q3/.
2. Shopify Inc., "Shopify merchants support world's largest workforce, contributing 5M jobs and $444B+ in economic activity in 2021," press release, April 28, 2022, https://www.shopify.com/news/shopify-merchants-support-world-s-largest-workforce-contributing-5m-jobs-and-444b-in-economic-activity-in-2021.
3. Tim Shufelt, "How Shopify made Kylie Jenner rich(er)," *Globe and Mail*, April 25, 2019, https://www.theglobeandmail.com/business/rob-magazine/article-how-shopify-made-kylie-jenner-richer/.
4. Tim Kiladze, "Solving Shopify's misery: How Canada's tech saviour lost its swagger — and why investors remain so scared," *Globe and Mail*, October 28, 2022, www.theglobeandmail.com/business/rob-magazine/article-shopify-stock-tech-crash/.
5. Tobi Lütke, "How Shopify is covered differently," X, October 27, 2022, https://twitter.com/tobi/status/1586040633893847040/photo/1.
6. Shopify Inc., 2022 *Annual Report*, https://s27.q4cdn.com/572064924/files/doc_financials/2022/ar/4cdd44db-ca94-4d2a-ae03-4dad70a72c58.pdf.
7. eMarketer, "Ecommerce Share of Retail Sales: 2021–2026," https://www.oberlo.ca/statistics/ecommerce-share-of-retail-sales.

8. Census Bureau, U.S. Department of Commerce, "Quarterly Retail E-Commerce Sales: 4th Quarter 2022," February 17, 2023, www.census .gov/retail/mrts/www/data/pdf/ec_current.pdf.
9. Daniela Coppola, "Countries with the highest share of retail sales taking place online 2022," October 11, 2022, Statista, www.statista.com /statistics/1042763/worldwide-share-online-retail-penetration-by -country.

1. AT THE EPICENTER: TOBIAS LÜTKE

An Unpromising Start

1. Laura Onita, "'We're the rebel army to Amazon's web empire': Shopify's Tobias Lutke on the $83-billion company he built," *Financial Post*, May 25, 2020, https://financialpost.com/technology/shopifys -tobias-lutke.
2. Kevin Scott, "Tobi Lütke: CEO and Founder, Shopify," *Behind the Tech with Kevin Scott*, Microsoft, January 3, 2023, https://www.youtube .com/watch?v=pkMjPQe_mpA.
3. Tobi Lütke, "I was grounded for weeks," X, December 10, 2023, https:// twitter.com/tobi/status/1733851786451054747.

The Apprentice

1. Tobi Lütke, "The Apprentice Programmer," *Tobi Lütke Blog*, March 3, 2013, https://tobi.Lutke.com/blogs/news/11280301-the-apprentice -programmer.
2. Ibid.
3. Ibid.
4. Trevor Cole, "Our Canadian CEO of the year you've probably never heard of," *Report on Business*, November 27, 2014, www.theglobeandmail .com/report-on-business/rob-magazine/meet-our-ceo-of-the-year /article21734931.

Entering the Workforce

1. Jason Calacanis, "Tobi Lütke — Founder & CEO of Shopify on future of retail," *This Week in Startups*, August 6, 2013, www.youtube .com/watch?v=mxBaDsosGPw.
2. Y Combinator, "User: xal," *Hacker News*, September 30, 2008, https:// news.ycombinator.com/user?id=xal.
3. Y Combinator, "YouPorn: Symfony2, Redis, Varnish, HA Proxy . . . (Keynote at ConFoo 2012)," *Hacker News*, March 24, 2012, https:// news.ycombinator.com/item?id=3750060.
4. Sean Silcoff, "Tobi vs. Goliath: How Shopify is bracing for a looming battle with Amazon," *Globe and Mail*, February 13, 2021, www .theglobeandmail.com/business/article-tobi-vs-goliath-how-shopify -is-bracing-for-a-looming-battle-with/.
5. Trevor Cole, "Our Canadian CEO of the year you've probably never heard of," *Report on Business*, November 27, 2014, www .theglobeandmail.com/report-on-business/rob-magazine/meet-our -ceo-of-the-year/article21734931.
6. Brad Stone, "How Shopify outfoxed Amazon to become the everywhere store," *Bloomberg Businessweek*, December 27, 2021, www .bnnbloomberg.ca/how-shopify-outfoxed-amazon-to-become-the -everywhere-store-1.1699910.
7. Cole, "Our Canadian CEO of the year."
8. Dan Martell, "The Future of Retail 'Arming the Rebels!' with Tobi Lütke @ Shopify.com," *Escape Velocity Show*, December 5, 2019, https://www.youtube.com/watch?v=-PZouDwpIYQ&t=3s&ab.

Gaming as Preparation

1. Lütke's auto-deleted April 2018 post remains online at places such as: Anton Sen, "How Playing Games Helped Me Succeed at Business," www.antonsten.com/fifa.
2. Sriram Krishnan, "Tobi Lütke," *The Observer Effect*, December 16, 2020, https://www.theobservereffect.org/tobi.html.

3. Daniel Coyle, *The Talent Code: Greatness Isn't Born. It's Grown. Here's How* (New York: Bantam, 2009).
4. Ben Gilbert and David Rosenthal, "Shopify IPO," *Acquired*, podcast, August 6, 2019, www.acquired.fm/episodes/the-shopify-ipo.
5. Brian Glass et al., "Real-Time Strategy Game Training: Emergence of a Cognitive Flexibility Trait," *PLOS ONE*, August 7, 2013, https://journals.plos.org/plosone/article?id=10.1371/journal.pone.0070350.

2. PRELUDE TO THE LAUNCH

Enter Fiona McKean

1. Tobias Lütke, "I met my Canadian wife Fiona playing Asheron's Call," X, November 12, 2018, https://web.archive.org/web/20220928005318/https://twitter.com/tobi/status/1062032289851301889.
2. Andrew Warner, "How Shopify Became Profitable by Helping Anyone Open an Online Boutique," Mixergy, July 9, 2010, https://mixergy.com/interviews/tobias-Lutke-shopify-interview.
3. Sriram Krishnan, "Tobi Lütke," *The Observer Effect*, December 16, 2020, https://www.theobservereffect.org/tobi.html.
4. Caitlin Dempsey, "What is a Snow Devil?" Geography Realm, January 29, 2020, www.geographyrealm.com/what-is-a-snow-devil/.
5. Trevor Cole, "Our Canadian CEO of the year you've probably never heard of," *Report on Business*, November 27, 2014, www.theglobeandmail.com/report-on-business/rob-magazine/meet-our-ceo-of-the-year/article21734931.

E-commerce before Shopify

1. Wikipedia, "Michael Aldrich," https://en.wikipedia.org/wiki/Michael_Aldrich.
2. Tucker Schreiber, "Proceed to Checkout: The Unexpected Story of How Ecommerce Started," *Shopify Blog*, November 25, 2016,

https://www.shopify.com/blog/69521733-proceed-to-checkout-the-unexpected-story-of-how-ecommerce-started.

3. Peter H. Lewis, "Attention Shoppers: Internet Is Open," *New York Times*, August 12, 1994, https://www.nytimes.com/1994/08/12/business/attention-shoppers-internet-is-open.html.
4. Paul Graham, "The Submarine," *Y Combinator Essays*, April 2005, www.paulgraham.com/submarine.html.
5. *SBN* Staff, "Visionary in obscurity: Charles Stack," *Smart Business*, July 22, 2002, https://sbnonline.com/article/visionary-in-obscurity-charles-stack-operates-in-two-business-communities-151-cleveland-and-the-internet-151-and-isn-146-t-well-known-in-either-this-time-around-that-146-s-going-to-change-he-hopes/.
6. Craig Smith, "The Birth of E-commerce: a Short History," LinkedIn, June 6, 2020, https://www.linkedin.com/pulse/birth-e-commerce-short-history-shopping-online-craig-smith/.
7. Digital Commerce 360, "Top Online Marketplaces Worldwide by GMV," https://www.oberlo.com/statistics/top-online-marketplaces-worldwide-by-gmv.

The Snowdevil Initiative

1. Guy Raz, "Shopify: Tobias Lütke," *How I Built This*, NPR podcast, August 5, 2019, https://www.npr.org/2019/08/02/747660923/shopify-tobias-l-tke (transcript: https://app.podscribe.ai/episode/1192113).
2. Laura Onita, "Shopify's 39-year-old billionaire founder 'Tobi' Lütke on the secrets of his success," *The Telegraph*, May 25, 2020, www.telegraph.co.uk/business/2020/05/24/shopifys-39-year-old-billionaire-founder-tobi-lutke-secrets/.
3. *OBJ* Staff, "Entrepreneurial lessons: Shopify CEO Tobi Lütke on his first sale," *Ottawa Business Journal*, October 25, 2017, https://obj.ca/entrepreneurial-lessons-shopify-ceo-tobi-Lutke-on-his-first-sale.
4. Matt Linderman, "Q&A with Tobias Lütke of Shopify," *Signal v. Noise*, June 3, 2010, https://signalvnoise.com/posts/2378-qa-with-tobias-ltke-of-shopify.

5. Tobias Lütke, "Snowdevil launches!" *Ruby Buzz Forum*, February 1, 2005, www.artima.com/forums/flat.jsp?forum=123&thread=91835.

3. LIFT-OFF!

The Launch of Shopify

1. Tobias Lütke, "Canada's new Ruby programmer," *Ruby Buzz Forum*, August 23, 2005, https://www.artima.com/forums/flat.jsp?forum=123&thread=124524#160922.
2. Andrew Warner, "How Shopify Became Profitable by Helping Anyone Open an Online Boutique," Mixergy, July 9, 2010, https://mixergy.com/interviews/tobias-lutke-shopify-interview/.
3. Scott Lake, "High Tech Coffee . . ." *Jaded Pixel Blog*, September 5, 2005, https://web.archive.org/web/20051215144624/http://blog.jadedpixel.com/articles/2005/09/05/high-tech-coffee.
4. Gail Goodman and Lily Lyman, "Tobi Lütke, Founder & CEO of Shopify | Core Summit 2019," Underscore VC, November 6, 2019, www.youtube.com/watch?v=PCyQ9acrz4Q.
5. Katherine Duncan, "How Shopify Became the Go-To Ecommerce Platform for Startups," *Entrepreneur*, March 13, 2012, https://www.entrepreneur.com/science-technology/how-shopify-became-the-go-to-ecommerce-platform-for-startups/222967.
6. Sarah Niedoba, "Shopify CEO Tobias Lütke on how to maintain a startup culture at scale," *Canadian Business*, August 9, 2016, https://web.archive.org/web/20160823064931/http://www.canadianbusiness.com/leadership/shopify-ceo-tobias-lutke-on-startup-culture.
7. Andrew Warner, "How Shopify Became Profitable By Helping Anyone Open An Online Boutique," Mixergy, July 9, 2010, https://mixergy.com/interviews/tobias-Lutke-shopify-interview/.
8. Shopify Inc., "Shopify Surpasses US$10 Million in Online Sales," press release, March 19, 2008, https://web.archive.org/web/20080324133457/http://www.prweb.com/releases/2008/03/prweb785404.htm.

9. Jamie Sutton, "How did Shopify get its initial traction?" Quora, 2013, www.quora.com/profile/Jamie-Sutton.

Fresh Founders

1. Sean Silcoff, "From hardware to software: Ottawa's push for a tech revival," *Globe and Mail*, September 18, 2015, https://www.theglobeandmail.com/technology/ottawas-resurgent-tech-scene/article26430302/.

Ramping Up

1. Katherine Duncan, "How Shopify Became the Go-To Ecommerce Platform for Startups," *Entrepreneur*, March 13, 2012, https://www.entrepreneur.com/science-technology/how-shopify-became-the-go-to-ecommerce-platform-for-startups/222967.
2. Andrew Warner, "How Shopify Became Profitable By Helping Anyone Open An Online Boutique," Mixergy, July 9, 2010, https://mixergy.com/interviews/tobias-Lutke-shopify-interview/.
3. Shannon McKarney, "Moving Day," *Pixelsoup Blog,* April 8, 2008, https://web.archive.org/web/20080410183824/http://jadedpixel.com/2008/4/8/jaded-pixel-has-moved.

4. TURBULENCE AND TAILSPIN

Shopify Nearly Goes Bankrupt

1. Diane Jermyn, "Fluke and luck: Shopify's co-founder profited from both," *Globe and Mail*, October 5, 2012, www.theglobeandmail.com/report-on-business/small-business/sb-growth/fluke-and-luck-shopifys-co-founder-profited-from-both/article4575360/.
2. Lauren Debter and Antoine Gara, "Shopify's Soaring Stock Creates Fistful of New Billionaires," *Forbes*, February 25, 2020, www.forbes

.com/sites/laurendebter/2020/02/25/shopifys-soaring-stock-creates-new-billionaires/?sh=1f046f284ff8.
3. Andrew Warner, "How Shopify Became Profitable by Helping Anyone Open an Online Boutique," Mixergy, July 9, 2010, https://mixergy.com/interviews/tobias-Lutke-shopify-interview/.
4. Ibid.

CEO Departs — Lütke Steps In

1. Trevor Cole, "Our Canadian CEO of the year you've probably never heard of," *Report on Business*, November 27, 2014, www.theglobeandmail.com/report-on-business/rob-magazine/meet-our-ceo-of-the-year/article21734931.
2. Tim Ferriss, "Tobi Lütke," *The Tim Ferriss Show*, podcast, February 11, 2019, https://tim.blog/2019/02/11/the-tim-ferriss-show-transcripts-tobi-lutke/.
3. Cole, "Our Canadian CEO of the year."
4. Ferriss, "Tobi Lütke."
5. Cole, "Our Canadian CEO of the year."
6. Ferriss, "Tobi Lütke."
7. Ibid.
8. Cole, "Our Canadian CEO of the year."

Global Financial Crisis and Recession

1. Sarah Niedoba, "Shopify CEO Tobias Lütke on how to maintain a startup culture at scale," *Canadian Business*, August 9, 2016, https://web.archive.org/web/20160823064931/http://www.canadianbusiness.com/leadership/shopify-ceo-tobias-lutke-on-startup-culture.
2. Dayna Winter, "My Starting Over Story: A Soap Making Hobby Became My Lifeline after Loss," Shopify Inc., May 16, 2022, www.shopify.com/blog/prairie-sage-soap.
3. Trevor Cole, "Our Canadian CEO of the year you've probably never heard of," *Report on Business*, November 27, 2014, www.theglobeandmail

.com/report-on-business/rob-magazine/meet-our-ceo-of-the-year/article21734931.

4. Tim Ferriss, "Tobi Lütke," *The Tim Ferriss Show*, podcast, February 11, 2019, https://tim.blog/2019/02/11/the-tim-ferriss-show-transcripts-tobi-Lutke/.
5. Matt Linderman, "Q&A with Tobias Lütke of Shopify," *Signal v. Noise*, June 3, 2010, https://signalvnoise.com/posts/2378-qa-with-tobias-ltke-of-shopify.

5. THE TURNAROUND

The API and Other Astute Moves

1. Shopify Inc., "Shopify Launches API Platform and App Store," press release, June 2, 2009, https://news.shopify.com/shopify-launches-api-platform-and-app-store.
2. Alex Ferrara and Trevor Oelschig, "Shopify Memo," Bessemer Venture Partners, October 12, 2010, https://www.bvp.com/memos/shopify.
3. Reid Hoffman, "Be a platform — Shopify's Tobi Lütke," *Masters of Scale*, February 13, 2020, https://mastersofscale.com/tobi-Lutke-be-a-platform/.
4. Shopify Inc., "Shopify Theme Store Launches," press release, April 22, 2010, https://investors.shopify.com/news-and-events/press-releases/news-details/2010/Shopify-Theme-Store-Launches/default.aspx.

Crossing the Chasm

1. Tim Ferriss, "Harley Finkelstein — Tactics and Strategies from Shopify, the Future of Retail, and More," *The Tim Ferriss Show*, podcast, December 11, 2020, https://tim.blog/2020/12/11/harley-finkelstein-transcript/.
2. Tim Ferriss, "The Tim Ferriss Show Transcripts: Tobi Lütke (#359),"

The Tim Ferriss Show, podcast, February 11, 2019, https://tim.blog/2019/02/11/the-tim-ferriss-show-transcripts-tobi-Lutke/.

3. Andrew Warner, "How Shopify Became Profitable by Helping Anyone Open an Online Boutique," Mixergy, July 9, 2010, https://mixergy.com/interviews/tobias-Lutke-shopify-interview/.
4. Kanishka, "How Tim Ferriss built a winning angel investing portfolio," *Angel Chronicles*, July 21, 2023, https://www.getpin.xyz/post/tim-ferriss-angel-investing-portfolio.
5. Tim Ferriss, "Tobi Lütke — From Snowboard Shop to Billion Dollar Company," *The Tim Ferriss Show*, podcast, March 21, 2019, https://www.youtube.com/watch?v=PQRXssjlk9U.
6. Ibid.
7. Tim Ferriss, "No More Excuses — How to Make an Extra $100,000 in the Next 6 Months," *The Tim Ferriss Show*, podcast, December 8, 2019, https://tim.blog/2009/12/08/no-more-excuses-how-to-make-an-extra-100000-in-the-next-6-months/.
8. Lora Kolodny, "Shopify, a Start-Up, Starts Its Own Business Competition," *New York Times*, February 2, 2010, https://archive.nytimes.com/boss.blogs.nytimes.com/2010/02/02/shopify-gains-customers-with-a-competition/.

A Diverse Team

1. Trevor Cole, "Our Canadian CEO of the year you've probably never heard of," *Report on Business*, November 27, 2014, www.theglobeandmail.com/report-on-business/rob-magazine/meet-our-ceo-of-the-year/article21734931.
2. Fahd Alhattab, "How to Foster a Culture of Development to Improve Your Team's Performance with Brittany Forsyth," *Unicorn Leaders*, podcast, October 13, 2022, www.youtube.com/watch?v=oaUege_VDiA.
3. Benjamin Crudo, "Shopify's Harley Finkelstein On The Future Of Retail," *Making A Diff*, December 20, 2021, www.linkedin.com/pulse/making-diff-harley-finkelstein-president-shopify-benjamin-crudo/.

4. Andrew Warner, "Shopify's 'Agile Business Development,' Explained," Mixergy, May 25, 2011, https://mixergy.com/interviews/harley-finkelstein-shopify-interview.
5. Dan Martell, "The Future of Retail 'Arming the Rebels!' with Tobi Lütke @ Shopify.com," *Escape Velocity Show*, December 5, 2019, https://www.youtube.com/watch?v=-PZouDwpIYQ.
6. Martell, "Future of Retail."
7. Cole, "Our Canadian CEO of the year."
8. David Sloan Wilson, "Evolving the Future of Corporations: A Conversation with Toby Shannan," *This View of Life*, podcast, May 25, 2020, https://thisviewoflife.libsyn.com/evolving-the-future-of-corporations-a-conversation-with-toby-shannan.
9. Sloan Wilson, "A Conversation with Toby Shannan."
10. Brandon Chu, "Craig Miller on Being Shopify's CPO, Marketing by an Engineer, Leadership, and Scale," *The Black Box of Product Management*, April 27, 2021, https://www.youtube.com/watch?v=6F1iN4sAVEs.
11. Ilana E. Strauss, "How Shopify beat eBay by betting on small business," *When It Clicked*, March 16, 2022, https://www.youtube.com/watch?v=rDcVQqy7yzE.
12. Craig Miller, "The P.S. that changed my life," *Medium*, November 11, 2015, https://medium.com/inside-shopify/the-p-s-that-changed-my-life-82a623c912e9.
13. Harvard Business School, "Sheryl Sandberg Addresses the Class of 2012," May 24, 2012, https://www.youtube.com/watch?v=2Dbo_RafutM&t=282s.

6. THE BOOST FROM VENTURE CAPITAL

1. Trevor Cole, "Our Canadian CEO of the year you've probably never heard of," *Report on Business*, November 27, 2014, www.theglobeandmail.com/report-on-business/rob-magazine/meet-our-ceo-of-the-year/article21734931.
2. Jason Calacanis, "Tobi Lütke — Founder & CEO of Shopify on

future of retail," *This Week in Startups*, August 6, 2013, www.youtube.com/watch?v=mxBaDsosGPw.

3. Tim Ferriss, "Harley Finkelstein — Tactics and Strategies from Shopify, the Future of Retail, and More," *The Tim Ferriss Show*, podcast, December 11, 2020, https://tim.blog/2020/12/11/harley-finkelstein-transcript/.
4. Byron Deeter et al., "Bessemer's Top 10 Laws for Being 'SaaS-y,'" Bessemer Venture Partners, 2008, https://www.ueinvestors.com/wp-content/uploads/2012/05/Bessemers_Top_10_Laws_for_Being_SaaS-y.pdf.

$120 Million

1. Alex Ferrara and Trevor Oelschig, "Shopify Memo," Bessemer Venture Partners, October 12, 2010, https://www.bvp.com/memos/shopify.
2. Bruce Firestone, "Connecting with clients before foraging for funds," February 15, 2011, *Ottawa Business Journal*, www.obj.ca/article/opinion-connecting-clients-foraging-funds.
3. Dan Martell, "The Ultimate SaaS Financial Guide with Mark MacLeod," June 7, 2021, *Escape Velocity Show*, www.youtube.com/watch?v=CySjqdmVwmM.
4. Tim Ferriss, "Tobi Lütke," *The Tim Ferriss Show*, podcast, February 11, 2019, https://tim.blog/2019/02/11/the-tim-ferriss-show-transcripts-tobi-Lütke/.
5. Martell, "The Ultimate SaaS Financial Guide."
6. Tobi Lütke, "Pick your compass metric," *Tobi Lütke Blog*, March 3, 2013, https://tobi.Lutke.com/blogs/news/11280913-pick-your-compass-metric.

Hypergrowth and Coaching

1. Harley Finkelstein, "My Dirty Little Secret: I Have An Executive Coach," *Forbes*, October 7, 2016, www.forbes.com/sites/groupthink/2016/10/07/my-dirty-little-secret-i-have-an-executive-coach/2/#73f833cac9fe.

2. Ibid.
3. Tim Ferriss, "Harley Finkelstein — Tactics and Strategies from Shopify, the Future of Retail, and More," *The Tim Ferriss Show*, podcast, December 11, 2020, https://tim.blog/2020/12/11/harley-finkelstein-transcript/.

Shopify the Venture Capitalist

1. Shopify Inc., "Let's build the commerce of tomorrow," June 2023, https://shopify.vc/.
2. Sean Silcoff and Temur Durrani, "Klaviyo stock takes off in IPO, giving investor Shopify hundreds of millions in paper gains," *Globe and Mail*, September 20, 2023, www.theglobeandmail.com/business/technology/article-shopify-klaviyo-ipo-nyse-stock/.

7. SHOPIFY GATHERS SPEED

1. Lukas Naugle, "Shopify CEO email to managers: We are not a family," LinkedIn, May 13, 2021, https://www.linkedin.com/pulse/shopify-ceo-email-managers-we-family-lukas-naugle/.
2. Trevor Cole, "Our Canadian CEO of the year you've probably never heard of," *Report on Business*, November 27, 2014, www.theglobeandmail.com/report-on-business/rob-magazine/meet-our-ceo-of-the-year/article21734931.
3. Sriram Krishnan, "Tobi Lütke," *The Observer Effect*, December 16, 2020, www.theobservereffect.org/tobi.html.

Agile Business Development

1. Mike Duboe, "Shopify President Harley Finkelstein on Catalyzing Entrepreneurship," *Greylock*, October 4, 2022, https://www.youtube.com/watch?v=A5Zn-aP8hrI.
2. Ibid.
3. Andrew Warner, "Shopify's 'Agile Business Development,' Explained,"

Mixergy, May 25, 2011, https://mixergy.com/interviews/harley-finkelstein-shopify-interview/.

4. Andrew Warner, "Shopify: Kill 'Deal Lethargy' with Agile Business Development," Mixergy, March 28, 2012, https://mixergy.com/interviews/harley-finkelstein-shopify-interview-2/.
5. Ibid.

A Secret Growth Hack

1. Greg Isenberg and Sahil Bloom, "Forget Zero Sum, Be Positive Sum with Harley Finkelstein," *Where It Happens*, February 10, 2022, www.youtube.com/watch?v=J4Yu_UTUZR8.
2. Bruce Firestone, "Connecting with clients before foraging for funds," February 15, 2011, *Ottawa Business Journal*, https://obj.ca/opinion-connecting-with-clients-before-foraging-for-funds/.
3. Tim Ferriss, "Tobi Lütke," *The Tim Ferriss Show*, podcast, February 11, 2019, https://tim.blog/2019/02/11/the-tim-ferriss-show-transcripts-tobi-Lütke/.
4. Isenberg and Bloom, "Forget Zero Sum."
5. Motley Fool Staff, "The Motley Fool Interviews Shopify Co-founder and CEO Tobi Lütke," The Motley Fool, August 4, 2017, www.fool.com/investing/2017/08/04/the-motley-fool-interviews-shopify-co-founder-and.aspx.
6. James Bagnall, "The strange alchemy of Shopify's millennials," *Ottawa Citizen*, May 28, 2018, https://ottawacitizen.com/business/local-business/the-strange-alchemy-of-shopifys-millennials.
7. Aaron Orendorff, "What Is a Shopify Guru?" *Shopify Blog*, January 1, 2018, www.shopify.com/ca/blog/3301562-what-is-a-shopify-guru.
8. David Sloan Wilson, "Evolving the Future of Corporations: A Conversation with Toby Shannan," *This View of Life*, podcast, May 25, 2020, https://podcasts.apple.com/us/podcast/evolving-the-future-of-corporations-a/id1484281813?i=1000475767808.
9. Ibid.

Marketing Outside the Box

1. Mark Witten, "Thinking outside of the retail box," *McGill News*, https://mcgillnews.mcgill.ca/s/1762/news/interior.aspx?sid=1762&gid=2&pgid=2007.
2. Brandon Chu, "Craig Miller on Being Shopify's CPO, Marketing by an Engineer, Leadership, and Scale," April 27, 2021, *The Black Box of Product Management*, www.youtube.com/watch?v=6F1iN4sAVEs.
3. Andrew Chen, "Growth Hacker is the new VP Marketing," *@andrewchen*, April 27, 2012, https://andrewchen.com/how-to-be-a-growth-hacker-an-airbnbcraigslist-case-study/.

The Back Office

1. Joe Michalowski, "Turning Finance into a True Strategic Business Partner: Russ Jones, Former CFO, Shopify," *The Role Forward Podcast by Mosaic Tech*, August 8, 2022, https://www.youtube.com/watch?v=nDAXih2qqPw.

8. THE SHOPIFY ENVIRONMENT

The City's Hippest Scene

1. Little Miss Shopify (Anna), "Ahora with CEO Tobi," *Life @ Shopify*, May 12, 2011, https://littlemissshopify.tumblr.com/post/5420911327/ahora-with-ceo-tobi#.

Offices in Paradise

1. Mark Anderson, "Canada's Smartest Company: Shopify," *Profit*, November 28, 2012, https://web.archive.org/web/20140709160714/http://www.profitguide.com/industry-focus/technology/canadas-smartest-company-44283.

2. Shane Parrish, "Tobi Lütke: The Trust Battery," *Knowledge Project Podcast*, April 2, 2019, https://fs.blog/knowledge-project-podcast/tobi-lutke/.
3. Ibid.
4. Tom Pitfield, "Shopify's Tobi Lütke on growing & disrupting in Canada," Canada 2020, November 14, 2016, www.youtube.com/watch?v=aFRyf5aOKH0.
5. Matt Linderman, "Q&A with Tobias Lütke of Shopify," *Signal v. Noise*, June 3, 2010, https://signalvnoise.com/posts/2378-qa-with-tobias-ltke-of-shopify.

Skip the Shit Sandwiches

1. Bianca Bartz, "A Look Inside Shopify's Culture with Daniel Weinand," *Hazel Blog*, March 9, 2017, https://web.archive.org/web/20170707145154/http://hazelhq.com/blog/daniel-weinand-shopify-interview/.
2. Gail Goodman and Lily Lyman, "Tobi Lütke, Founder & CEO of Shopify | Core Summit 2019," Underscore VC, November 6, 2019, https://underscore.vc/blog/no-nonsense-featuring-tobi-Lutke/.
3. John Gardner, "The Motley Fool Interviews Tobi Lütke, CEO of Shopify," The Motley Fool, September 11, 2018, https://www.fool.com/investing/2018/09/11/the-motley-fool-interviews-tobi-Lutke-ceo-of-shopi.aspx.
4. John Stackhouse and Trinh Theresa Do, "The Creativity Economy Part 2: From the Classroom to the Boardroom," *Disruptors*, podcast, April 27, 2021, https://rbc-disruptors.simplecast.com/episodes/the-creative-economy-pt2.
5. Bartz, "A Look Inside Shopify's Culture."
6. Shopify executives, "The Shopify Book Bar," Goodreads, https://www.goodreads.com/shelf/show/shopify-book-bar.
7. Sriram Krishnan, "Tobi Lütke," *The Observer Effect*, December 16, 2020, www.theobservereffect.org/tobi.html.

8. Jason Calacanis, "Tobi Lütke - Founder & CEO of Shopify on future of retail," *This Week in Startups*, August 6, 2013, www.youtube.com/watch?v=mxBaDsosGPw&ab_channel=ThisWeekinStartups.
9. Shane Parrish, "Tobi Lütke: The Trust Battery," *Knowledge Project Podcast*, April 2, 2019, https://fs.blog/knowledge-project-podcast/tobi-lutke/.

Recruitment: Key to Shopify

1. Bianca Bartz, "A Look Inside Shopify's Culture with Daniel Weinand," *Hazel Blog*, March 9, 2017, https://web.archive.org/web/20170707145154/http://hazelhq.com/blog/daniel-weinand-shopify-interview/.
2. Gail Goodman and Lily Lyman, "Tobi Lütke, Founder & CEO of Shopify | Core Summit 2019," Underscore VC, November 6, 2019, https://underscore.vc/blog/no-nonsense-featuring-tobi-Lutke/.
3. James Cowan, "Lessons in Scaling Startup Culture from Shopify's Harley Finkelstein," *Canadian Business*, April 18, 2016.
4. Tobi Lütke, "Your StarCraft accomplishments," X, October 14, 2019, https://twitter.com/tobi/status/1183807041678299137.
5. Tobi Lütke (a.k.a. xal), Reddit, https://www.reddit.com/r/starcraft/comments/dl302p/comment/f4my80i/.
6. Brandon Chu, "Craig Miller on Being Shopify's CPO, Marketing by an Engineer, Leadership, and Scale," April 27, 2021, *The Black Box of Product Management*, www.youtube.com/watch?v=6F1iN4sAVEs.
7. Cube Business Media, "Ask Me Anything — Harley Finkelstein from Shopify," SaaS North 2019 conference, posted November 13, 2020, www.youtube.com/watch?v=r7n1ihMPNEk.
8. Shopify Inc., "Dev Degree Program," https://devdegree.ca/.
9. Josh C. Simmons, "Why I Quit Shopify After Five Months," *The Blog Of Josh C. Simmons*, February 2022, https://www.joshcsimmons.com/posts/why-i-quit-shopify.

Engagement

1. Daymond John, "Harley Finkelstein from Shopify on Why E-Commerce is the Future of Business," *#Powertalks*, August 8, 2020, https://www.youtube.com/watch?v=kiTBL6-oSe8.
2. Little Miss Shopify (Anna), "The Comeback," *Life @ Shopify*, November 23, 2013, https://littlemissshopify.tumblr.com/post/67863079630/the-comback.
3. Meghan Rosen, "Hack Days, Shopify," https://www.megrosen.me/.
4. Tobias Lütke, "The Case For Swagger: Canadians Have a Lot to Be Proud Of," *Tobias Lütke Blog*, May 22, 2018, https://tobi.Lutke.com/blogs/news/the-case-for-swagger-canadians-have-a-lot-to-be-proud-of.
5. Tobias Lütke, "How to make sure your business is on the right side of history through code & culture," Business of Software 2011 speech, May 23, 2012, https://businessofsoftware.org/talks/ceo-shopify-how-we-can-build-businesses-that-people-in-100-years-wont-be-embarrassed-by/.
6. Dan Martell, "The Future of Retail 'Arming the Rebels!' with Tobi Lütke @ Shopify.com," *Escape Velocity Show*, December 5, 2019, https://www.youtube.com/watch?v=-PZouDwpIYQ.

9. EMPOWERING ENTREPRENEURS

The Unscaling Paradigm

1. Hemant Taneja, *Unscaled: How AI and a New Generation of Upstarts Are Creating the Economy of the Future* (New York: Public Affairs, 2018).
2. Isabel B. Slone, "How Allbirds Co-Founder Tim Brown Went from Pro Sports to Sustainable Shoes," *Canadian Business*, September 12, 2022, https://canadianbusiness.com/people/allbirds-co-founder-ceo-tim-brown/.

Celebrity Merchants

1. Natalie Robehmed, "At 21, Kylie Jenner Becomes The Youngest Self-Made Billionaire Ever," *Forbes*, March 5, 2019, www.forbes.com/sites/natalierobehmed/2019/03/05/at-21-kylie-jenner-becomes-the-youngest-self-made-billionaire-ever/?sh=34b824ac2794.

Dropshippers

1. Sirin Kale, "Shopify: the good shop to Amazon's bad shop," *Guardian*, June 14, 2020, www.theguardian.com/technology/2020/jun/14/shopify-the-good-shop-to-amazons-bad-shop.
2. Ibid.
3. Corey Ferreira, "What Is Dropshipping and How Does It Work?" *Shopify Blog*, October 19, 2022, www.shopify.com/ca/blog/what-is-dropshipping.

10. RETAIL OPERATING SYSTEM I

Changing Engines Mid-Flight

1. Ilana E. Strauss, "How Shopify beat eBay by betting on small business," *When It Clicked*, March 16, 2022, www.youtube.com/watch?v=rDcVQqy7yzE.
2. Shopify Inc., "Shopify Launches Revolutionary Point of Sale System," press release, August 12, 2013, https://news.shopify.com/shopify-launches-revolutionary-point-of-sale-system.
3. Shopify Inc., "Shopify Launches Shopify Payments," press release, August 12, 2013, https://news.shopify.com/shopify-launches-shopify-payments.
4. Shopify Inc., "Shopify Launches Shopify Plus," press release, February 4, 2014, https://news.shopify.com/shopify-launches-shopify-plus.
5. Shopify Inc., "Shopify Announces Multichannel Shopify and Updates to Shopify POS," press release, March 31, 2015, https://news

.shopify.com/shopify-announces-multichannel-shopify-and-updates-to-shopify-pos.

6. Shopify Inc., "Shopify Announces Shopify Capital," press release, April 27, 2016, https://news.shopify.com/shopify-announces-shopify-capital.
7. Strauss, "How Shopify beat eBay."
8. Ibid.

28,000 Lines of JavaScript Deleted

1. Rip Empson, "After 7 Years & 50K Storefronts Created, Shopify Launches Major Redesign To Simplify Online Store-Building," *TechCrunch*, April 11, 2013, https://techcrunch.com/2013/04/11/after-7-years-50k-storefronts-launched-shopify-launches-major-redesign-to-simplify-online-store-building.
2. Shopify Inc., "Shopify Releases Revolutionary New Online Store-Building Platform," press release, April 11, 2013, https://news.shopify.com/shopify-releases-revolutionary-new-online-store-building-platform.
3. Jaime Woo, "Rebuilding the Shopify Admin: Deleting 28,000 lines of JavaScript to Improve Dev Productivity," *Shopify Engineering*, blog, October 28, 2014, https://shopify.engineering/rebuilding-the-shopify-admin-improving-developer-productivity-by-deleting-28-000-lines-of-javascript.
4. Ibid.
5. Ibid.

Shopify Payments: The Fountainhead

1. Ben Thomson, "Shop Pay on Google and Facebook, Shopify's Evolution, the E-Commerce Shift," *Stratechery*, June 16, 2021, https://stratechery.com/2021/shop-pay-on-google-and-facebook-shopifys-evolution-the-e-commerce-shift/.

11. CEO OF THE YEAR

1. Trevor Cole, "Our Canadian CEO of the year you've probably never heard of," *Report on Business*, November 27, 2014, www.theglobeandmail.com/report-on-business/rob-magazine/meet-our-ceo-of-the-year/article21734931.

Lütke's Modus Operandi

1. Trevor Cole, "Our Canadian CEO of the year you've probably never heard of," *Report on Business*, November 27, 2014, www.theglobeandmail.com/report-on-business/rob-magazine/meet-our-ceo-of-the-year/article21734931.
2. Ibid.

The Art of Decision-Making

1. Andrew Warner, "How Shopify Became Profitable by Helping Anyone Open an Online Boutique," Mixergy, July 9, 2010, https://mixergy.com/interviews/tobias-Lütke-shopify-interview.
2. Gail Goodman and Lily Lyman, "Tobi Lütke, Founder & CEO of Shopify | Core Summit 2019," Underscore VC, November 6, 2019, https://underscore.vc/blog/no-nonsense-featuring-tobi-Lütke/.
3. Shane Parrish, "Tobi Lütke: The Trust Battery," *Knowledge Project Podcast*, April 2, 2019, https://fs.blog/knowledge-project-podcast/tobi-lutke/.

The Big Picture

1. Sriram Krishnan, "Tobi Lütke," *The Observer Effect*, December 16, 2020, https://www.theobservereffect.org/tobi.html.
2. Tim Ferriss, "Tobi Lütke," *The Tim Ferriss Show*, podcast, February 11, 2019, https://tim.blog/2019/02/11/the-tim-ferriss-show-transcripts-tobi-lutke/.

3. Tim Ferriss, "Tobi Lütke — From Snowboard Shop to Billion Dollar Company," *The Tim Ferriss Show*, podcast, March 21, 2019, www.youtube .com/watch?v=PQRXssjlk9U&ab_channel=TimFerriss.

Hands On

1. Shane Parrish, "Tobi Lütke: Empowering a World of Rebels," *Knowledge Project Podcast*, November 15, 2022, www.youtube.com /watch?v=hUug8tEWtoY.

First-Principles Thinking

1. Dan Martell, "The Future of Retail 'Arming the Rebels!' with Tobi Lütke @ Shopify.com," *Escape Velocity Show*, December 5, 2019, www.youtube.com/watch?v=-PZouDwpIYQ.

12. LISTING ON THE STOCK MARKET

1. Shopify Inc., IPO Prospectus, EDGAR Online, May 21, 2015, https:// s27.q4cdn.com/572064924/files/doc_financials/2015/q4 /5b53ab65-0602 -4968-9e7b-41c0de01de58.pdf.

The IPO and Subsequent Issues of Shares

1. Shopify Inc., IPO Prospectus, EDGAR Online, May 21, 2015, https:// s27.q4cdn.com/572064924/files/doc_financials/2015/q4/5b53ab65-0602 -4968-9e7b-41c0de01de58.pdf.
2. Sriram Krishnan, "Tobi Lütke," *The Observer Effect*, December 16, 2020, https://www.theobservereffect.org/tobi.html.
3. Nik Sharma and Moiz Ali, "Harley Finkelstein Talks Shopify Fulfillment (Part 2)," *Limited Supply*, podcast, October 5, 2022, www .youtube.com/watch?v=leZCkLDoiWk.
4. Brad Stone, "How Shopify outfoxed Amazon to become the everywhere store," *Bloomberg Businessweek*, December 27, 2021, www

.bnnbloomberg.ca/how-shopify-outfoxed-amazon-to-become-the-everywhere-store-1.1699910.
5. Shopify Inc., "How Shopify Went From Startup to IPO," May 2015, www.youtube.com/watch?v=EDleqidmsXA.
6. Stone, "How Shopify outfoxed Amazon."

The Attack of the Short Seller

1. CBC News, "Shopify shares fall 12% as short seller calls firm a 'get rich quick scheme,'" October 4, 2017, https://www.cbc.ca/news/business/shopify-citron-research-andrew-left-1.4327736.
2. Geoff Zochodne, "Shopify shares tumble after accusations of promoting 'get rich quick' schemes," *Financial Post*, October 4, 2017, https://financialpost.com/investing/shopify-shares-tumble-after-accusations-of-promoting-get-rich-quick-schemes.
3. Motley Fool Staff, "Shopify Inc. (SHOP) Q3 2017 Earnings Conference Call Transcript," Motley Fool, November 1, 2017, https://www.fool.com/earnings/call-transcripts/2017/11/01/shopify-inc-shop-q3-2017-earnings-conference-call.aspx.
4. Sean Silcoff, "Shopify stock falls on report from short-seller Andrew Left," *Globe and Mail*, March 26, 2018, https://www.theglobeandmail.com/business/technology/article-shopify-stock-falls-on-report-from-short-seller-andrew-left/.
5. Kevin Curran, "Shopify Shares Fall Fast Following Report from Short Seller," *TheStreet*, April 4, 2019, https://realmoney.thestreet.com/investing/stocks/shopify-shares-fall-fast-following-report-from-short-seller-14917578.

What They Did with Their Wealth

1. James Bagnall, "The strange alchemy of Shopify's millennials," *Ottawa Citizen*, May 28, 2018, https://ottawacitizen.com/business/local-business/the-strange-alchemy-of-shopifys-millennials.
2. Madeline Stone, "Meet 35 members of the 'Shopify Mafia' who embraced the e-commerce giant's entrepreneurial spirit and launched

their own companies," *Business Insider*, updated September 30, 2022, www.businessinsider.com/shopify-mafia-members-who-started-their-own-companies-2022-3.
3. Ibid.

13. RETAIL OPERATING SYSTEM II

Shopify Plus: The Big Players

1. Steve LeBlanc, "Padelford drafted by the B.C. Lions," *Canadian Champion*, May 5, 2000, http://images.ourontario.ca/Partners/MPL/MPL002504519pf_0057.pdf.
2. Zubin Mowlavi, "Loren Padelford, VP and GM of Shopify Plus," *Coffee & Commerce*, July 10, 2020, https://www.youtube.com/watch?v=Ez3YFJfEnok.
3. Ibid.
4. Ibid.
5. Ibid.
6. David Cancel, "The Science Of Sales With Shopify's Loren Padelford," *Seeking Wisdom*, October 31, 2017, https://www.youtube.com/watch?v=OBbEZCqURqU.
7. Ibid.
8. Ibid.
9. Jason Del Rey, "Shopify CEO Tobi Lütke | Full Interview 2018 Code Commerce," *Recode*, September 17, 2018, https://www.youtube.com/watch?v=6isvTuasA24.
10. Mowlavi, "Loren Padelford."

Social Commerce

1. GMA, "Comprehensive Guide to Social Commerce in China," Marketing to China, August 16, 2023, https://marketingtochina.com/social-commerce-in-china/.
2. Nicholas Grous, "Social Commerce: The Next Wave in Online

Shopping," ARK Invest, October 14, 2021, https://ark-invest.com/articles/analyst-research/social-commerce-the-next-wave-in-online-shopping/.

3. Kara Swisher, "The Rise of Shopify — Tobias Lütke," Startupfest 2016 event, August 24, 2016, www.youtube.com/watch?v=VSO7Py_XGZg.
4. Yiren Lu, "Can Shopify Compete with Amazon without Becoming Amazon?" *New York Times*, November 24, 2020, www.nytimes.com/2020/11/24/magazine/shopify.html.
5. Dan Whateley and Madeline Stone, "TikTok is moving to control all aspects of e-commerce on its app as it kills the 'storefront' integration with Shopify and other vendors," *Business Insider*, August 24, 2023, https://www.businessinsider.com/tiktok-end-shopify-integration-drive-sellers-tiktok-shop-e-commerce-2023-8.

The Bank of Shopify

1. Matt Turck, "Fireside Chat: Solmaz Shahalizadeh, VP of Data Science & Engineering at Shopify," *Data Driven NYC*, June 12, 2019, https://www.youtube.com/watch?v=9OAqk9w1jkA.
2. John Sime, "Exploring Shopify Capital's Effect on Business Growth," *Shopify Blog*, July 21, 2021, www.shopify.com/blog/capital-effect-on-business-growth.
3. Matt Turck, "Fireside Chat: Solmaz Shahalizadeh."
4. Jack Coogan, "HCG Fund Management LP to Purchase Loans Facilitated by Shopify Capital," *Business Wire*, June 27, 2023, www.businesswire.com/news/home/20230627501111/en/HCG-Fund-Management-LP-to-Purchase-Loans-Facilitated-by-Shopify-Capital.

14. THE HEROISM OF THE ENGINEERS

Shopify Dodges the BlackBerry Curse

1. Sean Silcoff, "Shopify grows up," *Globe and Mail*, December 2, 2016,

www.theglobeandmail.com/report-on-business/how-shopify-finally-got-smart-about-mobile/article33184093/.
2. Ibid.
3. Ibid.
4. Brandon Chu. "Craig Miller on Being Shopify's CPO, Marketing by an Engineer, Leadership, and Scale," April 27, 2021, *The Black Box of Product Management*, www.youtube.com/watch?v=6F1iN4sAVEs.
5. Ibid.

Keepers of the Code

1. Ben Smit, "Autonomy vs Alignment, with Jean-Michel Lemieux," *Teamgage*, May 3, 2022, https://www.youtube.com/watch?v=wvWy3JPITSw.
2. Keith Adam, "Bot Devs Confront SHOPIFY CTO — Jean-Michel Lemieux," *Worlds Collide*, December 24, 2021, www.youtube.com/watch?v=bzJfPeslk8I.
3. Tobias Schlottke, "Building a Scalable eCommerce Platform at Shopify," *Alphalist Blog*, December 3, 2020, https://alphalist.com/blog/building-a-scalable-ecommerce-platform-at-shopify.
4. "Jean-Michel Lemieux," LinkedIn, https://www.linkedin.com/in/jmlemieux-613/?originalSubdomain=ca.
5. Wikipedia, "Monolithic system," https://en.wikipedia.org/wiki/Monolithic_system.
6. Philip Müller, "Under Deconstruction: The State of Shopify's Monolith," *Shopify Engineering*, blog, September 16, 2020, https://shopify.engineering/shopify-monolith.

Battling the Bots

1. Keith Adam, "Bot Devs Confront SHOPIFY CTO — Jean-Michel Lemieux," *Worlds Collide*, December 24, 2021, www.youtube.com/watch?v=bzJfPeslk8I.
2. Ibid.

3. Daisuke Wakabayashi, "The Fight for Sneakers," *New York Times*, October 15, 2021, https://www.nytimes.com/interactive/2021/10/15/style/sneaker-bots.html.
4. Ibid.

Trolls, Fraudsters and Hackers

1. Tobi Lütke (a.k.a. xal), "Ask HN: How to deal with SYN FLOOD and extortion," *Hacker News*, March 24, 2009, https://news.ycombinator.com/item?id=530973.
2. HackerOne, "The Shopify Hacker-Powered Security Story," March 15, 2018, www.hackerone.com/sites/default/files/2018-04/Shopify%20Hacker-Powered%20Security%20Story_Case%20Study.pdf.

15. ESCAPE VELOCITY

Moving Upmarket

1. Tobi Lütke (a.k.a. xal), "Shopify Traffic Surge," Reddit, February 10, 2021, www.reddit.com/r/shopify/comments/lg9qaz/shopify_traffic_surge/gmur5q8/?context=3.
2. Shopify Inc., "Q4 2019 Earnings Conference Call," *Wall Street Reporter*, February 12, 2020, www.wallstreetreporter.com/2020/02/17/shopify-inc-nyseshop-q4-2019-earnings-conference-call-february-12-2020/.

Going International

1. Tom Giles, "Disrupting e-Commerce: A Conversation with Shopify | STYT," *Bloomberg Live*, October 30, 2019, www.youtube.com/watch?v=gCac723JDXE&ab_channel=BloombergLive.
2. Shopify Inc., "Global by Default: Shopify Markets Becomes New Global Commerce Hub for Merchants," product news, September 14, 2021, https://news.shopify.com/global-by-default-shopify-markets-becomes-new-global-commerce-hub-for-merchants.

3. Sebastian Herrera and Shen Lu, "Amazon's New Challenge: Bargain Retailers That Are Playing a Different Game," *Wall Street Journal*, September 22, 2023, www.wsj.com/business/retail/amazon-shein-temu-online-shopping-727570ea.

Cryptocurrency and Cannabis

1. Harrison Miller, "Bitcoin Price Surges Above $30,500; But Warren Buffett Still Thinks It's a Gamble," *Investor's Business Daily*, April 13, 2023, www.investors.com/news/warren-buffett-bashes-bitcoin-as-gambling-token-bitcoin-price-hovers-near-30000/.
2. Marc Andreessen, "Why Bitcoin Matters," *New York Times*, January 21, 2014, https://archive.nytimes.com/dealbook.nytimes.com/2014/01/21/why-bitcoin-matters/.
3. Temur Durrani, "Shopify unveils partnerships with Apple, Google and Twitter, offers crypto feature," *Globe and Mail*, June 22, 2022, https://www.theglobeandmail.com/business/article-shopify-cryptocurrency-wallets-nft/.
4. Ryan S. Gladwin, "Why Shopify is doubling down on crypto — even after the crash," *Fast Company*, May 27, 2022, www.fastcompany.com/90756233/why-shopify-is-doubling-down-on-crypto-even-after-the-crash.
5. Rick Watson, "Andy Jassy Says 'Simple To Put Up a Website;' Shopify Says 'Just Watch,'" RMW Consulting, December12, 2023, www.rmwcommerce.com/blog/andy-jassy-says-simple-to-put-up-a-website-shopify-says-just-watch.

Fuelling the Shopify Brand

1. Josh Kolm, "The idea behind Shopify's first brand campaign," *Strategy Online*, April 15, 2019, https://strategyonline.ca/2019/04/15/the-idea-behind-shopifys-first-brand-campaign/.
2. Harley Finkelstein, "Dear Entrepreneurs: We Build for You," *Shopify Blog*, February 17, 2021, https://www.shopify.com/ca/blog/entrepreneurship.

3. Shopify Inc., "Shopify launches Shopify Studios to tell true stories of entrepreneurship," press release, January 23, 2019, https://news.shopify.com/shopify-launches-shopify-studios-to-tell-true-stories-of-entrepreneurship.
4. Shopify Inc., "My Shopify Business Story," January–December 2019, YouTube playlist, https://www.youtube.com/playlist?list=PLlMkWQ_65HlcFkZN5hnh9o__oQxcR4_xLq.
5. Meagan Simpson, "Shopify CMO Out as Company Reorganizes Division," *BetaKit*, February 4, 2020, https://betakit.com/shopify-cmo-out-as-company-reorganizes-division/.
6. Amy Hufft, "How to Build a Brand Like an Entrepreneur," *The Gathering*, April 23, 2021, https://app.swapcard.com/event/the-gathering-global/planning/UGxhbm5pbmdfMzkoMjI5.
7. Ibid.

The Shopify Fulfillment Network

1. ShopifyDevs, "Shopify Fulfillment Network—Craig Miller (Shopify Unite 2019)," June 24, 2019, www.youtube.com/watch?v=YRRwW8fiHUY.

16. ENTERING THE BIG LEAGUES

1. eMarketer, "Strong & Competitive Market Position: Share of U.S. Retail Ecommerce Sales 2021," Shopify Investor Deck Q4 2021, October 2021, https://s27.q4cdn.com/572064924/files/doc_financials/2021/q4/Shopify-Investor-Deck-Q4-2021.pdf.

The Empire versus the Rebels

1. Isabelle Kirkwood, "Here's How Scott Galloway Thinks Shopify Could Supplant Amazon," *BetaKit*, August 30, 2019, https://betakit.com/heres-how-scott-galloway-thinks-shopify-could-supplant-amazon/.

2. David George-Cosh, "Ark Invest's Cathie Wood thinks Shopify could be next Amazon," *BNN Bloomberg*, April 14, 2021, https://www.bnnbloomberg.ca/ark-invest-s-cathie-wood-thinks-shopify-could-be-next-amazon-1.1590225.
3. Andrew Button, "Could Shopify Become the Next Amazon?" The Motley Fool, January 19, 2023, https://www.fool.ca/2023/01/19/could-shopify-become-the-next-amazon/.
4. Tobi Lütke, "#ask Tobi," X, October 11, 2019, https://twitter.com/tobi/status/1182697544167632898.
5. Kara Swisher, "The Rise of Shopify — Tobias Lütke (Shopify)," Startupfest 2016 event, August 24, 2016, www.youtube.com/watch?v=VSO7Py_XGZg.
6. Jason Calacanis, "Tobi Lütke — Founder & CEO of Shopify on future of retail," *This Week in Startups*, August 6, 2013, www.youtube.com/watch?v=mxBaDsosGPw.
7. Wunderman Thompson Commerce, "Where Shoppers Say They Start Their Product Hunt: Amazon > Search," Marketing Charts, May 22, 2020, https://www.marketingcharts.com/industries/retail-and-e-commerce-113138.
8. David H. Freedman, "Shopify Saved Main Street. Next Stop: Taking On Amazon," *Marker*, July 22, 2020, https://marker.medium.com/first-shopify-saved-main-street-next-stop-taking-on-amazon-7035620d19b8.
9. House Judiciary Committee, "Investigation of Competition in Digital Markets," July 29, 2020, https://www.govinfo.gov/content/pkg/CPRT-117HPRT47832/pdf/CPRT-117HPRT47832.pdf.
10. Ryan Tracy, "House Panel Says Big Tech Wields Monopoly Power," *Wall Street Journal*, October 6, 2020, https://www.wsj.com/articles/house-panel-calls-for-congress-to-break-up-tech-giants-11602016985?mod=article_inline.
11. Yiren Lu, "Can Shopify Compete With Amazon Without Becoming Amazon?" *New York Times*, November 24, 2020, www.nytimes.com/2020/11/24/magazine/shopify.html.

To Patent or Not to Patent

1. Jim Hinton, "Despite what its CEO says, Shopify's IP is worth a lot more than a 'good bottle of Scotch,'" *Globe and Mail*, April 18, 2021, www.theglobeandmail.com/business/commentary/article-despite-what-its-ceo-says-shopifys-ip-is-worth-a-lot-more-than-a-good/.
2. Sean Silcoff, "Tobi vs. Goliath: How Shopify is bracing for a looming battle with Amazon," *Globe and Mail*, February 13, 2021, https://www.theglobeandmail.com/business/article-tobi-vs-goliath-how-shopify-is-bracing-for-a-looming-battle-with/.
3. Hinton, "Despite what its CEO says."
4. Shiri Breznitz (host), "Intellectual Property and Entrepreneurship in Canada," Munk School of Global Affairs & Public Policy, March 24, 2021, www.youtube.com/watch?v=o3mr_kYgqoY.

17. COVID-19 AT WARP SPEED

"The Pandemic Just Turbocharged Them"

1. Brad Stone, "How Shopify outfoxed Amazon to become the everywhere store," *Bloomberg Businessweek*, December 27, 2021, www.bnnbloomberg.ca/how-shopify-outfoxed-amazon-to-become-the-everywhere-store-1.1699910.
2. Shane Parrish, "Tobi Lütke: Empowering a World of Rebels," *Knowledge Project Podcast*, November 15, 2022, www.youtube.com/watch?v=hUug8tEWtoY.
3. David H. Freedman, "Shopify Saved Main Street. Next Stop: Taking On Amazon," *Marker*, July 22, 2020, https://marker.medium.com/first-shopify-saved-main-street-next-stop-taking-on-amazon-7035620d19b8.

Shopify Shop

1. Rebekah Carter, "Shop App Review (February 2023)," Ecommerce Platforms, September 13, 2022, https://ecommerce-platforms.com/ecommerce-resources/shop-app-review.
2. Ariel Michaeli, "Two Years in, Shop Is Having Its Best Season Yet!" Appfigures, December 2, 2022, https://appfigures.com/resources/insights/20221202?f=5.
3. Ariel Michaeli, "Shopify Launches Shop, Takes Top Rank from Walmart, Challenges Amazon," Appfigures May 7, 2020, https://appfigures.com/resources/insights/shopifys-strategic-switchup.
4. Juozas Kaziukėnas, "Shopify Tests Universal Search," Marketplace Pulse, November 15, 2022, www.marketplacepulse.com/articles/shopify-tests-universal-search.

Code Red!

1. Alan Shimel, "Developer-First — Glen Coates, Shopify," *Techstrong TV*, July 1, 2021, https://techstrong.tv/videos/interviews/developer-first-shopify.
2. Harry Stebbings, "Glen Coates: Why Shopify Will Dominate Amazon," *20VC*, March 8, 2023, www.youtube.com/watch?v=iDKUI1CuoMA.
3. Shimel, "Glen Coates."

Buy-Outs and IPOs

1. Miguel Facussé, "I sold my Shopify store for nearly $1 million only 8 months after launching it," *Business Insider*, May 23, 2022, www.businessinsider.com/sold-shopify-store-1-million-8-months-after-starting-it-2022-5.
2. Andrew Silard, "How OpenStore increased Jack Archer's revenue from $1M to $10M," *OpenStore Blog*, September 13, 2023, https://open.store/blog/how-openstore-increased-jack-archer-revenue-10x.
3. Madeline Stone, "A 31-year-old who buys Shopify stores and flips

them makes $2 million a year in sales," *Business Insider*, August 31, 2022, www.businessinsider.com/buy-sell-websites-explains-how-he-did-it-2022-6.

18. THRIVING ON CHANGE

Digital by Design

1. Brad Stone, "How Shopify outfoxed Amazon to become the everywhere store," *Bloomberg Businessweek*, December 27, 2021, www.bnnbloomberg.ca/how-shopify-outfoxed-amazon-to-become-the-everywhere-store-1.1699910.
2. Reid Hoffman, "Be a platform — Shopify's Tobi Lütke," *Masters of Scale*, February 13, 2020, https://mastersofscale.com/tobi-Lutke-be-a-platform/.
3. Lenny Rachitsky, "Brandon Chu on building product at Shopify," *Lenny's Newsletter*, June 27, 2022, www.lennysnewsletter.com/p/brandon-chu-on-what-its-like-to-build#details.
4. Nik Sharma and Moiz Ali, "Harley Finkelstein Talks Shopify Fulfillment (Part 2)," *Limited Supply*, podcast, October 5, 2022, www.youtube.com/watch?v=leZCkLDoiWk.

Logistics: The Five Stages of Grief

1. Madeline Stone and Emma Cosgrove, "Shopify is cutting contracts with warehouses across the US, marking a shift in its push to challenge Amazon's massive fulfillment machine," *Business Insider*, January 21, 2022, www.businessinsider.com/shopify-overhauls-fulfillment-strategy-as-it-challenges-amazon-2022-1.
2. Madeline Stone and Emma Cosgrove, "In its quest to challenge Amazon's fulfillment business, Shopify is stumbling where it usually excels — in software," *Business Insider*, February 16, 2022, www.businessinsider.com/shopify-fulfillment-network-struggles-software-2022-2.

3. Rick Watson, "Shopify Engineering Shakeup Shows Tobi Resetting Shopify in Last Year," RMW Commerce Consulting, January 30, 2023, https://www.rmwcommerce.com/blog/shopify-engineering-shakeup-shows-tobi-resetting-shopify-in-last-year.
4. Nate Tabak, "Shopify CEO envisions fulfillment network on global scale," FreightWaves, October 29, 2020, www.freightwaves.com/news/shopify-ceo-envisions-fulfillment-network-on-global-scale.
5. Balaji Srinivasan, "Tobi Lütke & Kaz Nejatian on Shopify's Country-Sized Economy," *The Network State Podcast*, February 15, 2023, www.youtube.com/watch?v=DfrhCGpRCPI&t=4968s.

Shopify Is a Team Not a Family

1. Brad Stone, "How Shopify outfoxed Amazon to become the everywhere store," *Bloomberg Businessweek*, December 27, 2021, www.bnnbloomberg.ca/how-shopify-outfoxed-amazon-to-become-the-everywhere-store-1.1699910.
2. Luke Rosiak, "'Shopify Is 'Not the Government': Largest Company in Canada Lays the Smackdown On Woke Employees," *Daily Wire*, May 25, 2021, www.dailywire.com/news/company-lays-the-smackdown-on-woke-employees-shopify-is-not-the-government.
3. Tobi Lütke, "Thriving on Change," company news, September 29, 2020, https://news.shopify.com/thriving-on-change.
4. Brandon Chu, "Craig Miller on Being Shopify's CPO, Marketing by an Engineer, Leadership, and Scale," *The Black Box of Product Management*, April 27, 2021, www.youtube.com/watch?v=6F1iN4sAVEs.
5. Lütke, "Thriving on Change."
6. Ibid.

Telling Shopify's Story

1. Steve Bartlett, "Shopify President: How to Become a Millionaire for the Price of a Starbucks Coffee!" *The Diary of a CEO*, May 8, 2023, www.youtube.com/watch?v=F6PxgTV-BJk.

2. Ibid.
3. Danny Miranda, "Shopify President on Mr. Beast, Mentors, & Loss — Harley Finkelstein," March 24, 2023, *The Danny Miranda Podcast*, www.youtube.com/watch?v=PNwZOs9CpB4.
4. Shopify Rebellion, "Arm the Rebels," https://shopifyrebellion.gg/.

Departures and Reminiscences

1. Shane Parrish, "Tobi Lütke: Empowering a World of Rebels," *The Knowledge Project Podcast*, November 15, 2022, https://www.youtube.com/watch?v=hUug8tEWtoY.
2. Tobi Lütke, "Shopify Announces Leadership Changes," press release, September 8, 2022, https://investors.shopify.com/news-and-events/press-releases/news-details/2022/Shopify-Announces-Leadership-Changes/default.aspx.
3. Brandon Chu, "Craig Miller on Being Shopify's CPO, Marketing by an Engineer, Leadership, and Scale," April 27, 2021, *The Black Box of Product Management*, www.youtube.com/watch?v=6F1iN4sAVEs.
4. Ibid.
5. Ibid.
6. Ibid.

19. STAYING ALIVE

1. Madeline Stone, "In a Leaked Memo, Shopify CEO Tobi Lütke announces CTO departure and other engineering shakeups," January 27, 2023, *Business Insider*, www.businessinsider.com/shopify-ceo-tobi-lutke-leaked-memo-announces-cto-departure-2023-1.

A Different Kind of Company

1. Harley Finkelstein, "This year is my Shopify Bar Mitzvah year — I've been here 13 years, a third of my life," LinkedIn, www.linkedin.com

/posts/harleyf_this-year-is-my-shopify-bar-mitzvah-year-activity-7032034671337103360-DnkU/?originalSubdomain=mu.

2. Madeline Stone and Emma Cosgrove, "Shopify's midlife crisis: How a surprise pivot away from logistics capped the e-commerce giant's whirlwind year," *Business Insider*, June 29, 2023, www.businessinsider.com/shopify-logistics-deliverr-sale-flexport-layoffs-crisis-2023-6.
3. Tim Kiladze, "Solving Shopify's misery: How Canada's tech saviour lost its swagger — and why investors remain so scared," *Globe and Mail*, October 28, 2022, www.theglobeandmail.com/business/rob-magazine/article-shopify-stock-tech-crash.
4. Kaz Nejatian, "China's growth was fueled partially by 996 companies (9 to 9, 6 days a week)," X, October 16, 2021, https://twitter.com/CanadaKaz/status/1449445302973333513.
5. Stone & Cosgrove, "Shopify's midlife crisis."
6. Bobby Morrison, "180 Days at a founder led company," LinkedIn, April 12, 2023, https://www.linkedin.com/pulse/180-days-founder-lead-company-bobby-morrison/.
7. Ibid.

The Compensation Crisis

1. Shopify Inc., "Rewriting the story of compensation," company news, September 16, 2022, https://news.shopify.com/rewriting-the-story-of-compensation.

The Corporate Governance Crisis

1. Shopify Inc., "Shopify Announces Proposed Updates to its Governance Structure to Support Continued Long-Term Growth," company news, April 11, 2022, https://news.shopify.com/shopify-announces-proposed-updates-to-its-governance-structure-to-support-continued-long-term-growth.

The "Buy with Prime" Crisis

1. Richard Meldner, "Shopify Bans Use of Amazon's 'Buy With Prime' Service," *eSeller 365*, September 2, 2022, www.eseller365.com/shopify-bans-amazon-buy-with-prime-servide.

Insomnia

1. Shane Parrish, "Tobi Lütke: Empowering a World of Rebels," *Knowledge Project Podcast*, November 15, 2022, www.youtube.com/watch?v=hUug8tEWtoY.

20. REBOOTING THE ENGINE

Layoffs, Price Hikes and Cutbacks

1. Tobi Lütke, "Changes to Shopify's team," company news, July 26, 2022, https://news.shopify.com/changes-to-shopifys-team.

A Tighter Ship

1. Temur Durrani, "Fewer meetings and no more 'pineapple on pizza debates,'" *Globe and Mail*, January 6, 2023, www.theglobeandmail.com/business/article-shopify-2023-strategic-outlook.

High Rate of Innovation

1. Tobi Lütke, "Important team and business changes," company news, May 4, 2023, https://www.shopify.com/news/important-team-and-business-changes.
2. Tobi Lütke, "I've got something very exciting to announce," X, July12, 2023 https://twitter.com/tobi/status/1679114154756669441.
3. Harley Finkelstein, "Great to be back on stage and speaking with Richard. #nrf2023," Instagram, January 16, 2023, www.instagram.com

/p/Cneo9VouYbG/?utm_source=ig_web_copy_link&igshid=MzRlOD BiNWFlZA%3D%3D.

4. Bobby Morrison, "What a billion data points reveal about conversion and the future of commerce," Shopify Inc., June 2023, https://news .shopify.com/category/future-of-commerce.
5. Shopify Inc., "Shop Pay — the highest-converting accelerated checkout on the Internet — will be available to enterprise retailers not on Shopify," product news, June 21, 2023, https://www.shopify.com/ news/shop-pay-the-highest-converting-accelerated-checkout-on-the -internet-will-be-available-to-enterprise-retailers-not-on-shopify.
6. Bobby Morrison, "Hot take: B2B is the biggest commerce opportunity of 2024," Shopify.com, November 30, 2023, https://news .shopify.com/hot-take-b2b-is-the-biggest-commerce-opportunity -of-2024.
7. Danny Miranda, "Shopify President on Mr. Beast, Mentors, & Loss," March 24, 2023, *The Danny Miranda Podcast*, www.youtube .com/watch?v=PNwZOs9CpB4.
8. Ibid.
9. Vidhi Choudhary, "How Shopify's partnership with Drake lays the groundwork for future celebrity collaborations," Modern Retail, October 17, 2023, www.modernretail.co/technology/how-shopifys -partnership-with-drake-lays-the-groundwork-for-future-celebrity -collaborations/.
10. Eric Rosenbaum, "Shopify's president on why he prefers micro-influencers to grow his own side hustle," *CNBC Small Business Playbook*, May 7, 2023, www.cnbc.com/2023/05/07/why-shopifys -president-pays-micro-influencers-to-grow-his-side-hustle.html.
11. Jason Stapleton, "Monetize a Small Audience with Mike Schmidt," podcast, July 3, 2023, www.youtube.com/watch?v=lojAmqbLZqk.

Future Opportunities

1. John Lorinc, "Is live shopping the next big disruptor in Canadian retail?" *Report on Business*, March 22, 2023 (updated May 23, 2023).

EPILOGUE: WRAPPING UP

Role of Luck

1. Diane Jermyn, "Fluke and luck: Shopify's co-founder profited from both," *Globe and Mail*, October 5, 2012, www.theglobeandmail.com/report-on-business/small-business/sb-growth/fluke-and-luck-shopifys-co-founder-profited-from-both/article4575360/.
2. Tim Ferris, "The Tim Ferriss Show Transcripts: Tobi Lütke (#359)," *The Tim Ferriss Show*, podcast, February 11, 2019, https://tim.blog/2019/02/11/the-tim-ferriss-show-transcripts-tobi-Lutke/.
3. Jermyn, "Fluke and luck."
4. Guy Raz, "Tobi Lütke on Shopify and Starting Small," *How I Built This*, NPR podcast, May 13, 2020, www.youtube.com/watch?v=WxIO08ETcXQ&ab_channel=NPR.
5. Alexander Bastidas Fry, "Chance Favors the Prepared Mind," Lindau Nobel Laureate Meetings, July 5, 2012, https://www.lindau-nobel.org/de/chance-favors-the-prepared-mind/.
6. Jason Portnoy, "The Importance Of Being Lucky in Business," October 19, 2021, *Perfectly Mentored*, www.youtube.com/watch?v=CO6GuVk-Atk&ab_channel=JasonPortnoy.
7. Benjamin Crudo, "Shopify's Harley Finkelstein On The Future Of Retail," *Making A Diff*, December 20, 2021, www.linkedin.com/pulse/making-diff-harley-finkelstein-president-shopify-benjamin-crudo/.
8. ArtosisTV, "CEO of Shopify, Tobi Lütke joins TLO and Artosis to talk about #StarCraft," January 31, 2020, www.youtube.com/watch?v=EQei-JzY35g&ab_channel=ArtosisTV.

Let's Have More "Unternehmergeist"

1. Dan Martell, "The Future of Retail "Arming the Rebels!" *Escape Velocity Show*, December 5, 2019, www.youtube.com/watch?v=-PZouDwpIYQ&ab_channel=DanMartell.

2. Sean Silcoff, "Is entrepreneurship in crisis?" Collision Conference, June 21, 2019, https://www.youtube.com/watch?v=kv-VC61p1e4&ab_channel=CollisionConference.

Shopify's Externalities

1. Shopify Inc., 2021 *Annual Report* and 2022 *Annual Report*, https://investors.shopify.com/financial-reports/default.aspx#reports.

Promoting Entrepreneurship

1. Shopify Inc., "Percentage of Businesses That Fail," *Shopify Blog*, April 26, 2022, https://www.shopify.com/ca/blog/percentage-of-businesses-that-fail.
2. ShopifyDevs, "An AMA with Shopify's Tobi Lütke," May 24, 2017, Shopify Unite 2017, https://www.youtube.com/watch?v=wrZiOxwowXE&ab_channel=ShopifyDevs.
3. Josh Constantine (via Khai Ren), "Shopify CEO & President Speaking In Clubhouse," Clubhouse, February 10, 2021, www.youtube.com/watch?v=DYYff5nuKgo.

Review of Shopify's Growth Trajectory

1. Alex Ferrara and Trevor Oelschig, "Shopify Memo," Bessemer Venture Partners, October 12, 2010, https://www.bvp.com/memos/shopify.
2. Marc Andreessen, "Why Software Is Eating the World," Andreessen Horowitz, August 20, 2011, https://a16z.com/why-software-is-eating-the-world.
3. Ferrara and Oelschig, "Shopify Memo."

Index

Note: Page numbers in italics indicate a figure.

Active Merchant, 65
Affirm Holdings, 59
Agile Business Development, 63–64
Agile Software Development, 63
AI (artificial intelligence), 196–97
Airbnb, 72
Aldrich, Michael, 11
Alibaba Group, 13, 94
AliExpress, 94
Allbirds (retailer), 92
AMA (Ask Me Anything) sessions, 87, 155
Amazon
  "Buy with Prime" crisis at Shopify, 191–92
  as frenemy/competitor to Shopify, 154–59
  cooperation with Shopify, 114, 155, 191
  as e-commerce firm, 12, 13
  interest in its merchants, 167
  practices of and lawsuits against, 157–59, 165
  share of U.S. retail e-commerce, 154, *154*
  store on Shopify Plus, 144
  use by merchants and shoppers, 154, 156, 157
Amazon Pay, 114, 155, 191
Amazon Webstore, 114
Ananta, Fahd, 120
Anderson, Mark, 76–77
Android phones, and Shopify Mobile, 134, 135
angel investments and investors, 26–27, 32, 120–21
Annual Reports
  and core values of Shopify, 80, 81–82
  externalities of Shopify, 208
  and intellectual property (IP), 159–60
  and revenues, 102, *102*, 103, *104*
  stock floated, 115
API (Application Programming Interface), 33–35, 51, 211
Apple phones, and Shopify Mobile, 134, 135
apps
  and API, 33–34
  development, 33–34, 63
  increase on Shopify, 34–35
  for mobile phones, 35–36, 134–36, 163–65
  See also specific apps
App Store of Shopify, 34–35
ARK Investment Management, 128
ARPANET, 11
Arrive mobile app, 99, 164
artificial intelligence (AI), 196–97
Ask Me Anything (AMA) sessions, 87, 155
AuctionWeb, 12
Aurelius, Marcus, 209

B2B channel and features, 198
Backbone Angels, 120
Bagnall, James, 118–19
Bailey-Morey, Carrie, 21
Balsillie, Jim, 62
bank of Shopify, 129–32
Bathorium, 120
Berners-Lee, Tim, 11
Bessemer Venture Partners, 48–49, 50–51, 52–53
Bezos, Jeff, 12
black-hat hackers, 141
blog of Lütke, 19–20
"blueprint," as idea, 106
Bombas (retailer), 156
Books.com, 12
books recommended, 29, 69, 71, 80, 81, 96, 110, 181, 209
bots and anti-bot tools, 138–40
Breznitz, Shiri, 160
Bridgehead coffee shop (Ottawa), 14, 19, 23
Brooklinen (retailer), 198
Brown, Tim, 92
Brundage, Harry, 119–20

Build a Business contest
  description and background, 36–39
  entrepreneurs as mentors, 65
  prizes, 37, 38, 39
Bulut, Peter, 162–63
Burns, Tom, 136
"Buy with Prime" crisis at Shopify, 191–92

Canada, x, 10, 148–49
  See also Ottawa
cannabis sales, 148–49
Carleton University, 86
cart abandonment, 198
CCO (Chief Culture Officer), Weinand as, 79, 82, 212
CDO (Chief Design Officer), Weinand as, 23, 76
celebrity merchants, 93, 144–45
"centerpiece" approach at Shopify, 65
CEO (Chief Executive Officer), Lake as, 23, 27
CEO (Chief Executive Officer), Lütke as
  "big picture" issues, 107–8
  CEO of the Year, 105
  decision-making, 107
  early transition and learning, 29–31, 32
  first-principles thinking, 109–10
  hands-on style, 109
  influential books and approaches, 29–30, 69
  mentioned, 1, 183
  preparation through gaming, 6–8
  search for at Shopify, 27–29
  skills and talent of Lütke, 32, 50, 105–6
  "systems thinking," 110–11
CFO (Chief Financial Officer), 46, 73, 183
Chan, Erin, 120
ChatGPT, 196
Checkout Apps, 195
Chen, Andrew, 72
Chen, John, 168
China, 13, 94, 128, 134–35, 146, 202
Christensen, Clayton, 96
Chu, Brandon, 83, 85
Cialdini, Robert, 29–30
Cirne, Lew, 5
client support team.
  See support team
cloud computing, 90
cloud service provider, 145
CMO (Chief Marketing Officer)
  Miller as, 45, 46, 71–72, 135, 149
  Weiser as, 149, 150
CNBC channel, Finkelstein on, 176–77
Coates, Glen, 165, 166, 183, *187*
Coinbase Commerce, 147
Coinbase Global, 147
Commerce Components, 195, 198
Commerce Infrastructure of Shopify, holdings in 2023, 58–59
Committed Monthly Recurring Revenue (CMRR), as compass metric, 53–54
companies on Shopify.
  See merchants
COO (Chief Operating Officer)
  Finkelstein as, 43, 175, 176
  Nejatian as, 183, 184, 185–86
  Shannan as, 44, 175, 178
COVID-19 pandemic
  checkout issues, 165–66
  description and Shopify revenue, 161
  health guidelines, 172
  impact on Shopify, viii, x, 161–62, 169, 187
  remote work for staff, 170
  response to, 162–63
  Shopify Shop app, 163–65
  staff issues, 174–75
CPO (Chief Product Officer)
  Lütke as, 175, 183
  Miller as, 136, 175, 179–81
CRO (Chief Revenue Officer), Morrison as, 183, 186–87, *187*, 198
Crowdfunder app, 92
crowdfunding, 91–92
cryptocurrencies, 147–48
CTO (Chief Technology Officer)
  Lütke as, 1, 23, 27
  others in, 29, 136, 178, 183
culture and values at Shopify, 79–83, 185–87, 212
customer service.
  See support team

DDOS trolls, 140
Debow, Daniel, 183
Deliverr, 173, 174
denial-of-service (DOS) and distributed denial-of-service (DDOS) attacks, 140
design of/in offices, 23–24, 74, 76, 77–78
Destination90 program, 172
developers and designers
  API and apps, 33–34, 35
  and retail operating system, 100
  Shopify as venture capitalist, 57–60
DHL Express, 72

Dickson, Richard, 198
Digital Millennium Copyright Act (DMCA), 141–42
direct-to-consumer sales, 92–93, 163
distributed denial-of-service (DDOS) and denial-of-service (DOS) attacks, 140
DMCA trolls, 141–42
DODOcase, 38
Drake, and Shopify Collabs, 200
Drake Related store, 200
dropshipping, 94–95
DSers app, 94
Dunbar, Andrew, 141, 183, 184

eBay, 12
e-commerce (online marketplace)
  antitrust cases, 158–59
  and API, 33–35
  big leagues and Shopify, 154–57
  competitors of Shopify, 51–52
  history before Shopify, 11–13
  of large companies and merchants, 126
  on mobile phones, 35–36, 133
  and offline commerce, 97
  open banking, 201–2
  patents and intellectual property (IP), 159
  products with and without barcodes, 156
  projections and potential, x–xi
  share of U.S. retail sales, 154, *154*
  and social media, 127–29
  venture capital, 49–50
Edwards, Douglas, 181–82
Electronic Mall, 11
employees of Shopify. *See* staff at Shopify
engineers, 133, 137–39
enterprise-level companies, 123–24, 126, 143
  See also large companies and merchants
entrepreneurs
  bank lending to, 98–99
  and client support team, 67–68
  competition on Shopify, 37–39
  direct sales to consumers, 92–93
  dropshipping, 94–95
  impact of Shopify on, 207–9
  Lütke turning into, 10–11, 13–14
  marketing about, 150
  opportunity through Shopify, 17, 21, 90
  promotion of, 208–9
  staff of Shopify as, 82, 83, 85
  support group in Ottawa, 21–22
  unscaling by, 90–92
  See also merchants on Shopify
entrepreneurship, Lütke on, 206–7, 209
entrepreneur spirit (*unternehmergeist*), 206–7
Erika (grandmother of Lütke), 13
esports organization of Shopify, 177–78
Everstores, 167
executive team
  additions and changes, 39, 47, 50
  coaches for, 54–55, 56
  description of early team members, 39–47
  meetings with staff, 87
  new talent after COVID-19, 183–87, *187*
  remote work, 184
  shake-up and turnover, 175, 178, 182–84
  shares in Shopify, 118, 119
  See also staff at Shopify; individual positions (such as CEO); individual team members
Export Development Corporation (EDC), 131

Facebook, 117, 127, 129
Factorio (computer game), 8
Facussé, Miguel, 167
Fauser, Cody, *vi*, 20, 29, 54, 74, 100
  and API, 33–34, 211
Feastables.com, 199
Felicis Ventures, 49, 53
Ferrara, Alex, 49, 50–51
Ferreira, Corey, 95
Ferriss, Tim, 36–38
financial aspects of Shopify
  accounts, 73
  angel investments, 26–27, 32
  annual revenues, *viii*
  bank of Shopify, 129–32
  capital gains, 57, 59
  Class A shares, 112, 115, 189, 190
  Class B shares, 112, 189
  cryptocurrency and NFTs, 147–48
  developers and apps, 34, 35
  development and fixes, 73–74
  early days of Shopify, 18
  financing and loans for merchants, 129, 130–32
  "founder's share" of Lütke, 189–90
  funds raising, 28

future opportunities, 201–2
investments in 2023, 57–60
monthly subscription fee, 26
near-bankruptcy, 25–27
open banking, 201–2
pricing model, 25–26
private equities, 57
profits, vii, ix, 32–33
revenue by cohort, 103, *104*
revenue during COVID-19, 161
revenue growth, *102*, 102–3
Series A funding, 49, 52–53, 100
Series B funding, 52–53, 100
Series C funding, 53, 100
shares of Shopify, 104, 112–13, 116–19
Shopify as venture capitalist, 57–60
stock market listing, 112
stock price, 114, 115, 116–18, 187, 192, 193, 195
venture capital and capitalists, 27, 28–29, 48–54, 112
See also IPO of Shopify
financial crisis and recession (2008 and 2009)
description, 31
impact on Shopify, vii, 31–32
profits of Shopify, vii, ix, 32–33
Financial Services of Shopify, holdings in 2023, 57
Finkelstein, Harley, *vi*, *177*, *187*
as angel investor, 120
and Build a Business contest, 65
business development of partner ecosystem, 62–65
as "chief storyteller," 176
coach for, 55, 56
and Collabs, 199, 200–1
as COO, 43, 175, 176
description and background, 40–42, 43, 55
as executive, 40–43, 56–57, 61–62, 175, 211
in Fresh Founders, 22, 42
on growth of Shopify, 48
and IPO, 113–14
learning and development of, 61
on luck in business, 205
and management, 55–56
in marketing campaign, 149
and Mattel, 198
own online store on Shopify, 42–43
as President, 175–76, 183
on recent executive, 184
recruitment of staff, 83, 85
on remote work at Shopify, 171, 172
on Shopify as marketing scheme, 116
T-shirt printing business, 41–43, 91, 149
upmarket clients and international expansion, 144, 145
work ethic, 176–77
work relationship with Lütke, 61–62
Firestone, Bruce, 51, 66
FirstMark Capital, 49, 53
"first-principles thinking," 109–10
Flex Comp system, 188–89
Flexport, 194–95
Flippa marketplace, 168
Forsyth, Brittany, *vi*
coach for, 55
description and as employee, 39–40
as executive, 39–40, 74, 175
and staff, 80, 82, 86
and work culture, 79, 212
foundations, and shares of Shopify, 119
4261607 Canada Ltd., as founding name for Shopify, 18
Francis, Ben, 94–95
Frasca, Joe/Joseph, *vi*, 47, 74, 175
Fraud Protect for Shopify Payments, 140–41
fraudsters and fraudulent payments, 140–41
Frenzy mobile app, 99
Fresh Founders, support for Shopify, 21–22
fulfillment. *See* Shopify Fulfillment Network (SFN)
Functions, 197

Gadget startup, 119–20
gaming
esports organization of Shopify, 177–78
as interest of Lütke, 4, 5–6, 9
as preparation for Shopify, 6–8
Gates, Bill, 159
Georgian Partners, 53
Germany, 2–3, 145–46
Glass, Brian, 8
Global Commerce of Shopify, holdings in 2023, 58
Global-e Online, 58, 59, 146
Globe and Mail newspaper, 28, 105–6
Godin, Seth, 65
Google AdWords, 14
Google Cloud, 145

Goulet, Anne-Marie, 183
governments, and entrepreneurs, 206–7
Graham, Paul, 12
Great Lakes Brewing (retailer), 162–63
Gregg, Cam, 54, 56
Grous, Nicholas, 128
Grove, Andy, 29
growth of Shopify
  and big leagues of e-commerce, 154–57
  compass metric for performance, 53–54
  early days, 22–24, 33
  and first-principles thinking, 110
  future and potential, xi
  impact on Snowdevil, 18, 19
  Lütke on, 54
  main triggers and events, vii, viii, 33, 161–62, 169
  marketing trials by Lütke, 48
  number of merchants, viii–ix, *ix*
  Shopify as growth company, 27, 28, 48
  trajectory review, 209–14
  See also financial aspects of Shopify
gurus as staff, 67–69
  See also support team
Gymshark, 94–95

Hack Days, 87–88, 135
HackerOne, 141
hackers on Shopify, 141
Handshake, 165
Hansson, David Heinemeier, 15
hardware and software, as expenditure, 90–91
Hashemi, Mohammad, 119–20
HCG Fund Management LP, 132
Heinz, 163
Hertz, Jess, 183, *187*
Hoffmeister, Jeff, 183, *187*
Hostyn, Sasha, 177
Hufft, Amy, 150–51
Hydrogen, 197, 200
Hyun, Byun-woo, 177

Insight Venture Partners, 53
intellectual property (IP) and patents, 159–60
Internet, early commerce, 11–13
  See also e-commerce
"Internet, Everywhere," as location, 170
iPhones, and Shopify Mobile, 134, 135
IPO of Shopify (Initial Public Offering)
  description and promotional tour, 112, 113–14
  impact on Shopify, vii, 114–16
  IPO Day at NYSE, *vi*
  and shares of Shopify, 112–13
IPOs of merchants, 168
I Quit (TV marketing), 150

Jack Archer brand, 167
Jaded Pixel Technologies, as earlier name for Shopify, 18
JD.com, as online marketplace, 146
Jenner, Kylie, and Kylie Cosmetics, 93
Jones, Russell, *vi*, 46, 73–74

Kanata technology park, 76
Kickstarter, 92
Kitchener-Waterloo area, and Shopify Plus, 124
Klaviyo, 59
Klister Credit Corp., 121
Lake, Scott
  and beginning of Shopify, 18
  as CEO, 23, 27
  with Lütke as entrepreneur, 10–11, 209–10
  and Snowdevil, 10, 11, 14, 17
large companies and merchants
  development and expansion of Shopify Plus, 124–26, 143–44
  direct sales to consumers, 163
  in early days of Shopify, 25–26
  in-house e-commerce presence, 126
  new tools of Shopify, 197–98
  scaling up problem within Shopify, 122, 123–24
  wholesales, 198
  See also enterprise-level companies
Lazaridis, Mike, 62
Left, Andrew, 116–18
legal team and documents, 74
Lemieux, Jean Michel, *vi*, 136–37, 138–39
"Let's Make You a Business" campaign, 149–50
Levesque, Luc, 22, 106, 183
Life Story technique, 83, 84, 85, 86
livestream shopping, 202–3
Lobay, Christopher, 135
Locations feature, 72
Lower48 IP LLC, lawsuit against Shopify, 160
Lu, Yiren, 129, 158
luck, role and types, 204–5

lunchroom at Shopify, 77
Lütke, Tobias
on AI, 196
as angel investor, 120
apprenticeship as programmer, 2–4
as CEO (*See* CEO, Lütke as)
characteristics and description, 5–6, 105–6
compensation at Shopify, 188
as CPO, 175, 183
as CTO, 1, 23, 27
on culture of Shopify, 79
on customer satisfaction, 66
as early entrepreneur, 10–11, 13–14
on entrepreneurship, 206–7, 209
and financial aspects of Shopify, 73
"founder's share" of Shopify, 189–90
gaming as interest, 4, 5–6, 9
gaming as preparation for Shopify, 6–8
honours and awards, vii
insomnia problems, 192
and IPO, *vi*, 113–14
learning disability, 1, 2
and luck, 204–5
office of, 78
on podcasts, 107–8
positions at Shopify (generally), 1, 183 (*See also* specific positions)
and product development, 108, 136, 175
as programmer, 2–4, 108
relationship with F. McKean, 9–10, 13, 17
shares in Shopify, 112, 113, 118, 119, 189–90
snowboards as business and interest, 10–11, 14–15, 17
and staff issues, 174–75
standards for executives and staff, 178
work before Shopify, 3–5, 10
work in adult entertainment industry, 4–5
on working with Finkelstein, 61–62
youth and education, 1–3, 6, 13

Macdonald, Gary, 120
MacLeod, Mark, 52, 53
Magento Commerce, 51
"making commerce better for everyone," 82, 96, 146, 152, 162
Malthus, Thomas, 206
marketing at Shopify, 48, 71–72, 149–51
Marketing Technology of Shopify, holdings in 2023, 57–58
Mattel, 198
McChrystal, Stanley, 69–70
McKarney, Shannon, 23
McKean, Bruce, 25, 27, 119
McKean, Fiona, 9–10, 13, 16, 17, 113
McKean parents, 9, 13, 27
McLean, Malcom, 110
McNamara, Adam, 120
medium-sized businesses. *See* small- and medium-sized businesses
Merchant Solutions, and annual revenue, *102*, 102–3
merchants on Shopify
and apps on Shopify, 34, 35–36
and "Buy with Prime," 191–92
celebrity merchants, 93, 144–45
churn rate and retention, 51
competition with Amazon, 156
as core value of Shopify, 81–82
and COVID-19, 162–63
financing and loans by Shopify, 129, 130–32
first shops on Shopify, 20–21
geographic distribution, viii–ix
growth into larger companies, 98 (*See also* Shopify Plus)
interest from venture capital and buy-out firms, 167–68
IPOs of, 168
jobs supported, ix
number of, viii–ix, *ix*
payment processing, 97–98
physical stores or offline commerce, 97
price rises, 194
staff as store owners, 82
surge during COVID-19, 165–66
templates of Shopify, 35
tips from support team, 67
unscaling and SaaS, 90–92
See also large companies and merchants; small- and medium-sized businesses
Michaeli, Ariel, 164
micro-influencers, and Shopify Collabs, 200–1
Miller, Craig, *vi*
as angel investor, 120–21
as CMO, 45, 46, 71–72, 135, 149

as CPO and in product development, 136, 175, 179–81
description and background, 45–46, 179
and fulfillment network, 152
journey at Shopify, 179–82
leaving Shopify, 175, 182
recruitment of staff, 83
remote work, 170
on retail operating system, 97, 99–100
and SEO, 45, 71, 212
shares in Shopify, 119
and Shopify Mobile, 135
on Slack issues, 174
Mirzaee, Aydin, 21
mobile phones
apps for, 35–36, 97, 134–36, 163–65
in e-commerce, 35–36, 133
problems at Shopify, 134–36
Shopify Shop app, 163–65
use on Shopify, 133–34
Montemurro, Ralph and Michelle, 157
Morgan, Lewis, 94
Morgan Stanley, and IPO, 113
Morris, Robert, 12
Morrison, Bobby, as CRO, 183, 186–87, *187*, 198
MrBeast, and Shopify Collabs, 199–200
Multichannel Shopify, 98, 127–29
Musk, Elon, 159, 199
"My Shopify Business Story," 150

Nejatian, Kaz, 183, 184, 185–86, *187*, 194
Nest cams, 99
NetMarket online mall, 12
New York offices of Shopify, 184
NFTs (non-fungible tokens), 147
Northpine Foundation, 119
NYSE, *vi*, 116, *187*

Oberlo app, 94
offices of Shopify
design and physical space, 23–24, 74, 76, 77–78
downtown Ottawa as choice location, 75–76
early and small offices, 14, 19, 23–24, 76
"Internet, Everywhere" location, 170
later and bigger offices, 76–78, 79
in New York, 184
relocations, 75, 78
Omidyar, Pierre, 12
online content and creators, and Shopify Collabs, 198–201
online marketplace. *See* e-commerce
online stores
first stores on Shopify, 20–21
as opportunity and focus, 17, 96
software development by Lütke, 17–18
See also merchants on Shopify
Ontario Municipal Employees Retirement System, 53
open banking, 201–2
OpenStore firm, 167–68
Operation HOPE, 207
The Opinicon lodge, 16
Ottawa (Canada)
downtown's description, 75–76
early days of Lütke in, 14
executives' departure from, 184
as home for Shopify, 28–29, 50–51
move of staff to, 10, 18, 20
staff from, 85–86
support for entrepreneurs, 21–22
See also offices of Shopify
Own the Room (TV production), 150
Oxygen, 197

Padelford, Loren, 122–26, 144, 213
partners and partner ecosystem
business development, 62–65
examples, 62
investment in, 57
and revenues, 34, 35
patents and intellectual property (IP), 159–60
patent trolls, 160
Patricio, Daniel, 82
"Pay by Bank" solution, 201
Performance Court office tower, 78
Phillips, John
and changes to executive team, 39
description and as angel investor, 26, 32, 121
Lütke as CEO, 29, 30, 32
as mentor to Lütke, 30, 32
shares in Shopify, 112–13, 119, 190
Pinterest, 127
pivot, as ability at Shopify, 63–64, 162
PizzaNet, 12
Plaza 234 office tower, 79
point-of-sale, for Shopify, 97, 193
Pow Wow Pitch, 207

President of Shopify, 175–76, 183
private foundations, and shares of Shopify, 119
product development
approaches of Lütke, 108, 136, 175
challenges in, 179–81
innovations in 2020s, 195–201
See also specific products
product divisions and managers, 166
product team, and client support, 70
programmers, 74, 84, 171
Lütke as programmer, 2–4, 108
Project Santos, 155

Random Hacks of Kindness hackathon, 130
Red Bull, as client, 126
Report on Business magazine, Lütke as CEO of the Year, 105–6
retail operating system and bank of Shopify, 129–32
description, 96
revamp of software, 100–2
rollout, 97–100, 122
utilities and features, 97–99, 102–4, 124–29
revenue. *See* financial aspects of Shopify
Rhenti platform, 120
Rosenberg, Jonathan, 181
Rovio, 52
Ruby on Rails, 15, 17–18, 19, 20, 101, 171
Ryoo, Kyung, 84

SaaS ("software as a service"), 90, 91, 93, 94
Sandberg, Sheryl, 47
Schmidt, Eric, 181
Schumpeter, Joseph, 206
search abandonment, 196
Sebastian, Colin, 116
Senkut, Aydin, 52
SEO (search engine optimization), 45, 71, 212
Shahalizadeh, Solmaz, 129–30, 131–32
Shannan, Toby, *vi*
and client support team, 66, 67–70, 211
as COO, 44, 175, 178
description and background, 44–45
as executive, 43–45, 66, 178
influential books and approaches, 69
on Lütke, 105–6, 178
Shapero, Amy, 161, 173
Shein, 146
shipment of orders, 151–53, 172–74, 194–95
Shop Cash, 195
Shopify
branding, 150
corporate governance crisis, 189–90
culture and values, 79–83, 185–87, 212
diversity in, 82
domain name, 18
externalities, 207–8
financial aspects (*See* financial aspects of Shopify)
first workspaces, 19
flow of information and internal podcasts, 87
focus and mission, 82, 96–97, 103, 111, 162
going digital, 170–72
growth (*See* growth of Shopify)
as growth company, 27, 28, 48
honours and awards, vii–viii
jobs supported, ix
landing page, 20
launch, 17–21
lawsuits against, 160
legal documents, 74
liaison roles within, 69–70
logo, 20
"making commerce better for everyone," 82, 96, 146, 152, 162
merchants and stores (*See* merchants)
name's origin and changes, 18
open-source environment for work, 171
patents and intellectual property (IP), 159–60
pivot as ability, 63–64, 162
publicly traded companies of, 59–60
release date, 19
staff (*See* staff at Shopify)
story of (*See* story of Shopify)
technical aspects (*See* technical aspects of Shopify)
votes in, 112, 113, 189–90
Shopify 2, 100–2
Shopify Audiences, 197–98
Shopify Book Bar, 81
Shopify Buy Buttons, 99
Shopify Capital, 98–99, 129–32, 162
Shopify Collabs, 195, 198–201
Shopify Collective, 195
shopify.com, as domain, 18
Shopify Credit, 195
Shopify Dev Degree program, 86
Shopify Editions, 195, 197
Shopify Email, 72, 162

Shopify Fulfillment Network (SFN)
  delays and issues, 172–74
  divestment, 194–95
  plan and early development, 151–53
Shopify Global ERP Program, 144
Shopify Inc., as name for Shopify, 18
"Shopify Mafia," 119–20
Shopify Magic, 196
Shopify Markets, 146
Shopify Markets Pro, 146
Shopify Mobile, 35–36, 97, 134–36
Shopify Pay (now Shop Pay), 99, 163, 195, 198
Shopify Payments, 97–98, 102–4, 145–46, 191–92
Shopify Ping, 72
Shopify Plus
  clients, 126, 144–45, 163
  description and features, 98, 122, 143–44
  expansion and going upmarket, 123–26, 143–44
  new tools, 197–98
  service levels, 98, 194
Shopify POS, 97, 193
Shopify QR codes, 99
Shopify Rebellion, 177–78
Shopify Shipping, 71–72
Shopify Shop, 163–65, 195
Shopify Studios, 150
Shopify Theme Store, 35
Shopify Translate & Adapt, 146
Shopify Ventures website, holdings in 2023, 57–60
Shop Mini, 195
ShopMrBeast.com, 199
Shop Pay (was Shopify Pay), 99, 163, 195, 198
Shop Promise, 152, 195
  badge, 173–74
Sidekick, 195–97
Siemens, apprenticeship of Lütke, 2–4
Silas, Tia, 183, *187*
Silicon Valley, 28–29
Sime, John, 131
Simmons, Josh C., 86
6 River Systems, 153
S.J. Major Ltd. heritage building, 76–78
Slack channels, 174–75, 194
small- and medium-sized businesses
  bank lending to, 98–99
  competition with large companies, 90–91
  crowdfunding, 91–92
  direct sales to consumers, 92–93
  examples, 92, 93, 94–95
  on Shopify, ix
  Shopify as opportunity, 17, 21
smartphones. *See* mobile phones
Smoofer (retailer), 42–43
snowboards and snowboarding, 10–11, 14–15, 17
Snowdevil company (4261607 Canada Ltd.), 10–11, 14–15, 17, 18, 19
social commerce, 127–29
social media websites and marketplaces, 98, 127–29
"software as a service" (SaaS), 90, 91, 93, 94
Stack, Charles, 12
staff at Shopify
  "acqui-hiring," 84–85
  as angel investors, 120–21
  benefits and perks, 24, 77, 78, 87–88, 178
  "bursts" and in-person experience, 171–72
  change and chaos adaptability, 81
  coaches for, 54–55
  compensation crisis, 187–89
  and culture of Shopify, 79–82, 185–86, 212
  and design of offices, 77–78
  Destination90 program, 172
  early staff, 22–23, 24
  engagement, 86–89
  as entrepreneurs, 82, 83, 85
  environment at work, 4
  expansion, 23, 53, 54, 70
  feedback to, 80
  founders of acquired startups as staff, 84–85
  interviews and "Life Story," 82–84, 85, 86, 123
  issues during COVID-19, 174–75
  layoffs of 2022, 193
  learning and development, 61
  meetings, 87
  as owners of Shopify businesses, 82
  recommended books, 80, 81
  recruitment, 82–86
  remote work, 68–69, 70, 170–72, 184
  risks and failures, 80
  salary and equity mix, 188–89
  screening, 22
  shares and holdings in Shopify, 118, 119, 187–88
  Slack channels, 174–75, 194
  startups of, 119–20
  in support team (as gurus), 67–68
  talented staff, 77
  teams with leaders, 69, 87
  "trust battery," 80

turnover rate and
retention, 51, 85
See also executive team
StarCraft (computer game), 6–7
Starr, Jürgen, 3–4
startup companies, acquisition and staff from, 84–85
Stoic philosophy, 209
stores on Shopify. *See* merchants
story of Shopify
overview, vii–xi
background, 6–15
beginning, 17–23
in big leagues of e-commerce, *154*, 154–57
future opportunities, 201–3
going digital, 170–72
going upmarket, 143–45
innovations in 2020s, 195–201
international expansion, 145–46
launch, 17–21
logo, 20
luck's role in, 204–5
and media, 176–77
name of company, 18
support group for Shopify, 21–22
"thrive on change" as value, 175
support team (client support team)
description and role, 66, 67, 68, 69–70, 211
early days, 66
gurus as staff, 67–69
layoffs and changes, 193, 195
liaison roles within Shopify, 69–70
remote work, 171
as small teams, 69
Sutton, Jamie, 21
"systems thinking," 110–11

talent acceleration team, 55, 66–67
TalkShopLive video commerce platform, 203
Taneja, Hemant, 90, 91
Taylor, Bret, 183
Team Trees project, 199
technical aspects of Shopify
and AI, 196
API (Application Programming Interface), 33–35, 51, 211
batman.js, 101
bots and anti-bot tools, 138–40
"Chaos Monkey" of 2023 (robustness testing), 194
checkout issues, 165–66
codebase redesign, 137–38
code red (directive), 165
crowdsourcing, 22
ease of use for merchants, 20–21
fulfillment network, 151–53, 172–74, 194–95
future opportunities, 201–3
machine-learning models, 130, 131–32
multilingual and multi-currency features, 145–46
new features in early days, 33–34
Ruby on Rails, 18
software building, 19–20
software revamp (Shopify 2), 100–2
trolls, fraudsters, and hackers, 140–42, 160
UI design work, 18
Technology Partners team, 144
Temu, 146
Tessier, Joshua, 120
Thawar, Farhan, 121, 183
third-party developers. *See* developers and designers
Thistledown Foundation, 119
Thompson, Ben, 103
Tictail, 164
transfer learning, 7
trolls, 140, 141–42, 160
Trout, Trisha, 31–32
Tucker's Marketplace (Ottawa), as office, 23–24, 76
Typo (blog-hosting platform), 18, 19, 20

Unicorn messaging channel, 88–89
universities, partnership programs with, 86
unscaling, description and as paradigm, 90–92
unternehmergeist (entrepreneur spirit), 206–7
UPS, 72
U.S.-dollar accounts of Shopify, 73
user-interface (UI) designers, 18
USPS, 71–72

Vaynerchuk, Gary, 65
Venmo app, 202
venture capital and capitalists for Shopify, 27, 28–29, 48–54, 112
venture capitalist, Shopify as, 57–60
Viaweb, 12
Vohra Miller Foundation, 119
Volt, 201

Volusion, 51
votes in Shopify, 112, 113, 189–90

Warby Parker (retailer), 93
Watson, Rick, 129, 161, 174
Waverley House Foundation, 119
website of Shopify, info on and Help Center, 70
Weinand, Daniel, *vi*
  addition to Shopify team, 18
  background, 15, 210
  as CCO, 79, 82, 212
  offices design and as CDO, 23, 74, 76
  and staff, 80, 82, 83, 86, 88
Weiser, Jeff, 149, 150, 183
whales. *See* large companies and merchants
white-hat hackers, 141
Woo, Jamie, 101–2
Wood, Catherine, 128, 155
work environment at Shopify
  engagement, 86–89
  recruitment, 82–86
  work culture and core values, 79–83, 185–87, 212

X, 127, 151

YouTubers, and Shopify Collabs, 198–99